3 WEEKS

DON'T CALL US OUT OF NAME

Don't Call Us

Beacon Press

Out of Name

Lisa Dodson

THE UNTOLD LIVES

OF WOMEN AND GIRLS

IN POOR AMERICA

BOSTON

Beacon Press
25 Beacon Street
Boston, Massachusetts 02108-2892
www.beacon.org

Beacon Press books
are published under the auspices of
the Unitarian Universalist Association of Congregations.

Grateful acknowledgment is made to Annette Van Howe, whose generous
bequest to Beacon Press helped make the publication of this book possible.

03 02 01 00 99 98   8 7 6 5 4 3 2 1

Text design by Wesley B. Tanner/Passim Editions

Library of Congress Cataloging-in-Publication Data
Dodson, Lisa.
        Don't call us out of name : the untold lives of women and girls in
    poor America / Lisa Dodson.
            p.   cm.
        Includes bibliographical references.
        ISBN 0-8070-4208-0 (alk. paper)
        1. Poor women—United States. 2. Poor children—United States.
    3. Welfare recipients—United States. 4. Public welfare—United
    States. 5. Women—United States—Social conditions. 6. Women—
    United Sates—Economic conditions. I. Title.
    HV1445.D63 1998
    305.42'086'942—dc21   98-16520

Contents

Preface

More than twenty years ago, I worked in a factory in Charlestown, Massachusetts, packing crates of candy. I was a member of the union and worked with its local leadership's efforts to improve the factory's sweatshop conditions, but most of what I learned about factory work came from the hours I spent listening to the women who worked there with me. They were quite a combination of people: Italian women from Boston's North End and Waltham, Irish women from all over the city, some Portuguese workers, and then the tough young newcomers—Irish and African American girls from Boston's segregated neighborhoods. These women worked hard all day, packing and lifting crates in steady rhythm with conveyer belts that carried the chocolates through refrigerated rooms. At night, they went home to take care of their families.

Many people were laid off each year. They went on and off welfare propelled by cycles of hiring and layoffs. One day our supervisor, Joe, posted a sign saying, until further notice, our division of 250 women had to work a sixty-hour week, a speedup which was then followed by a six-week shutdown. About forty mothers walked out. Many of them went on welfare. I can remember thinking that these were not your average welfare recipients.

After my stint in the candy factory, I worked night shift in an electronics factory while finishing school. There, I listened to more women discuss their lives. They talked about men, mothers, cooking, family troubles, and children. And they talked about pivotal events in their lives, moments which they believed transformed them. Black and Irish women chatted together smoking cigarettes in an old bathroom, talked about being beaten, about watching children go to kindergarten, and about losing someone you love. Italian and Puerto Rican women traded spicy recipes and spicier stories about rendezvous with lovers. They talked about evictions, places to buy cheap fresh fruits, and how the day boss liked to rub up against the new girls who never said anything about it. I objected to this silence, but they told me to be real. These young women wouldn't speak out because they were "public trainees." They had just come off welfare.

Later, I worked in a community known as the "death zone" because of a high mortality rate among the people who lived there. As an obstetrics/gynecology nurse, I listened to adolescent girls and women speak about intimate choices, about men in their lives, about having babies or trying to stop babies from coming. One woman asked if I would persuade the doctor to call her workplace to see if she could get permission to sit down while she cut up chicken parts. She was only four months pregnant, but nine hours of standing and her feet were already a mess. We called. They fired her instead. She came back to the clinic on welfare, anxiously holding out a Medicaid card.

And I remember as though it happened yesterday when a stone-closed teenager of fifteen, Bernadette, decided to tell me that it was her foster father who had impregnated her. She finally spoke up because this man had started to molest her thirteen-year-old foster sister. "It disgusts me that he should start with her," Bernadette told me, "she's only a child."

Some patterns emerged as I listened. Without any particular expectation of justice, these women and girls were weighing the cost of their every move and the effect that it would have on a whole constellation of people to whom they were tied. I remember my young self encouraging women not to think so much about their duties to others, to think more about their *own selves*, to get mad, to insist on a humane life. One day a woman, pregnant with her third child, patted my hand to settle me down. She told me that this was her life and that her most essential obligation was to tend to a difficult family and to mediate the brutality around them.

I was many years into these private lessons before I realized that I needed to do more than listen. I saw that the hard labor which lifts up families and communities in low-income America requires some serious publicity to bring it to national attention. But as this book developed, I gave up the idea that it would fit into the conventions of a public policy discourse. The interviews, surveys, observations, and focus group studies compiled in this research offer an excess of data about growing up female in poor America. But as it turned out, this is not a book about welfare reform, teen pregnancy, and work programs.

This is a book about people, about women who are savvy, complex, and challenging. It's about people who insistently bring with them their attachments, attitudes, and loyalties, their colors, intonations, and their own American histories. I could not find a way to truncate their content, to prune them into the familiar, not without diminishing these women, without whitewashing them or amputating the parts of their lives which they told me they hold most dear.

In the places where the information in this book was gathered—in parks, hallways, hair salons, health clinics, corner stores, and at the kitchen tables of low-income America—women tend to talk about people. They speak about parents, children, partners, losses, and loyalties. They debate local changes in their communities, schools, and streets. They reflect about the way people behave, about race relations, intolerance, rich peoples' ways, and they consider the future of a democracy.

Some of these women persist in detailing a history of individual pain, stuck deep in their personal trauma. Others brag about their ability to withstand, to be tough and irreverent. Some speak of their lives as part of a shared legacy, an ethnicity, a race, or a religion, while others speak only of fierce individuality.

What they do not talk much about are welfare reforms, get-to-work rules, family caps, or the latest cutback schemes. They dismiss that "stuff" as foreign and obdurate. "You mean, the government's laws," they clarify for me. Or "that's just those politicians' game," or "it's the white man's plan." Such public policy "stuff" is not viewed as rational nor hopeful, and is never seen as having anything meaningful to do with peoples' lives. Millions of women and more millions of children simply go on about their business, adjusting to what they view as irrational policies, creatively, anxiously, and generally by ignoring the chilling ways of power.

In time this book became a crossing, a class crossing, taking readers into brief fellowship with people who are seldom invited to speak what they know. It is a book about the lives of daughters, mothers, and sisters who endlessly handle the mundane and sometimes the monstrous tasks of being female and poor in America. And in doing so, they are raising a large part of a nation.

Introduction

*"Well . . . giving back is something I learned at my mother's
table. It was just what you do. I mean, I didn't always like to help
out but it's the only way."*

*"Yeah and it's what we've got. It's how we get by. Sometimes, it's
all we've got."*

"And too . . . it is how we keep our community on the rise . . ."

—1993 INTERPRETIVE FOCUS GROUP

Ellen, 1992

Ellen Smith is playful with me this second time we have lunch together in the spring of 1992. She pokes gentle fun at me as I repeat the list of rules: "Skip any question you wish, stop me and question me if you wish, tell me if you want the tape recorder turned off . . ." Ellen intervenes, "I know, I know . . . you want me to tell you about it *my* way. Well don't you worry, I will." Without any further prompting, she picks up her history where we left off two days before, well into her adolescence.

Ellen says she was not surprised by Marcus's desertion, over sixteen years ago, when she was eighteen years old. He had become withdrawn when his job "and his pride" left town, before their son Calvin had even learned to walk.

"All his bad habits came out then, more and more. Finally that's all there was . . . a man who had nothing but bad words and temper. He started to blame me, like it was all my fault where we were. I was not about to tell him I was already pregnant again." Ellen chooses to keep to herself the final events which led up to his departure. "I was mad and hurt, yes, but I know he didn't know what to do . . . he gave up on us and on himself."

Shortly after Marcus left, Ellen was put out of his aunt's apartment, where they had been living. She was seven months into her second pregnancy. At first, she stayed with relatives and with friends. Then two weeks before she went into labor, she entered a homeless shelter with Cal. At the age of nineteen she gave birth to twins, a boy and a girl. Ellen laughed at me. "Well *how would you feel*, three babies in diapers and living in shelter where you had to spend the day outside, not go back in until dark. My sister would come in on the train, she'd skip school to sit with me and walk them around. We sang and played with Cal and we prayed for salvation."

Ellen got through that period "one bit at a time." She went back to school and received her high school diploma, took classes in accounting, and started a job. One fine day she moved with her three small children into a one-bedroom apartment, "with only *my name* on that lease," Over the next eight years she gained and lost employment, went on and off welfare, battled depression, and hardest of all, tried to cope with a suicidal child. "Cal saw the worst of everything we went through and he suffered the most, not only because it was so bad, but I used to get so angry at him when he would misbehave," she tells me.

Ellen tried to maintain some stability in her family, but her anxiety about Cal's illness and her exhaustion from caring for three small children while trying to work gradually overcame her determination. She went into a period of severe depression that all but paralyzed her for most of a year. Her doctor recommended that she have a hysterectomy, Ellen is not sure why, and while still recovering, she had an acute allergic illness. At that point, "I just gave up and sent my boys away to relatives. My daughter Deborah wouldn't leave me. She was eleven and she stayed." Whenever Ellen sent her daughter away, Deborah would simply get on a bus or a train and appear on her mother's doorstep. Ellen acquiesced, and she reports of her daughter, "she saw me through it."

"You have to remember, that it was not all bad. We had fun. We used to go to the park, to the movies, and just play. I loved my children more than myself," Ellen tells me, but she also describes getting lost, losing that part of her self that was clear and devoted to her children. She lost her "sense" temporarily, she says, when she tried to start another relationship which ended badly. She lost heart when fired from another job, after chicken pox "ate up all my sick days but my kids were still sick."

Ellen speaks of searching for a way through all the hardship and humiliation of poverty and child raising in America. "I would try to be the parent my great-grandmother believed in. She said, 'Show love to the child . . . always show love to the child.' She believed that love is passed along. And I would try." But Ellen found herself particularly hard on Cal who was temperamental and volatile. Cal challenged her every day. She resorted to spanking him, then to spanking him with a hairbrush, and then one day, "I caught sight of myself, my face, while I was hitting him. I saw it in the mirror. I looked like I wanted to hurt him."

Ellen reflects at some length on all the pressure which surrounds a young woman with no money, small needy children, a one-bedroom apartment, no man to help or to hold her, and a society that "treats her like dirt." She knows that very bad things can happen to a woman in this position because some of them have happened to her. But she will never forget the look of herself, hitting her son. "I went to a counselor at Fuller [the public mental health center], and told him I was not worthy to be a mother, I was nothing, I should have my children taken from me." The social worker to whom she was assigned disagreed. For two years he worked with Ellen and her children, using their love for each other to help them get through this period.

"It's all connected, you realize. My parents had left me in my grandmother's care to find work." Ellen's parents lived in four different states before she was ten, searching for employment and sending money home to her grandmother. "I didn't live with them until I was nine. I used to cry and pray my mother would come for me. And then when I was left again, and again . . . it makes you weak."

Ellen believes that she, like so many children in low-income America, was always expected to understand that other needs came before her own: her parents' need for jobs, her husband's need for work and pride, and the needs of a society which placed little value on the life of a child. Much of the time there was no one to notice one little girl in the middle. "I was never that important to anyone, I thought. And even so, I had to be so strong for my kids. But I wasn't always." Now, years later, Ellen is confident and proud of herself and her children. She describes hammering her way through the welfare years, holding onto her own ideas and aspirations. "They offer you no hope, nothing, they think you are nothing. It is easy to start believing them. I used to ask them, 'How many mothers did you *encourage* today?'" Encouragement is what all people need, Ellen tells me, when facing difficult and lonely transitions, encouragement and practical support. "Don't you need support and encouragement to handle bad times in your life?" she asks me.

In her struggle to manage the world she faced, Ellen held fast to the idea of becoming a well-educated woman. She told her children that they were all going to become educated, and that in time they were all going to college. But before she could begin to win this dream, she had to learn to read. "I had kept that as one of my secrets," she tells me. "But it is a secret I wanted to let out." So, at twenty-four, the mother of three and a high school graduate, Ellen finally learned to read.

Ellen was thirty-three the first time I interviewed her. In the eight years since she had first learned to read, she had completed an associate's degree, in bits and pieces, and then a baccalaureate degree from the University of Massachusetts. She was considering applying to law school. Cal was college-bound and still getting counseling. The twin sixteen-year-olds were both honor students in Boston's selective public "exam" schools. Yet, as Ellen reflected upon her children's progress she immediately reached beyond these standards to another measure of success. "How are my kids doing? Well, they are fine. And no boy of mine hits, and no daughter of mine will stay with a man who hits her."

At that first interview, I found that Ellen understood the nature of my inquiry before I was half done explaining it. "You want to know about women's real lives," she told me. It was a search that made all the sense in the world to Ellen. She had struggled against overwhelming odds to survive the life of a poor woman in America raising her children on her own, and she knew her experience is at odds with many official accounts. She advised me to look back, to look back to childhood, and then farther back to mothers and grandmothers. She believed I'd discover meaningful patterns there, that poor women's real lives lie in those patterns of survival "where women raise children with no money." Only then can we look forward too with the knowledge we need to do better by girls and young mothers, and the children they raise.

"I just ask, what are we thinking about?" Ellen told me. "Is this a good way to raise our children?" And where will this take us, as a society, she asked me in several different ways each time we met. Did I understand the thinking behind government policies, welfare reform, and a society which ignores child poverty amid great wealth?

Ellen was one of the numerous tough-minded participants in this study who tended to question me as much as I questioned her. She wanted to grasp the thinking of "those people" who get to make decisions because they have so many advantages. And more than that, she asked that I help her seek out an ethical explanation for what is going on. What kind of people can ignore what is happening to millions of mothers and children? "I just ask what are we thinking about?" Ellen repeated.

POOR AMERICA

Close to 37 million people live below the federal poverty level in America and the majority of these are women and children.[1] In terms of family types, single-mother families experience the greatest poverty and are the fastest growing poor family structure. In the academic literature, this trend is referred to as the "feminization of poverty," the disproportionate share of poverty experienced by women and the children whom they raise.[2] In 1970, 48 percent of all poor families were single-mother families. By 1993, families headed by single mothers had grown to 60 percent of all poor families with children.[3] As alarming as these figures are, some argue that the federal guidelines which determine the poverty level obscure the real scope of this American experience.[4]

Many Americans find it hard to believe that a family can maintain children on such low incomes as set by the federal poverty level. Regular polling of representative samples of the American public reveals that most Americans consider the federal level as set too low, and other expert panels would also adjust the level upward.[5]

The official estimate of child poverty is 20.5 percent for all children under the age of eighteen years.[6] But some experts challenge that rate. Donald Hernandez, Chief of the Branch of the U.S. Census on Marriage and Family Statistics, examined child poverty by the distribution of children by *relative income levels*, described as the percentage of children living in luxury and middle-class comfort, versus those living in relative poverty and near-poor frugality. His data suggest that the experience of growing up deprived of basic needs is much larger than officially acknowledged, with 29 percent of American children living in relative poverty and another 11 percent in near-poverty.[7] Yet whether it is one-fifth or close to one-third of American children, by any estimate, millions of American families with children live in poverty. Growing up deprived of basic material support in the midst of great national wealth is now a mainstream experience for American children.

Race and ethnicity are major variables in American poverty. Using the federal poverty measure, in 1996, 45 percent of people considered poor are white people and 49 percent are African American or Latino. (The remaining 6 percent are Asian, Native American, and other peoples of color.)[8] Yet, while numerically many of these families are white, in 1994 African American and Latino families experienced close to *three times* the rate of poverty of white families in America. Thus while peoples of color—even as a combined subgroup—make up a minority of the U.S. population, they compose 52 percent of all poor people and 22 percent of nonpoor people in this country.[9]

Experiences of poverty in the United States are not confined to single-mother families, but this family form is the most likely to be poor. Thirty-nine percent of all families living in poverty are headed by married couples while single mothers head 54 percent of all poor families.[10] Thus, while poverty or relative poverty is now a condition shared by many American families, single-mother families are most likely to be poor.

While family composition, particularly the increase in single-mother families, has been a major focus of the social policy debate, there are other major variables which account for the millions of poor American families. Kathryn Edin and Laura Lein have explored some of these variables in *Making Ends Meet*, which takes a close look at the challenges facing women who are trying to move away from public aid.[11] Their findings concur with those who assert that in America, wage levels for unskilled and entry-level employment have stagnated and do not support a family.[12] Several additional factors affect the poor in America. First, most low-wage employment invests very little in building human capital or in developing the skills of employees.[13] Second, job-advancement opportunities for most service sector and low-wage jobs are very limited, and such employment may be seasonal, part-time, and provide no medical benefits nor offer family leave policies for parents to care for sick children.[14] Third, even if an adequate family wage were available, national policy has not addressed the cost, quality, and availability of child care to ensure that low-income parents are able to enter the work force.[15] Fourth, the ever-increasing cost of housing and an inadequate stock of subsidized housing consumes a disproportionate share of many low-income family wages.[16] Fifth, dwindling public support nationwide for post-secondary education has increasingly obstructed post-secondary education as an opportunity for better employment and for individual development of low-income people.[17]

Yet, along with these powerful influences upon the conditions and opportunities of low-income America, the dramatic growth in child poverty is also clearly associated with the great increase in both divorced and never-married, mother-only families. Correlated with national trends in divorce and nonmarriage, half of all American children born by the 1980s will spend part or all of their childhood in a single-parent family, and many of these children will experience part or all of their childhood in or near poverty.[18]

Low-income parents face a great challenge in keeping their children safe, hopeful, and engaged in schooling and other opportunities. Adult vigilance and community services are important forces to counter the increasingly dangerous societal pressures of unstable and overcrowded housing, street crime, teen childbearing, and larger numbers of students dropping out of school. Yet public services in low-income neighborhoods, public schools, after-school programs, athletic and extracurricular options, transportation and local employment opportunities are far inferior to those enjoyed by middle-class youth.[19] Thus the external disadvantages faced by low-income families coupled with the daily stress of raising children without money, often alone, exaggerate the demands placed upon low-income parents. More low-income children are in out-of-home placement and are working below grade level than are nonpoor children.[20]

For all these well-documented economic and social hardships, poverty in America is most often posed as a problem with people, as a deficit in character and competence.[21] The late-twentieth-century debate on single-mother families and child poverty has focused upon a "welfare culture" and an American underclass, generally described as dysfunctional, nonworking, and immoral.[22] An important counteranalysis has pointed to an increasingly stratified economy and to the persistent loss of decently paid industrial employment as the core of American family poverty.[23] These industrial shifts, coupled with historically salient effects of race, ethnicity, and gender on economic opportunity exaggerate the exclusion of large parts of the population from economic advancement. Despite these well-documented trends, American public policies continue to focus on the notion of failed people.

Paupers, Tenement Dwellers, Welfare Mothers

The belief that poverty is essentially individual failure can be traced back into American history. Early American policymakers fretted about a connection between aid to poor persons and the growth of "pauperism," much as current policymakers focus on the insidious "dependency" effects of welfare today. Early Anglo-American immigrants, who carried with them the ideology of English poor laws as they headed to the "new world," believed that a community should assess the merit of an indigent person before offering aid. Widows and orphans were to be pitied and helped, to a point. But others were relegated to a poorhouse and some were literally run out of town.[24] Employment then, as now, was seen as the remedy for pauperism, and one's attitude toward work was understood to be a clear measure of one's worthiness. Yet there was not always work to be had. And women with small children were sometimes forced to give them up, to indenture them or be cast adrift.

In his landmark work, *How the Other Half Lives*, published at the end of the nineteenth century, Jacob Riis focused upon the life of the urban poor, the "tenement dwellers."[25] Essentially, he considered the conditions of poverty and lack of employment as related, but he did not see lack of employment as the central cause of ongoing poverty. His focus was on the behavior of poor people, whom he regarded as weak-willed, flawed, and unable to control their passions and desires. This "flawed character" explanation for poverty took hold with a fierce tenacity. By the mid-twentieth century, aided by the contributions of Oscar Lewis,[26] the ideology of a culture of poverty became entrenched in America. This paradigm pointed to the persistent deficiencies of poor people, and what was most impressive to adherents, proclaimed that these deficiencies are passed on and on, creating a veritable culture of subclass citizens.

The development of an American ideology of "the deficient poor" was also imbued with racial and ethnic identities. In his description of tenement culture, Riis pointed to race and ethnicity as the cause of pathology in Jews, Arabs, Italians, and Asians. Eighty years later Edward Banfield's description of Negro men as primitive and Negro women as passive, and his claim that these deficiencies were passed on to their children, was then followed by Daniel Patrick Moynihan's analysis of the low-income Black family as both matriarchal and largely, pathological.[27] Susan Thomas has traced the growth of this poverty ideology throughout the twentieth century. She suggests that, simultaneous with the growing popularity of the idea of poverty as a condition which is rooted in a genetic or cultural deficiency, was the identification of the chief culprit in this process as female.[28] And this female was often portrayed as a woman of color.

Mimi Abramovitz points out that, throughout history, American public policy has examined females for their proper gender behavior, not their material condition.[29] Women and girls who were poor were scrutinized for their compliance or failure "to properly carry out their assigned productive and reproductive tasks." The outcome of this scrutiny determined access to community largess or "outdoor relief," the precursor to welfare. Females deemed "worthy" were, by and large, white widows who were local residents of a given community. Women (and others in need) who were not well known to the local government were suspect. Indentured women, African American and other women of color, and unmarried mothers were generally deemed undeserving, out-of-hand. As Randy Albelda and Chris Tilly point out, while deprivation and stigma were the norm for white poor people even while receiving public aid, immigrants and people of color were routinely denied any public aid. This affected the status of former slaves particularly. "For decades after the Emancipation, local welfare authorities simply classified blacks and other people of color as 'undeserving.'"[30]

Alongside racial and ethnic prejudice, Abramovitz argues that a careful analysis of historical regulations of poor people suggests an effort to maintain a certain kind of female behavior and thus to conserve the established order of society, traditional families, and social structures.[31] Women whose status deviated from that social order were, some argue, necessarily isolated and condemned. Some contend that this role of state policy continues today.[32]

Ruth Sidel has studied the contemporary pejorative characterization of women and teenage girls in poor America. "They are pictured as virtually irredeemable, lazy, dependent, living off the hard earned money of others. They are poor single mothers. They are welfare recipients."[33] They are, Sidel and others argue, demonized, portrayed as less than decent citizens and certainly less than decent mothers. And this pervasive public image of the irresponsible "welfare queen" serves to segregate women and girls who are poor and to justify a different set of regulations to monitor and admonish them. Isolation of this class of females is made easier, some argue, by the disproportionate presence of single mothers of color who need assistance and an American history of segregation and slavery. As Wahneema Lubiano sees it, "the [African American] welfare queen represents moral aberration and an economic drain." And she is frightening. "She is the agent of destruction, she is the creator of the pathological, black urban, poor family from which all ills flow. . . . Ultimately, she is portrayed as threatening 'the American way of life.'"[34]

Sidel goes on to suggest that it may be *useful* to portray these women and girls as bad, even dangerous people. As she puts it, "If welfare recipients are so unworthy, perhaps such harsh treatment, such punishment is warranted, even necessary, in order to modify their social and reproductive behavior." To save a nation, tough policy would certainly be warranted.

And recent public policy to address the growing proportion of American single-mother families has been pretty tough, indeed. In the last decade the goal of "reforming" welfare has evolved into a clearly articulated effort to end it. Accompanying this mission is the common usage of derogatory, even beastly terminology for women and girls who need public aid. Referred to as "wolves" and "alligators" in congressional debate, "crack mothers" and "parasitic girls" who bear children as "cheap jokes," in the press, the public has grown accustomed to this image of women and girls in poor America, a picture of incompetence, criminality, and dysfunction.[35]

Ellen Smith challenged this image as a distortion of her people and of herself, and she asked me to say so. Along with hundreds of other women and girls who participated in the research which went into this book, Ellen described a separate place, an American outback in which millions of people devote themselves to the work of raising families and building a society in the face of material hardship and social stigma.

This book is a synthesis of different research studies: a Life-History Study with grown women; a High School Study with young women; a Girls Project survey and focus group study; a Women in Transition study; and Interpretive Focus Groups with women and girls who analyzed the data with me (see the methodology section for a full description). The research includes years of observations, conversations, and working relationships in health centers, schools, sheltering programs, and in community centers. It follows chronicles of girlhood, experiences of adolescents, accounts of raising babies in the cold arms of welfare, and the observations of human service workers, social workers, teachers, and youth workers. It also includes the reflections of grown women who look back at American poverty origins and look ahead at the legacy we are forging today. The research reveals tales of resistance by women who have learned how to stand up to a society which does not know them. In the company of many, this research goes beyond surveys, tallies, personal accounts, and population trends to examine the version of women and girls that currently underlies American social policy. Against the challenge of primary knowledge, critical insight, and informed interpretations, an old stereotype simply falls to pieces. Before I was finished, hundreds of white, African American, Latino, Haitian, Irish, and other women and girls would impress upon me a very different version of being female and poor in America.

CHAPTER ONE

Daughters' Work

*"Well I guess you could say I'm the other mom. I cook, clean, watch
the kids. I help figure out what we're paying this month. When my
mom's at work, I do the [health] clinic with the kids, and in the summer take them to camp in the mornings, and all that. It's hard sometimes . . . especially with school and all."*

—DARLENE, FRESHMAN, 1993 HIGH SCHOOL STUDY

O ver years of listening to women and girls, I came across a person
I began to think of as the "family worker." She first emerged in
scores of interviews with women describing their lives as little girls and
adolescents. In these Life-History interviews, I asked grown women, in
their twenties, thirties, and forties, to step back into childhood and recall those days. I asked them to picture the buildings they frequently
entered, the streets and corridors they walked down. I asked about the
people to whom they listened and those they sought out when troubled.
I inquired into day-to-day friendships, connections, and kin. And I
asked about activities and routines, "the things that would take up
your time, most days."

In their answers to these questions, I began to notice casual but frequent references to obligations put on girls in low-income families.
Some referred to these entrenched duties as "house chores" and others called it "girl's work." It was a catchall category of baby-sitting,
housecleaning, errand running, attending to people, and sometimes
meeting complex family problems. In time, all duties ran together for
me, became more than particular duties and more than individual
work done for particular families. What emerged from these women's
histories was the image of someone who is working hard for reasons

well known to her family and to herself, yet obscure to the world outside of low-income America. The work of low-income daughters has
little recognition in the public discourse about girls' lives. Standing in
the shadow of research on sexual activity, lost self-esteem, premature
childbearing, eating disorders and the loss of voice, is the rarely discussed hard service low-income daughters commit to their struggling
families.

And the truth is, this work does not stand out obviously in most
women's memoirs. In contrast to their memories of love and of traumas, their recollections of people "who stood by you" and "people
who scum you," graduations and unexpected pregnancies, these
women's childhood work, even in excess, is half forgotten. Yet, the de-
scriptive data which detail this work appear to be strong. Over the
course of many interviews and discussions, the "family worker"
seemed to be the role for young girls in low-income families.

As I attempted to quantify the time that individuals had devoted to
family work, it became clear that some of the work of low-income
daughters has not yet received a terminology. Women recounted emotional obligations and pressures which were hard to explain yet were
remembered as the greatest drain on their energy and time. Girl's work,
it emerged, was not only a matter of performing time-consuming
housework and child care. It also seemed to demand the offering of
oneself personally and intensely, siphoning off strength which might
have been devoted elsewhere.

Subsequently, I turned to girls currently living at home. With the
High School Study and in the Girls Project survey, I began to interview
girls who were in high school, to ask them about the obligations and
chores they have at home. These interviews were slow going. The adolescents were far more interested in talking about high school issues,
social anxieties, personal relationships, sex, and conflict with authorities. But I persisted in asking about the pragmatic details of family life.

I was able to survey a class of juniors from a public high school in Boston who were willing to talk. And, subsequently, I had the opportunity to conduct in-depth interviews with other young women who were in their senior year of high school.

I found that most girls do very much the same work in their families as their mother's generation did before them. The only real change, they pointed out, is the descent of the economic and social conditions in which they live. Things have gotten tougher for many families so there may be more work to do.

The three most prominent kinds of work which emerged as girls' family work are providing child care, performing house chores, and trying to help with troubles and instability faced by their parents. The Life-History Study revealed that women had spent many hours as girls providing family care. The High School Study indicated almost 80 percent of girls provided between two and four hours of work each weekday and, additionally, on most of their weekends. More than half of high school girls contributed five to twenty hours of child care (excluding care for their own children) weekly, 80 percent did regular housecleaning, and half did the family laundry. Thirty percent provided regular help with an ill or incapacitated relative or family member, and one in four girls were routinely cooking for their families. All girls helped with food shopping. Overall, the time girls provided for housework and child care ranged between sixteen and twenty hours each week. Yet this kind of work is generally so little noticed, even these girls tend to understate it.

One high school senior, Edwina, generalized that she did "a little" around the house and "more with child care." When looked at in detail, this seemed a modest self-assessment. The oldest of four children, Edwina finished school at 1:00 P.M., then worked at her clinic job until 4:30, and was due home at 5:00 when she began watching over her eight-year-old brother and six-year-old sister. While her mother left dinner prepared before going to her nurse's aide job, it was Edwina's and her fifteen-year-old sister's job to feed their siblings, clean up, wash the children, and put them to bed. Edwina would sometimes help her sister with homework and then finish other house chores. She would start her own homework at 9:30 or 10:00, but she reported, "I fall asleep a lot and I'm slipping behind."

For some, this role of family worker starts early on. Annette is now in her early twenties. But she recalls becoming her mother's main source of help at the age of eight, and she realizes now that this role had a powerful effect on the course of her life.

"My mother came home from the hospital with my baby brother and she was very sick. I never *felt* the obligation of having to take care of the baby or [her older] brothers. But with all the other work combined . . . I would miss days of school in the fourth grade to do the housework. By the time I was thirteen, I would rather stay home and help my mother than go to school. She needed me."

And what about her brothers and her father? "Men take care of the business outside, in the street," Annette said, and besides, "I just loved my mother. She was not strong in a fighting sense but she was kind and loving. I was her helper, her counselor, her translator. She needed me, you know . . . who else would help her?" Yet for Annette and many other daughters, this role of mother's helper comes with a long-term cost. Annette gained no confidence in school nor did she spend much time developing a peer group. She grew into adolescence without a real presence anywhere but at home. Never a discipline problem, Annette was promoted each year to the next grade, but "the fact is, I couldn't read English *or* Spanish." She left school on her sixteenth birthday and was married before her seventeenth. By the time she turned twenty-one, Annette was a divorced unemployed mother of two children.

HOUSE CHORES

"Without Apologies": Arlette, Roxbury, 1992

On our second afternoon together, Arlette and I walk down Columbus Avenue in Boston, to a side street, pushing her two-year-old Damika's carriage. Columbus Avenue near the intersection with Washington Street is always noisy and busy, and this steaming July day it is boiling over. Trading Damika's carriage back and forth, as the child sleeps the heat away, we head for "the Academies" Housing Development. During the next few hours we will wander in and out of Arlette's little apartment, to a park, and to the local corner store to buy more ice-cold sodas and soak up the air conditioning.

Arlette is an eighteen-year-old African American woman who introduced herself to me after a workshop that I gave at a local health center. I spoke there about women's health issues, and as always I told the women present that I would welcome a conversation with anyone who might be interested in being interviewed about handling single motherhood. These were interviews, I informed them, which would be anonymous and paid by the hour.

The first time Arlette and I went over the interview guide, she nodded, accepting it, with some additions. She wanted to spend more time talking about her childhood, about the family move from South Carolina to Boston and the way life is for children who are suspended between Boston and the South. "It is not the same life there, you know. You have to do things differently. You walk slower, spend more time outside. You treat the older folks with respect there." Arlette went on to talk about the painful transition to Boston's neighborhood schools where "country" children are mimicked for their accent, by whites, Latinos, and Boston-born African Americans. But more than anything, Arlette wanted to talk about the "disrespect" she experienced from teachers, police, and other adults in her youth. (Her words came back to me a year later when 35 percent of 250 girls in a survey said that most of their teachers neither listened to them nor respected them, and 75 percent said that police harass teens. Some girls said teachers don't even bother to learn names anymore, "like we aren't people.")

Arlette is still angry about this kind of treatment. She believes that her performance in school and outside school merit respect. She points to her sleeping daughter and asks, "Does that child look dirty to you? Does she look sickly or hungry? Does she have marks on her? Does she have raggedy clothes?" These were mocking questions. Arlette gave birth to Damika when she was sixteen. She made up the school term over the summer and "walked with her class" at graduation, with Damika dressed to shine, by her side.

I wanted to know the mundane. What does it take to keep a child scrubbed and fed and safe in a congested and deteriorating housing development which is slated to be razed within three years?

Arlette's answer takes us back again to South Carolina, to the place where her house chores started. We move back and forth, from a farm house to city apartments, until Arlette's history of chores seems to run together across the states and then, to join the stories of work told by other girls who came to Boston from Puerto Rico, New York, Mississippi, Haiti, and Los Angeles.

"You always have chores because there was the gardens, the dishes, and clothes. The boys would come in so hot and tired you just fed them and they went to sleep. I remember that my older sisters and mama didn't eat till they were done. In Boston, there was no garden to work, but you had to walk a long ways to get your food." With no car, Arlette and her sisters walked to the laundromat, to the grocery store, to the clinic, and to school. Cleaning the family clothes was an all-day job, which she completed while accompanied by her nieces and nephew whom she watched for her sisters.

"You don't really want to hear about this. It's boring stuff. You just do it," Arlette tells me. She seems to resist reducing her time to the chores she performed, but once she begins to detail her days, the memories intrigue her. "We worked at home down south and here, but the chores were different. My brothers had a lot of work at the farm, but nothing up here." Arlette reflects that her sisters were just as responsible for the family and house chores in Boston as ever they had been on the farm. "Look, as long as you have a family, there's a lot of work that's just got to get done every day. Who do you think's going to do it?"

The gender division of housework is a constant in most of these girls' stories, with some older brothers pitching in on cooking and older child care. Most young women interviewed claim that they will make their sons contribute much more to the household than their brothers were made to do. But some women admit that, already, their little daughters are far more likely than their brothers to be doing house chores.

One mother of teens explained, "You plan to tell them both to do it, but then you get so you are just so glad that child [her son] is *alive* at the end of the day when he is out." She told me that she pushed her daughter more, and expected and received more help from her. And other teen girls seemed to accept this expectation as standard for their gender, as simply part of the course of life.

I ask Arlette if she had ever felt angry or restless about all the work she was expected to do. She tells me a tale I will hear many times.

Yes, she tells me, in some ways it made her angry because there was so much to do. She would have little time or privacy for homework or any other activity devoted to herself. She believes, looking back, that her childhood was truncated, cut off early on before she was ready to let it go. And she missed the attention and focus of parents. Hers always seemed too busy and distracted. Her father, a minister, wanted Arlette to spend time on church activities after her house chores. He had no patience with her desire for privacy or socializing with friends. Arlette's mother would simply list the chores she expected her daughter to do and remind her that, back down South, she would be working twice as much. So Arlette resented her parents and their expectations, but she concludes that they raised one very competent daughter.

Arlette believes that by twelve or thirteen years she was as capable as many grown women. She organized and sang in a youth choir, learned to speak out in church, tended small children, and helped run a house. She was able to rise early and work until dark, making family celebrations alongside her mother and sisters. When a parishioner fondled her breasts at thirteen, she threw him down the stairs of her apartment building, "and if my sister hadn't been stopped, that man would be sitting down to pee after that day."

At eighteen, Arlette regards herself as a capable woman who must build her own life. She is very angry with her parents who "threw her out" when she announced her pregnancy. She believes that her childhood made her strong enough to face whatever comes to her in life, but Arlette also seems lonely and a little frightened now. She is alone with a baby, on welfare, and estranged from her family. Though she never says so, she clearly wants her family back. At the same time, their "disrespect" and rejection still gall her. Would she do something differently now, looking back? "I probably would have not had a baby. I love her more than anything else, but I can't leave her with anyone I don't trust. But I am not saying I am sorry I had her, no sir. I'm not going around apologizing for my baby."

At the end of our visit, Arlette shakes my hand formally, but she doesn't move away. We both wait. I watch as she seeks out words to express a feeling common to many of the adolescent girls whom I met. "I can't understand why people don't see me for *all* that's me . . . not just some trifling girl with a baby. I'm more than that you know?"

FAMILY CHILD CARE

> *"After taking care of my sisters' kids for so long, taking care of my own baby was easy."*
> —TWENTY-SEVEN-YEAR-OLD NILDA, RECALLING HER
> YEARS OF TEEN PARENTING, 1993 LIFE-HISTORY STUDY

The most common kind of support which low-income girls give to their families is caring for other children. Even those girls who perform only moderate housework and whose families have ample adult resources routinely care for cousins, siblings, nieces, and nephews. Older daughters are considered the "second" or "little momma" to younger siblings and are responsible for watching, disciplining, and nurturing them.

Older teens speak with great authority about a child routinely left in their care and are often called into family council about that child's problems or needs. While some younger daughters fondly recall "being babied" in their families, these same girls when older were likely to be the second mother to their nieces and nephews, as the need for caretaking passed on. While the demands of such early induction into a mother role had a powerful impact in their lives, most girls seemed to accept, if not value, their role in providing child care.

Clara, who participated in a focus group which analyzed the role of daughters, believes that her experience "half-raising" her little sister is common. When Clara was seven and while her mother was still pregnant, she was told that she would become the older sister in the family, and that this was a proud position to uphold. From an early age, Clara had observed her own mother, also an older sister, aiding and advising her aunts and uncle. She couldn't wait for the chance to do the same. "I was so impatient for that child that my mother took me with her when she went into the hospital. They tell me that when my sister was

born I told my stepfather that I should hold her first because I was going to be in charge of her." Clara is amused at the memory of her own
self-importance. But in truth her role as caretaker and authority was
cast in steel and required by her mother and stepfather. "They knew
that as long as I was around, Cassie was going to be watched. They
could get on with other business."

Did so much child care get in Clara's way or hinder her own life?
Clara acknowledges that she would get sick of her sister. She admits to
slapping her sometimes when the child would whine. Occasionally, she
dragged her sister along when she socialized, and looking back she now
believes it was probably not a good idea to expose her little sister to
older kids. But Clara assumed that her duty as an older sister was to integrate Cassie into her whole life.

Clara's attitude toward providing child care was largely shared by
the other adolescent girls interviewed. They expected, even enjoyed,
some child care responsibilities and believed that this experience made
them far more capable when they had their own children. But when
helping with child care meant filling the shoes of a primary parent, girls
were almost always resentful, believing they had lost part of their own
childhood. And in the fractures and upheaval which visit many low-income families, young children are often left in the substitute care of
older siblings. Adolescents spoke with resentment, sometimes rage,
about the arrival of new babies, either born or adopted into the family, whose presence meant that a daughter in the family became a
mother without choice, expected to sacrifice her childhood for the new
family member.

In one focus group, Sheila, age sixteen, describes a situation which
the other girls know well. She was a junior and planning to attend college when her mother told her that, despite misgivings, she felt obligated to adopt the two-year-old and one-year-old children of Sheila's
older brother. He had left the area, and the babies' mother could not
care for them at all. Sheila knew full well that when her mother told

her this, "it wasn't *she* was going to adopt them, it was *we* were."

Sheila isn't sure if she would ever have been able to finance her plans to attend Northeastern University, but she feels her family life became chaotic with the arrival of her brother's two babies. When her grades plunged she turned all her attention to a new boyfriend. "I love my niece and nephew all right, but they drive me crazy. They tear the place apart and my mother doesn't know I'm there any more."

Sheila's mentor believes that Sheila will have a child of her own before she graduates from high school. This mentor was herself a teen mother many years ago. She says, "It is somehow a response to losing your place in the family, or in the world. You find a boyfriend and think he is the sun itself and then you have a baby." Her mentor sees Sheila as having lost her place as a child in her family. While already a willing contributor to family work, the arrival of two babies blew Sheila's girlhood away. With nothing but work at home and little attention from her distracted mother, Sheila was ready to bail out in search of another attachment.

Most of the adolescent girls interviewed believe, like it or not, that child tending is inevitably a task that must fall to females. When one focus group was asked if child care was work they shared with brothers, the girls laughed ruefully. "My mother just couldn't trust him with the children," one fifteen-year-old said. "He really likes them and all, but doing all that has to be done . . . forget it." The other five girls in the group—two African American, two white, and one Dominican— all shook their heads as if I'd asked a pretty foolish question.

Postscript on Sheila

Sheila did have a baby and did not return to her senior year of high school. She was unprepared for the role of motherhood and has taken to leaving the baby with her mother, who has reluctantly left the job she held for a decade in order to tend to three children under the age of five. She will have to apply for welfare to survive. Sheila is sometimes missing for days at a time. When she was last seen by a youth counselor, she was unresponsive, depressed, and she showed no interest in nor affection for the baby son who lay on her lap. Sheila's mentor believes that Sheila will lose custody of her child, "and then she will *really* start hating herself."

Quick Note: 7:50 A.M. in Dorchester, 1995

I reach our meeting place before Maria, so I take a seat on a park bench to wait. The morning traffic rushes by, everyone hurrying to work, just as Maria and I will have to do if she doesn't get here soon. Across the busy street children are playing in the schoolyard, enjoying their last few minutes of freedom before the morning bell rings. I watch a tall man walking down Tremont toward the park. A Black man, he walks very slowly because he is holding the hand of a diminutive girl, perhaps seven years old. She is chatting to him without let up. He carries a large book bag in his other hand. As they pass by my bench, I realize this is not really a man but a tall boy, maybe fifteen years old, and this is not his daughter but his little sister, to whom he listens, nodding frequently. At the corner, a group of young men on bicycles pull up beside them. All known to each other, they joke together. I hear one boy call him "Mr. Mom." The tall boy laughs right back, but "Little Bit," as they are all calling her, takes offense on her brother's behalf. The tiny girl points into the face of the jokester and lets loose on him. I hear the words "dropout" and "no-account," each punctuated by a small stamping foot. The young men laugh, but they also pull back a few steps. She is a small girl, but there is nothing fragile about her words or her attitude.

The young men move on, cycling fearlessly out into traffic and calling back over their shoulders. "She's just like your mama," one yells, and the tall boy laughs in agreement. The brother and sister cross the street to her grammar school. Quickly, he extricates himself, pulling his own books out before handing his little sister her book bag and glancing at the tight knot of little girls racing toward them. Little Bit stands watching her brother now moving off easily on his own.

"Don't you be late," she calls after him, the little finger pointing again. "No ma'am," he calls back. She watches him disappear down the crowded sidewalk, a frown on her face. Her little friends watch too, as though this is a morning ritual. Little Bit tries to keep him in her sight, but he is soon gone. She shrugs, turning to her friends. All together, sucking in a quick breath, they plunge into their morning discourse.

THE HARDEST WORK OF ALL: HOLDING BACK CHAOS

"I don't like to back down. Then they think you're weak. I'm tough
'cause I had to be."
—IRENE, SOUTH BOSTON, 1994 HIGH SCHOOL STUDY

Irene is not enthusiastic about the idea of being interviewed, but she has decided to give it a chance. By our third conversation, she lets me in just a little. "Well," says this seventeen-year-old Irish Catholic, "I grew to love my little brother more when I started raising him, but I hated him too, sometimes."

Irene's mother became ill shortly after Irene's violent, alcoholic father finally left their South Boston home. Irene regarded her mother as weak and had long felt it necessary to defend her, as well as her seven-year-old brother, Billie, from her father. But she also loved her tender mother and tried to pass on the maternal care she had received to her troubled little brother. Taking care of him was hard on Irene. The responsibility fell to her just as she was beginning to find her own ground as a young woman and was entering a public high school after leaving Catholic middle school. Why, I ask Irene, did she leave Catholic school. "I hit a nun," she tells me. I quickly look at her to see if she is kidding.

"Well, I spoke rude to her . . . really rude . . . and she said, 'That's it, you're out the door,' and so I thought, what the hell have I got to lose now? So I gave her one. She was one mean bitch, that sister. I would never have hit any of the other nuns." Irene moved to a racially mixed school in Dorchester, Massachusetts ("I didn't know anything about Blacks and the Spanish"). She faced a new school with no friends, her father's departure, and her mother's illness all at the same time that she took over her role as family worker and caretaker for her little brother.

"I was pretty tough, you know, I'm not a wimp. I guess I'm more like my bastard father. But it got crazy with my mother sick and Billy being so bad with everything." Irene's brother "kind of regressed, they called it," when his mother was hospitalized and then came home to be bedridden for almost a year. With their father's absence and few relatives to help out, Billy started to wet his bed, suck his thumb, and have nightmares. Irene sat up with him, nursed her mother, and went to school in a ragged daze each morning. Rage, an emotion which comes readily to this physically powerful young woman, came even more quickly now. "All you had to do was look at me wrong and I would jump you."

Irene describes herself as one tough girl. In contrast to some daughters, she fought every step of the way against a life she resented, and inevitably, her bellicose spirit landed her in trouble. After she sent a neighbor to the hospital ("Remember, she started with me when she mentioned my mother that way. And she was two hundred pounds and twenty-five—she was twice my size!"), Irene started court-ordered counseling.

"I figured out some of my problems, which are none of your business. But I know I try to be tough all the time so I don't feel weak or small." Irene believes she has been overwhelmed by the losses and the demands put on her. And she is suspicious of adults who tell her what to do, who try to control her, or who question her, just as I was doing. Irene had looked me over more than once and decided I was going to be easy to shock. She tells me how often she would get into fights, how she could beat up most boys, how she had no patience for "wimps and fools." I ask her if she can imagine that her struggle and pride hold lessons for other girls, other "nonwimps and nonfools." She laughs. "That's why I finally said yes," she tells me. "You kept saying how you were going to take the stories to other girls, and get people to listen. And you know it's not only the Black kids who have problems around here. Some of us have just as much going on as they do." I tell her that many of us, Black and white, would agree with that assessment.

A year after the worst of times Irene is doing better, but she failed a year in high school and has a police record. And she admits with regret that she hurt some people. Irene tells me that she went to the hospital to apologize to the woman she "fought." Softly, she tells me, "She wasn't even mad at me, like she knew about how it is . . ."

Irene met the "crazy" demands life put upon her, but not passively. She wants now to "stop all of that shameful fighting," but still not lose the spirit which drove her to fight back in ways that got her into trouble. She thinks hard about the daughter she hopes to have one day. "She will have a life and everyone else can eat shit if they don't like it. She is going to play and play. No nun's going to put her down. No man's going to hit her. We are going to play together." Irene, who has not played much for a long time, seems to hold tight to this idea. She plans to guard it well for her imagined daughter.

When I ask Irene how her teachers and all the other adult authorities view her now, Irene can't resist. "Well, I think they think I'm headed straight for hell," but this time she smiles.

Much like Irene, a number of other girls interviewed described their duties as family mediators and protectors, both for younger people and for mothers who sometimes desperately need an advocate. Of the fifty women in the Life-History Study, fifteen played a role in helping mothers break from an abusive partner, and some physically intervened to protect siblings and mothers. Of all the family work they do, this kind was reported as the most demanding. It is also a critical contribution to keeping families intact. Yet seldom is this role examined as part of the labor of young people devoted to the survival of their families.

"How do I handle the stress? Mostly singing as loud as I can with the radio so I can't hear anything else. But sometimes I get into bed and rock myself like a baby."
    —*Sixteen-year-old Dana, 1995 High School Study,*
        on stress of helping her mother leave a batterer

These narratives of girlhood reveal that the experience of a family crisis is complicated not only for the individuals involved but also in terms of the community's response. Not all family trauma is received equally by the larger world, and this has a profound effect upon the children in the family. Girls report a generally sympathetic response to a sudden death, a fire, or other dramatic loss. These events are remembered as times when distant relatives appeared, and neighbors, even strangers, offered support and sympathy. Everyone seems to join the family effort to recuperate. But what stands out in the conversations of girls, and in the recollections of grown women, is the response of outsiders to family crises which don't go away.

Girls describe filling a role of mediation, advocacy, and caretaking in a family in which the adult strength has broken down. This disintegration comes about in various ways, but the most common stories concern domestic violence, parental substance abuse, or when a mother becomes physically or mentally unable to perform. Such conditions differ from the drama of a sudden death or a gutting fire because they are ongoing, often escalating, and they evoke much less public sympathy. No random act of God, these "family pathologies" tend to drive people and public aid away. As girls explain it, when parents are addicted to drugs or drink or mothers are battered, relatives and neighbors lose patience and disappear, angry at the adults in the family who seem unable to overcome problems. And yet when *all* the adults abdicate, first the overwhelmed or sick parents and then the rest of the adult community, they leave children trying to hold a family together.

Between one-third and one-half of participants in the Life-History and High School studies, at some point in their childhood, lived with a mother who was abused by a partner. While in some cases such abuse did not continue, largely because mothers ejected abusive men, those girls who lived with battered mothers describe the depth of their suffering. And some women, reflecting back on the course of their lives, believe that the experience of witnessing their mothers being beaten ended any sense of safety they had possessed in their childhood. They recall a sense of terror, helplessness, and rage.

Espiranza is now thirty, but she still thinks back to when she was in grammar school and vividly remembers the beatings her mother sustained. For Espiranza and all the other girls recalling this history, it was not only a beloved mother at stake, but a child's whole world. Espiranza's lips tremble a little as she speaks of it. "I felt worse than when he hit me. I felt as though he was breaking me in two when he would punch my mother." Espiranza and her brother and sister eventually united to intervene, a story I was to hear many times. One night they grabbed kitchen knives and attacked their father, telling him they would cut him up if he didn't stop.

Escape is a more common response to domestic abuse, and I heard many such accounts from daughters. Espiranza's mother learned to drive on the sly and even managed to buy a car in secret. She hid the keys under her mattress, and one night after her husband had fallen into a drug-induced sleep, she piled her children into the car with a few bags of clothes. "She rolled down all the windows as we drove away and the wind was blowing in and she was laughing . . . and we just drove away."

Other daughters recall night terrors, frantic escapes, and family melees. And beyond these obvious traumas in their memories of domestic violence, something more subtle is revealed. That is an eclipse of childhood. In these homes where girls repeatedly had to face terror and violence, girlhood was obliterated. "You're always on the lookout," says nineteen-year-old Roxanne, who left her violent stepfather's home three years ago. "And always scared, but angry too, at him for doing it and her for taking it."

Domestic violence can paralyze a family. Daughters and sons are pulled into the family lies which explain how mothers receive their wounds. The girls and women interviewed recall how they would sometimes hide younger siblings, flee the house, or huddle with brothers and sisters, planning the bloody vengeance they would take. Some daughters elected to stay home from school or feigned illness to keep watch over mothers and fathers. While brothers were more likely than their sisters to jump in to protect their mothers, sisters report being emotionally absorbed, taking care of their mothers, and trying to solve a desperate situation.

Veronica, now in her thirties, reports that the last year she lived at home she helped her mother get rid of her violent father. She fought her father. She went to the police and pushed her mother to testify. She stood up in court at thirteen and told a terrible history. And as soon as he was truly gone, fourteen-year-old Veronica left home for the streets, friends' apartments, boyfriends, or shelters. The life of a nomad suited her, she says, "after watching and worrying about my mother and brothers for years. Once he was gone, I could just leave. I didn't have to stay to protect them." For Veronica, "the street" was a welcome change.

The path which Veronica's life took after she left home reflects a maverick spirit—the same spirit which may have been the key to her role in "saving" her family. But she had lost any illusions that adults were there to care for her. While she loved her family ("I would visit them often"), for Veronica safety meant taking her young life into her own hands. She was to become successful in illegal trades and a woman who chose to have and raise her children alone. "The idea of parenting with a man was a joke to me."

As these women shared memories of their hard times, they would catch each other's eyes and nod. Daughters' days in families under extreme trial were known, not merely as individual memories, but as a shared legacy. One which called for another kind of girl to emerge, and she is not a slight, soft girl and she does not always live by the rules.

WHEN MOTHERS FAIL

> *"I have no respect for her, she was drunk and depressed and she left me to my fate."*
> —TWENTY-ONE-YEAR-OLD PAULA,
> 1993 LIFE-HISTORY STUDY

The use of drugs and alcohol by parents, particularly by mothers, was the next most commonly reported family trauma which catapulted girls into early, angry womanhood. Nine of the fifty women interviewed in the Life-History Study who reported that their mothers had problems with alcohol or drugs also reported that their mothers were depressed, mentally ill, or battered. Whether their mothers were incapacitated by substances or paralyzing depression, the girls experienced this as abandonment and they were largely unforgiving. In three cases, where mothers had sought and maintained recovery, with their children also getting help, there was a family reconciliation. But six report that, while they were children, they were sent to live with other family members or to foster care, four of them permanently.

Paula hated her mother's weakness. She grew up knowing she was

the product of her mother's rape and believing that event was the catalyst for her mother's depressions. Now, at twenty-one, she believes her
own experience of being molested by her baby-sitter's son ("My
mother would leave me there even when I was screaming that he hurt
me") and subsequent rapes in her teens were somehow attached to a
stigma, a tattoo that she was a "rape-child . . . not like a 'love-child,'
but a rape-child." Paula has been learning in therapy that her mother
was clearly depressed all her life from her own unresolved abuse experiences and was incapable of protecting her daughter. But learning this
has not changed the contempt she feels toward her mother. "I always
had to be able to cope, 'cause she couldn't. I helped out my brother and
I raised my damn self."

Paula is now raising two-year-old Lucy, by herself. She is going to
community college and trying to deal with her problems. We meet on
a summer day and talk while Lucy plays nearby. Paula watches her
every move. I ask whether she feels she can protect herself and Lucy.
Paula describes the evils, the torments, which will visit any man who
comes near her daughter. Then she calls Lucy over to change her diapers. "Assume the position," she tells her daughter, using the very
words which she has told me haunted her childhood. Lucy lies down
and opens her legs, and her mother gently tends to her. It's a familiar
scene, but her words, even said jokingly, have chilled the summer day.

A daughter's hardest work may be the job of taking over when parents and other adults disappear. The women and girls interviewed for
this book recount that more than the long hours of house chores and
more than unexpected child-care obligations, the demand that a
daughter face adult terrors consumes and changes a girl. Such girls have
little time to focus on school, to build friendships, or to reach out into
the world. They describe themselves as having been lost in crises which
their parents could not manage and that no other grownups had inter-
ceded on their behalf. The majority of girls interviewed did not face this

extreme family life. And some parents who were very disturbed managed to overcome their troubles and restore the family to a balance. But childhood is gone for daughters and sons when they are abandoned to clean up the damage inflicted by an adult world which cannot or will not protect children.

Building Theory: A Different Kind of Girlhood

Shareese, Rosa, Keesha, Monique, Theresa, and Shannon, Girls Project, May, 1994

"If I was to have a daughter," Shareese says, "I wouldn't lock her up like some parents do. If you lock a girl up all the time, like don't let her go out or do anything, she is ready to rebel." Shareese is seventeen and a veteran in this peer group of six girls who are juniors and seniors in high school. She has become very comfortable analyzing the questions which are raised by the adult facilitators. Generally, the other girls agree with her opinions, but they are also willing to take issue with her.

In this day's focus group, the girls are asked how they would raise a daughter; how they would emulate, and how they would differ from their own parents.

Keesha agrees with Shareese. "My grandmother keeps telling my mother I have too much freedom. She's from down South, and she wants my mother to keep me in, busy with the kids and cooking. My mother says, 'No ma, she's got to have her own way a little.' They argue about it."

"That's just the same with us," adds Rosa. "My grandmother came here from Puerto Rico when my mother was ten. She kept my mother on a short leash, I can tell you. My mother fights with her now, she says I should be able to have friends and go out . . . well a little." Theresa, also Puerto Rican agrees, laughing, "Yeah, just a little."

And what, I ask, is the big deal with these girls going out? They laugh indulgently.

Shareese explains: "Parents are always worrying you'll come home with that seed planted inside you. My dad says, 'Now don't you be messing around out there girl. I'm not ready to be a granddaddy.' And I say to him, "You already a granddaddy with Earl's baby.' But they think the baby comes home with the girl, you know, like my brother's girlfriend is raising that baby with her family."

And are they right about that fear of pregnancy?

Shareese keeps going. "Well, girls get pregnant out there for sure. But if a girl is going to be messing around, then so be it." Shareese believes that locking girls up will not stop something as easy to accomplish as "planting a seed." And she believes that the pressures put on girls, to make the right choices, to perform well, to "be good" are a constant theme in many families. "Like, in Black families, the girls are supposed to be dependable, we are supposed to be strong and grown up. But I know that in Rosa's family, it's the same 'cause when I go to her house, it's the same thing there."

Rosa and Shareese are good friends and have been for years. When they go over to Rosa's house, Shareese asks how many chores she has to do and "how many kids are there" because Shareese knows they will be expected to take over the moment they walk in. "I think I play with her little sister more than my brother . . . but she [Rosa] takes him a lot too . . . I guess we trade." At this they both laugh, bickering about whose sibling is a better deal.

Shannon has a piece to say too. "We have to do all the baby-sitting, me and my cousins who are the girls. Like the guys are right outside, sitting on the steps or hanging, you know, and we're supposed to get the kids fed, and keep them in line, pick up after them."

Keesha has another point to make. "My family is always telling me how I have to be a good example to the younger kids. Like I have to show them the right way and if I mess up then they are going to, too.

It's like I have to be a role model all the time." All the other girls agree. Rosa adds, "Especially when you spend so much time raising these kids and then, if you make a mistake . . . like my aunt did. She was like a big sister to me 'cause she is much younger than my mother. And she spent all kinds of time with me, more than anybody. And when she dropped out of school and all and went with this man, it was like she was thrown out of the family. I didn't see her for two years."

Did her "bad example" hurt Rosa? "I just missed her that much. I was eight, and I would go and sit on her stoop even when I knew she was gone. When she came back, I followed her around morning till night. I felt like my own sister had come home." And is it a burden to be a role model?

Rosa is ambivalent. "In some ways it is. You know, you're just a kid yourself and then you're supposed to be thinking about everyone else. But it makes you responsible, too."

But Shareese thinks that having to set an example is a demanding role. "I feel like I am always being criticized. Like what I do is never enough, and I had to stop being a child when I was ten years old." Her friends nod.

Shareese's mother had her third child when Shareese was ten, and the birth of her little brother quickly propelled her into an adult role. When her mother returned to her evening job, Shareese helped with night feedings, diaper changes, and basic baby care. Shareese's stepfather contributed some care, but he worked ten-hour days and would sleep through the baby's crying. Shareese's mother told her she had to "be a big girl now."

In private conversation, Shareese considers this time to mark the end of her childhood. She feels that after she was directed into this "little mother" role, she was never allowed out again. She clearly remembers the night that she began menstruating at the age of twelve. She waited until her mother came home from a hard night of overtime. Her mother was exhausted, but she smiled when she saw Shareese sitting in the rocking chair holding her little brother. When Shareese told her that "the blood has started, Ma," her mother sat down on the couch and started crying. Shareese, unaccustomed to her mother's tears, asked her what was wrong, was something wrong. And her mother just cried. Later she told her daughter that it meant the end of childhood, but Shareese says, "She knew I had already lost that a long time ago." Shareese thinks that was the real cause of her mother's tears, that there was no time left to turn back the clock.

Sometimes, this group of girls agree, too much pressure at home will make a girl run away. If parents are strict, critical, worried about their daughter's every move, and they also expect a lot of help from her, she will "just jet on them." It is a hard kind of girlhood, with little or none of the luxury of time and freedom which some children enjoy. The girls in the group, however, speak wisely and kindly about the experience. They refer to their parents, mostly mothers, with great respect, and in some cases, unabashed love. Keesha speaks openly of hearing "my mother's voice coming to me, and I feel like the sun is warming me just with the sound of her." Keesha's friends smile at her pleasure.

As we pored over the stories of girls, the work they do, it seemed inexorable that family needs dominated their early years. I asked, how could these young women balance the pull toward family work and the need for an education? What I hear from them is the familiar, almost orchestrated, response: "Education is the most important thing in your life." But, I ask, do you all spend a fair amount of time on homework and working with teachers? Do you all plan to go to college? All six in this group are good students, but all agree they do very little homework. Rosa speaks for the group: "They don't give us much homework to do. And when they do, it is really hard to do it. At home, there isn't any place to do it . . . it's loud, and there are so many kids at my house." Keesha adds: "Once I leave this school, I deal with what's out there."

I read a poem to the girls, one written by another Rosa:

"Why I didn't do the homework
Because the phone is ringing
the door is noking
the kid is yumping
the food is burning
time runs fast."[1]

After I read it, the girls nod to each other. "Yeah," Shareese says, *"you got to make up your own words for how it is, 'cause other people's words don't get to it."*

Maribella, Dorchester, 1993 and 1995: "A Success Story"

"She was one of our real successes . . ."
—BOSTON HIGH SCHOOL TEACHER,
1994 HIGH SCHOOL STUDY

Seventeen-year-old Maribella recalls that, during her junior year, she was inundated with advice from her history teacher, her job supervisor in a lab, her mentor, and a youth counselor. She was told to keep up her good grades, prepare to take the SATs, visit and start applying to colleges, and above all, to avoid a pregnancy. Maribella's mother, who was born in Puerto Rico, never directly contradicted these credible adults, but she projected a different message. She was afraid of the prospect of her daughter moving away, even to another part of the city. The idea of Maribella going to an unknown, perhaps unsafe, place kept her mother up at night. She had a ninth grade education, and the imperative of college was unfamiliar to her. It seemed enough, and she was quite proud of the fact, that Maribella was graduating from high school. Furthermore, Maribella's mother was a single parent, and Maribella's salary from the laboratory was needed to supplement the income of the family of four, which included Maribella's two younger sisters. Maribella was a second mother to her younger sisters, one of whom was getting out-of-hand as she entered adolescence.

One youth counselor has dubbed the dynamic which occurred in Maribella's family "the subtle sabotage." It emerges as a successful daughter moves toward the end of high school, when parents who have always been very supportive of all opportunities which have come to their daughters begin to withdraw their support. For Maribella, as is often the case, the sabotage doesn't stop with parents.

Maribella's boyfriend, Ediberto, almost twenty, was hoping to find a decent job after finishing a youth program in the construction trades. He was ambivalent about Maribella's plans to go to college and become a teacher of special-needs children. While he was very proud of accomplished Maribella, college was a world he did not know. He admitted to his own counselor that he feared that college might change Maribella. She might meet other men, or she might begin to view herself as being better than Ediberto. He had struggled to graduate from high school, not so much academically, but against the pull of a group of his friends who had dropped out to "work the free market." Ediberto's counselor had worked with him to focus on his own considerable success and not to thwart Maribella. But the counselor also confided that he was worried. "This is a perfect setup for a birth control 'accident' which would settle her life."

Maribella's two close girlfriends were split on the subject of her future plans. Her lifelong friend told Maribella that she was a fool to "play with this" when she had a wonderful man who respected her. Her more recent friend, also a successful student, told Maribella to "hold onto what you want, 'cause no one else will get you there but you."

Maribella speaking about her own desires is a cascade of contradictions. She moves back and forth between people she loves and respects. She speaks of loyalty, obligations, and hopes, spinning out a picture that is discordant and complex. She believes she will have to pick between people or, what is more poignant, between versions of her life. Her own version has not yet emerged.

Postscript on Maribella: Two Years Later

Maribella finished high school well and entered a local college to study nursing, a field with more loans and scholarships available than in special-needs education. She remained living at home and she kept her job in the laboratory, working on weekends and during school vacations. Her relationship with Eddie continued but became strained as he was unable to find employment and Maribella was busy all the time.

After Maribella received low grades in the second term of her first year, which annulled her scholarship, she dropped out of nursing school. "I was a good student in high school," she tells me, "but I was not prepared for college. I had to take remedial math and science to continue. I couldn't keep up, my grades dropped down."

During the year Maribella was in nursing school, one of her younger sisters ran into trouble. She was skipping school and had befriended some tough, court-involved peers. When she returned to full-time work in the laboratory, Maribella was able to be home in the evenings and on weekends to help her mother cope with her sisters. But four months later, Maribella found she was pregnant. Eddie was delighted at first, but gradually he became despondent. He was still unable to get employment, and he was no longer eligible for a youth counselor. Believing him to be in danger of getting into serious trouble, Eddie's family and Maribella convinced him to enter the military.

Maribella had to leave her job at the lab because the chemicals were making her constantly ill. She gave birth to her daughter Milagros early in 1995. Six months later, her seventeen-year-old sister had a baby boy.

Maribella was delighted with her beautiful daughter, and she is helping her mother raise her little nephew, whose own young mother is not up to it. Maribella says, "He is like my baby's brother, really." Maribella has been depressed over the way things worked out and now feels resentful of Eddie's absence. But she is also positive that she will go back to school. By the end of 1995, she was taking remedial math and applying for financial aid to return. And maybe she will go back.

Ms. Nelson, Maribella's high school mentor, believes that Maribella would have succeeded at college and earned a specials-needs education degree. She believes Maribella would have terminated a "good but adolescent" relationship with Eddie and avoided early motherhood, "given half a chance." She has no patience with what she considers a simpleminded political response to the problems of girls like Maribella. "It's a pass-the-blame-around game. Blame her mother, or her sister, or her father. We all know the whole family is up against odds you can't beat."

Her tenure as mentor is over, but Ms. Nelson has decided to stay in Maribella's life. She is Milagros's godmother. "I want to see that girl get rid of all the weight people have put on her, see her and that baby have a chance."

Like Ms. Nelson, others who serve as mentors, teachers, and youth counselors, have come to the conclusion that relentless forces are at work in these girls' lives. Ms. Nelson believes that the demand for daughters' work is economic, the result of a lack of money. Where there are no nannies, no cars, no child-care centers, no washers or dryers or dishwashers, no vacations, no house cleaners, no takeout dinners, a daughter's labor must substitute. As Arlette says, "How do you think all that gets done?" Girls do it alongside women. Many of them are good at running homes and are proud of their competence. Many of them are counselors, advocates, translators, and mediators all rolled into one young and invisible girl. "They don't notice us till we get pregnant," said a fifteen-year-old I met in a Boston middle school.

WOMEN BUILDING THEORY ABOUT GIRLHOOD

While conducting my final review of data collected in the High School Study and Girl's Project survey and focus group, I sought out the counsel of other women. We met in two Interpretive Focus Groups made up of parents, social workers, and teachers who are working with girls in the Boston schools. These were easygoing discussions; some women brought experiences from their own lives into the mix, while others focused on daughters, nieces, students, or girls they see daily.

Most of the women were intrigued by the data. "It seems we bring our girls up to be strong, but that's no news," remarked Letitia, an African American woman in her thirties. "It seems though that we maybe bring them up to put other people before themselves, and that's something to think about."

Many daughters, we concluded, are family workers whose contribution is critical, who actually help raise families alongside their parents and thus support the life of the community. This conclusion reflects literature which examines family survival strategies, a discussion which is particularly well articulated in the African American community.[2] Sharing the care of kin-children, where daughters help take care of siblings and the children of adult relations or siblings, is a well-known practice that crosses over to many different cultures and communities. But the effects upon *daughters' lives*, the obvious and insidious ways in which this family role may influence and limit their future, seem largely ignored.

Many parents, at a loss for other kinds of support, may be unknowing conspirators in the forced maturation of little girls. Yet, parents may also want to hold them back, afraid of the consequences of a truncated childhood. As Marianna, who is Puerto Rican, asked, "If we make them grow up quick 'cause childhood is just a luxury, how come we're so shocked that they get ready to move out, move on, and make families of their own?"

Our Interpretive Focus Groups considered the contradictory messages which face low-income girls. A "good girl" is obedient to her parents' wishes and needs. If her family is under great stress, those needs are great. And meeting them will require her to play an adult role. Once the trouble is past, the discussants observed, parents often want their "girls to get back in their place," but it may be too late. Girls who have been managing the troubles of an adult world are in an important sense no longer children and often cannot resume the place of a child.

Deborah, a white woman of thirty-five, suggested that some of the early responsibilities were good in that they made low-income girls a lot more self-reliant and resilient than their middle-class counterparts. From a vantage of observing different "branches" of her own family, a middle-class branch and the more low-income roots, she believes that many middle-class children, both white kids and kids of color, are immature and are taught to think about nothing but themselves. She believes that the motto of the middle class is to put yourself first and that middle-class children have been encouraged to "forget about others, even step on others because that will get you ahead in America." She thinks the responsibilities of low-income children toward their families actually build stronger families. "I love the part about all the sibling connections," she said. "My [Italian] family expected us to love and care for each other . . . when we weren't fighting. I see so many kids in suburban schools, they hate their siblings, they were never taught that you stand by your people." This statement evoked some protests.

For example, one twenty-four-year-old African American woman, Vanessa, pointed out, "If you are taught to put everybody before yourself, how do you ever get out? How do you achieve something? And look at where it gets you. I always think of Clarence Thomas and his sister . . . Emma Mae [Martin]. Look where he got to, and she stays home with sick relatives and kids . . . and she's just another black woman living on the dole." Muttering, she added, "And he goes on and marries a white woman at that." The group laughed with her.

Most of the African American and Latino women in the Interpretive Focus Groups were emphatic that this early training in taking care of the family is emphasized in communities of color, where the economic experience of being "put outdoors" as Nobel Laureate Toni Morrison has expressed it, is exaggerated by racism. An African American woman, DeVita, summarized: "You are told that the white world is going to cut you down . . . not in so many words maybe, but you know it before you're off that milk bottle. So you've got to stand by your own. Survival is on your back. But some of this is really sick, you know." Nearly two decades ago, Joyce Ladner found that "Black females are socialized by adult figures in early life to be strong, independent women, who because of precarious circumstances growing out of poverty and racism, might eventually have to become heads of their own households."[3] Common talk in Boston neighborhoods certainly supports her finding today.

One adolescent member of the group, Shanda, spoke of the African American community as "counting our riches in our people, not in all the things that suburban [middle-class white] people want." She went on to explain that this is related to placing great value on children. Vanessa, who is also African American, but older, understood this young woman and the "race pride" behind her words, but she winced as she heard them. "When I see some young girls with their babies, I think they bought a bill of goods. How can that be good for that girl and that baby? We need to make another way for them."

Helene, a Jamaican woman, who has raised three daughters as a low-income single mother, regarded the issue to be one of "family values." By this she meant the backward message many families give to their daughters about their place in the world. This woman believes the real damage done to girls is that their relationships, and not their education, are emphasized at home. "Like your research says, we always tell them how they have to be a helper, have to be strong and carry on. We are hard on them because they have to be role models for other kids. But we don't spend enough time telling them that they need to go to college, to get a profession . . . like that Maribella . . . she should tell *everybody* else to get lost." But she added reflectively, "I know she couldn't bring herself to do that . . . *it would be a betrayal.*" This

woman went on to speak of the contradictions which play out in female lives. She described the pressures from inside, to embody the family and culture, and those from outside, to be successful according to
external measures, standards that have to do with individual achievement. She believes girls have to understand both and somehow juggle
all of it.

And is all this connected to early sexual activity and early pregnancy?

"Of course it is," Pilar, a Latino woman of twenty-eight responded,
almost angrily. "If what you've been taught is how to care for kids, how
to run a house on nothing, and that's what everyone has valued in you,
what do you expect?" Her answer reminded us of Arlette, whose pregnancy was antithetical to her religious family. She had admitted that, if
she was going to be taking care of family and children anyway, why not
have the baby be her own? Fanning the sleeping Damika in her carriage, Arlette had murmured, "At least she is mine."

Carol, a white woman who taught in a Boston high school, referred
to family demands on girls as the "over-scheduled daughter syn-
drome." She has worked for years in a city school which has been slated
for renovations and has deteriorated all the while. Determined not to
lose her educational goals, despite the battered conditions in which she
teaches, Carol had attempted to work with several teenagers on a literary journal. Many girls signed up, but their scheduling conflicts, most
of which arose from family obligations, were astonishing. Carol told
me that these racially and ethnically diverse girls truly seemed to want
to be involved, and that they came to the literary project meetings
whenever they could, but that the time they actually had to contribute
was simply not enough to keep the project afloat. Carol has come to
believe that *time* in the lives of young low-income people, time to pursue their own interests, talents, and aspirations, is the ultimate luxury.

Years after these focus groups were concluded, I listened to the same tale told by Blanca Bonilla, a Puerto Rican woman and family center coordinator, who was developing a softball team for young Latinas in Boston. It was a cultural coup to get these young girls onto an athletic team, Blanca told me. "They tried so hard, they showed up so regularly. But you know, one of our best players would bring *three children* under the age of four to every game and every practice." This girl of fourteen had complete responsibility for these little cousins every day of the summer, while their parents worked. "If they couldn't come, she couldn't play. If one was sick, she didn't play. I believe we need child care for any activity which these girls are involved in, or they won't be there. And then, they don't get a chance."

Liliana Silva, who served as facilitator for girls' groups in this study and has worked with urban girls for many years, suggests that many of the popular youth organizations are actually built around boys' lives. They are structured on the assumption that, if you get the youth to leave the pull of peers behind, you've won the major battle. But she argues, many girls don't have to struggle to free themselves from the "pull of street." Instead, they come connected to so many other lives that it seems as though you are managing a small nation, not working with one girl. And down to the bone, this may be true for many. The roles they fill in their families are often so multi-layered that it is hard to distinguish this one girl from the people and obligations that surround her.

VALIDATING DAUGHTERS' WORK

There is little scholarly research which either explores the theme or quantifies the extent of daughters' labor in contemporary, low-income America. In fact, as some economists and feminists have long argued, the labor of family-keeping is universally ignored in any broad economic discourse. The work of caring for people in families is sometimes conversation at the margin of serious policy, maybe acknowledged, but quickly shelved as serious discussion gets underway. Yet some research has theorized that "housework" alone is labor which, without any monetary value attached to it and largely woven into the female (and thus free) workload, remains a massive but invisible economic variable.[4] The cost in both time and dollars has been variously estimated as larger than a total national product or in any case, on average, as larger than the value of an average male income.[5] If you add to housework the work of kin-care, not only of child raising but also of elder and sick family care, the actual value of such family labor—should such work have to be purchased on the open market—would topple any economy. Yet, as feminist theorists have noted, "caregiving is the quintessential piece of women's unpaid work."[6]

In analyzing the ways in which "caring" is work which has long been socially assigned to women, Margery Garrett Spring Rice argues that this labor transcends the gender-role division. Based upon research with working-class women, she points out that "caring is not simply something women do for themselves, to achieve femininity. It is something women do for others, to keep them alive."[7] Janet Finch and Dulcie Groves suggest that what particularly characterizes the nature of family labor is that such work is without a standard and responds to the changing needs of others. It is an "unspecific and unspecifiable kind of labour, the contours of which shift constantly."[8] Because such work is dedicated to the well-being and development of people, there are no particular rules or plans. It is whatever must be done to keep people healthy and safe and to manage the world around them.

In poor America, keeping people safe and families intact is excessively difficult. It is often more than one mother can manage. Beyond the material hardships and the upheavals which take place far more frequently in low-income families, publicly aided families must also incorporate considerable time every week into meeting the regulatory demands of state structures. Meeting eligibility requirements, monitoring the moving target of changing legislation, managing the case-review demands of housing, health, food stamps, and income assistance are all part of poor family labor. It must be so because without such work done routinely and accurately, there is no family left to care for.

My work suggests that it is often daughters who, after mothers, contribute much of this uncounted work. It is often daughters who accompany little children to the long waits at health clinics, who help parents fill out ever-changing forms or translate paperwork, or who stay home to be there when the public-housing manager finally comes to fix the toilet. It is often daughters who seek out the offices and advocates to get access to special programs, tutors, and summer camps. Along with my colleagues, I have watched hundreds of young people throughout Boston spending time pursuing subsidized opportunities for themselves, for other siblings, and even for parents. These are tasks which make family life possible. But they take up considerable time, and the outstanding cost lies in what girls *cannot do*, while they are "taking care of business."

In examining the dropout behavior of urban youth, Michelle Fine and Nancie Zane report that, while both girls and boys in low-income urban America drop out at a higher rate than other youth, girls report more "family concerns" as the cause of their detachment from school. Specifically they report that 37 percent of the female dropouts cited family issues as the cause of disconnecting from school, while this was true for only 5 percent of the male dropouts.[9] Others who have focused upon the connection between dropping out and childbearing have noted that many girls leave school first and become pregnant later, suggesting that they were already detaching from schooling as a pathway to adulthood. While dropping out of school largely has been viewed as juvenile delinquency, this research suggests that girls may be caught between the demands of family needs and the institutionalized demands of the larger world.

Certainly, with no national value assigned to the family labor provided even by middle-class American women in "nuclear" families which reproduce that most heralded of family forms, it is not surprising that such labor is entirely overlooked in the lives of low-income girls. Yet keeping families going in the face of unending hardship is labor which is essential to low-income community survival. Alongside overworked parents, invisible girls take care of family life in poor America, and they do so at no small cost to themselves.

CHAPTER TWO

Boyfriends, Love, and Sex

"We've been talking about telling the truth about having sex . . . not just talking trash. Like last time we said that we don't know when we're ready for sex, that guys hit on us and girlfriends say, 'It's sooo this and that.' And like, parents say, 'It's sin, you're too young' . . . and the movies show it all pretty and perfect . . . and we don't know what's going on . . ."

—SIXTEEN-YEAR-OLD TARA, 1993 HIGH SCHOOL STUDY

Love, boyfriends, and sexuality are topics which dominated the adolescent girl talk that underlies these studies. During structured interviews, in long rambling walks down city streets, and in group discussions led by the girls, these themes insistently emerged. While girls spoke of their dreams and longings, they also grappled with the everyday world of adolescent life in America, with life in school hallways and on "the street." Most conversation about intimacy outside of family life became talk about sex. Similar to the gender division of labor in the household described by most girls, were the clear-cut differences in the rules of courting behavior for boys and girls. Girls described being taught by adult family members about how girls should behave, what they should expect, and what they must guard against. Extra-familial intimacy and love were largely articulated by girls as romantic and sexual love. Friendship, often a cornerstone in girls' lives, was casually referenced as a backdrop for the real drama, the epic relationship with men.

Girls spoke of love as dangerous, of boys as "dogs" and "gangbangers," and of sexually predatory behavior. Even so, they longed for a boyfriend who would be different, who would "be there for me." Clearly reflecting family lore, they spoke at length about female roles, describing what a woman must face, must demand, and must accommodate when she is with a man. Their description of men was of powerfully sexual creatures, who have impulses beyond their control and are led by "raging hormones." Yet they also described boys as vulnerable, even childlike. Many girls spoke as though it were understood that most of the work of maintaining a relationship was women's work, along with child and family work.

Adolescent girls detailed a context for their sexual development. They described a social environment in which sexuality is emphasized and attractiveness is considered *the* critical female asset. Culture, race, and one's status in a group were factors which influenced their idea of attractiveness. Strong and "healthy" girls, particularly African American and Irish, eschewed "wimpy" and very feminine images. Other girls, Black, white, and Latina, expressed strong judgments about girls who did not dress up, put on makeup, or spend time and money on their appearance. The picture of pretty was not universal, but concern about being attractive seemed to be.

There was much ambivalence about attracting males too, a longing to attract and a sense of peril intertwined. Girls talked of other girls who dare you, of boys who sometimes woo and sometimes threaten you. They spoke of God's judgment, of a grandmother's virtue, of "guys with tight butts." They spun out tales of juggling pressures and peers while seeking out their own way. Always present in these coming-of-age stories was the elusive notion of having a choice.

"When is a girl ready for a boyfriend?" "Why does a girl decide to have sex?" "When is she really ready?" "Was it her choice?" The answers of girls and women to these kinds of questions were convoluted. As girls and women described it, developing into a woman was complex and contradictory. It involved mediating the moral teachings of adults, the influence of friends, daily life in a sex-charged youth culture, and one's own curiosity, fears, and desire. One seventeen-year-old said, "I think that it was me who decided that day, but you know, I

knew he wanted to so bad and . . . if I wanted to keep him. I would hear
my grandmother's voice in my head saying 'They are just after one
thing, you give it and it's gone.' But I loved him . . . so it was me, but it
wasn't me . . . if you understand."

For this young woman, as for many others, the desire to possess a
boyfriend was transcendent in this period of life. It was a transitional
period, a time when ties to family were naturally strained, and many
girls were chaffing at the ongoing demands which their low-income
families placed upon them. A desire for "someone who is there for me,"
someone who sought them out as an individual, who pulled them away
from those family ties was a powerful draw. As they described it,
boyfriends represented a tangible way to separate, a discernible egress,
a way actually to *become* someone else.

TaShawna, Brenda, Elana, Tara, Noel, and Felicia: High School Study, November 1993

"We like to talk about sex here 'cause it's on our minds," TaShawna
tells me. She has a wicked, "I'm-gonna-shock-you," gleam in her eye.
TaShawna is sixteen, African American, and a junior in a Boston public high school. She speaks her mind and is highly respected in this six-
member girls' group. Facilitated by Liliana Silva, these young women
have been meeting weekly since the fall of 1993, when they began their
junior year, and will continue to meet until most graduate in 1995.

"You like to talk about sex," Brenda responds, "but some of us
have more thoughts on our minds." Brenda is sixteen also, Irish American and equally outspoken. TaShawna and Brenda roll their eyes at
each other. They have been through this before. Usually, it is humor-
ous, eloquent Noel who will step in and mediate their power play.
Noel, born of Jamaican parents, identifies herself as "just Black and a
human being, if anyone needs to know." But today it is Elana who intervenes in her self-deprecating way. "I like to talk about anything. I
just like to be in the group." Elana is white, sixteen, but she looks

three years younger. She reveals her neediness so publicly it embar-rasses the other young women. They are protective of her and often say "you're all right Elana," but without conviction. Liliana and the girls have grown to suspect that Elana has been sexually abused, that maybe it's still going on.

Leaning into the group circle, her face open and lit with a full smile, TaShawna reinstates her challenge. "Well, I am not ashamed to be in-terested in sex and I'm not ashamed to admit it."

Tara, TaShawna's cousin and also a junior, speaks next with quiet authority. "But we've been talking about telling the truth about having sex . . . not just talking trash. Like last time we said that we don't know when we're ready for sex, that guys hit on us and girlfriends say, 'It's sooo this and that.' And like, parents say, 'It's sin, you're too young' . . . and the movies show it all pretty and perfect . . . and we don't know what's going on . . ."

Tara has been in a loving and long-term relationship with a boyfriend. That relationship and Tara have become something of a model for the other girls. This day, Tara sits very still as she speaks, looking at no one in particular. Only Liliana knows she is pregnant, and she wonders whether Tara is quietly preparing to tell the group.

In the responses of hundreds of young women and girls, three themes about love and sex prevailed. First, girls expressed the opinion that most female sexual induction is more a response to social and male pressure than it is an expression of physical desire or autonomy. Most girls, and many grown women too, believe that females are socialized to accommodate sexual pressure, and that to withstand that pressure well into adolescent years, one must become something of an outsider.

Many of the girls who participated in this research gave accounts of a persistent sexual pressure, a kind of hypersexual pubescence. As older teens described it, youngsters are pushed by youth entertainment, by peers, and even by inappropriate adult behavior to identify themselves as sexual while still very young. Some girls ". . . go straight from dolls to sex; there's nothing in between." These little girls, a sixteen-year-old said, "have no sense at all. They're nine, ten—real babies—and then they're all dressed up in sexy stuff, talking trash."

This young woman's view was shared by many. In the variety of data gathered, girls described an environment in which early sexual-ization seems to be universal. One focus group of eight sixteen- and seventeen-year-olds put together a list of ever-present sexual influences in their lives. These included youth music, youth television, movies, girls' clothing, everyday advertising, common conversations, and just walking down the corridors of their high school as "all filled with sex." They also identified much of this presentation as being deceptive. "These kids [watching television] see the lights get all soft and [the actors] are getting all hot and it's all perfect and pretty. They say 'I want to get me some.' But there are no condoms or fumbling or anything . . . it's all fake."

Girls also asserted that sexual abuse is prevalent. Childhood abuse, molestation by strangers, and date or peer rape were regarded as force-ful elements in the sexual landscape which a girl must manage. The risk of sexual abuse was seen as an inherent part of a girl's sexual develop-ment.

Above all other themes, however, the prevailing power was the longing for a boyfriend. Despite their agreement that sexual accom-modation is expected, despite an ever-present awareness that sexually abusive males around, girls sought a partner. Most regarded this quest, with all the pitfalls known and the losses anticipated, as worth almost any cost.

SEXUAL ACCOMMODATION

Many girls talked about a paradox, an essential discord between young male and young female social-sexual imperatives. Girls, they pointed out, face the age-old judgment that "good" girls should withhold sex. Boys, on the other hand, are supposed to "hit" or "score," and often, in order to establish themselves as men. "It's a man's world out there," many girls said. "She's a whore and he's a man for doing just the same thing." "Society is two-faced, but we've got to live with it." "Girls got to value their bodies, guys don't have to care, it's like notches in their belts." "If you want him to stay, you don't have a choice. If you're not giving to him, someone else will." Girls expressed this fundamental conflict in gender imperatives in dozens of ways, but the consensus was that, if you want to be with boys, who must themselves prove their manhood, you will have to "give-over."

Despite general agreement among girls that these rules are unjust, many saw little way around them. As one girl said, "I don't know who wrote the rules, but they suck. But if you want to play, that's the way it is." Accommodating the sexual demands of a male, whether they arise from physical needs ("you know, their hormones are raging") or from the male's need to affirm his status among his peers, is thought to be common female practice.

And there was little mercy for *anyone* in these rules. One sixteen-year-old wrote: "A guy, to be a real guy, is always 'supposed' to have more sex. They get praised for it, it's their ego. Girls are 'supposed' to remain faithful. It isn't fair." And a seventeen-year-old wrote: "A guy's reputation is built on his sexual promiscuity. He's nothing without it."

What is rare is an expression of rebellion against these gender rules. Some tried to turn the rules upside-down: "Guys brag about it, they have a mouth so they brag. If a woman has sex with more than one guy, we call her loose. Guys don't have to worry about that. Guys think it's a man thing, but a woman could do the same. They could go brag like the guys . . . until women backfire, it'll always be the same." A few girls attempted to construct sexual abstinence as a message of independence, framing it as a religious conviction or a strong family belief. One sixteen-year-old, Patricia, who felt socially isolated by her abstinent status, eventually turned abstinence into part of her social identity and won respect for her ability to not "follow the flock." Other girls, like TaShawna, openly acknowledged enjoying sex and rejected the idea that this was a sign of female immorality or an acquiescence to become "somebody's thing." The girls who declared their own sexual terms were also more likely to express positive attitudes about males and about themselves as young women. Whether abstinent or active, clarifying one's own choice seemed the healthy place to be.

Regardless of their attitude toward these gender rules, most of the girls who participated in this three-year study talked about having sex in the context of rules. And the rules, even if unfair, were accepted by most. One fourteen-year-old wisely wrote on a survey, "I think guys are praised when they have sex because it is this 'man thing' and if a guy is a virgin, he gets teased. They have to lie. *Guys need something to make them feel like they're somebody.*" Finding something to make you "be somebody" is sometimes hard for these young people, both young women and young men. Some girls, who recognized the world was largely empty of opportunity for many male peers, understood themselves sometimes to be the "booty," the prize which asserted male power. Older women who reviewed this data asserted that, while they understood the complexity these girls report about relationships with boys, acquiescence was "dangerous play." Above all, what emerged is that these girls live in a nest of pressures, and many women see a boy's need to assert power through sex as reflected in a girl's need to gain socially and to separate from family through a romantic and sexual relationship.

A common attitude girls expressed toward the sexual act was ambivalence. Of the over one hundred sexually active girls who participated in the Girls Project, 60 percent said that they were "not ready" to have sex when they first started. Many of these young women acknowledged that they did not really enjoy sex, that they had sex to gain or appease a boyfriend and to fit in with their peers.

The girls and women in the Interpretive Focus Groups who examined the Girls Project responses were not at all surprised by them. They regarded sexual appeasement as very common behavior for girls and women. While they considered appeasement to be very different from being forced to have sex, they were also troubled by the impact of sexual accommodation. As one forty-year-old woman said, "When my daughter was putting up with his shit, his abuse you know, I was mad at her 'cause I knew it was bad for her respect and my granddaughter was learning that it was, like, this is OK . . . but I know she seen me put up with it too, so who am I to tell her what a woman should do?"

Debbie, Dorchester, 1994

> "Being ready doesn't always matter. It's not like you say, 'Today, I'm ready.'"

Debbie is a twenty-two-year-old student at Bunker Hill Community College when she agrees to talk with me. She tells me, "You can use my name and everything about me because I want people to know." I tell her that I will tell her story truthfully but that I'm not comfortable identifying her. "That's OK," Debbie says. "My thing is, if this can help some other girls out there, to not go through all of this."

We decide to walk around the Bunker Hill monument, but by the end of three hours we have covered most of Charlestown. By 1994, walking has become a common way to spend time with a woman who wants to talk.

Debbie comes from a struggling working-class family. Her parents had "a typical marriage, I think. They didn't like each other that much. They got married when he was nineteen and she was eighteen and being Catholics and all . . . you just stick it out." Debbie remembers being a big, strong girl, "a tomboy." Her older sister was responsible for baby-sitting and housework when her mother worked. Her father, who was employed in the limping Massachusetts manufacturing industry, was periodically out of work. During his unemployed stints, he did little with his daughters. "Maybe if he'd had a boy he might have spent more time with us, but maybe that was just his excuse." Debbie thinks that maybe she tried to be the boy. Her older sister was in the mother-back-up role, and her younger sister was always "the baby." Debbie remembers trying out for every sport and "hanging with the guys a lot more than other girls did."

Debbie tells me her mother was not a happy woman. She discovered that her mother had been abused as a child and thinks this experience may have been the root of her depression. But then again, "I mean living with my father is enough to make anyone depressed." Debbie's father would drink more when he was unemployed and "he was a mean drunk." She explains that her father did not batter his family, but he would "slap my mother around . . . and if we got in the way he'd wail on us too." So, why didn't she consider him to be a batterer? "Well, it's not like we ended up in the hospital like other mothers did. My uncle, my father's brother, *he* used to batter. He sent my aunt to the hospital twice a year at least."

Debbie says her parents became increasingly angry with her when, in the eighth grade, she began to do poorly in school and started drinking and taking drugs. Her family was "the churchgoing kind, every Sunday, all dressed up and talking to everyone. They were ashamed of me 'cause people knew I was getting bombed and staying out."

Debbie thinks of a high school sports coach as one of the only adults who ever really reached out to her. He seemed to recognize that Debbie was walking on thin ice. He also recognized her potential for success in almost any team sport. "He told me that I was a team player, that I didn't showboat or act all stupid. I loved the feeling of a team, together. I quit smoking and drinking that year 'cause of him."

When Debbie was a sophomore, her older sister graduated from high school, got married to her new boyfriend, and moved to the army base where he was stationed. Before she left, she told Debbie that it was her turn to take responsibility, that she had to "stop being such a flake now."

Debbie admits that she had no idea how much of a help her sister had been to the family, until her departure. When Debbie assumed the second-mother role, she had to drop two of four sports, watch her little sister most afternoons, and prepare dinner for her family. She hated being home. "All I did was sit on the couch and pig out," she tells me. Being able to remain on the softball and basketball teams might have sustained her, except that "all my parents did was say how I was a slug, a slack-off. And then, I was getting fatter, you know, and so I didn't play as well. So my team lost confidence and the coach was disappointed." When I point out to Debbie that she seems to regard these losses as being all her fault, she admits that she tended to give credit to her team and take the blame on herself. "That's one of the things my shrink has been making me think about," she says, "how I think I'm to blame."

Toward the end of that sophomore year, Debbie became sexually active but not as a result of sexual desire. "The 'desire,' if you call it that, was to be with a guy and hang with him, and we'd get a high and . . . I was happy around guys. We'd horse around and play rough. I guess sex just goes with that." Does she think that she was ready for sex when she first started? Debbie tells me that "being ready" is a pretty obscure idea. "Being ready doesn't always matter. It's not like you say, 'Today, I'm ready . . . Yippee!" She sees the transition from being "a virgin" to being a sexually active fifteen-year-old as a chain of events, not as a cataclysmic moment. "If you want a boyfriend, you want him to be with you, you got to have sex with him sooner or later. Be real."

Debbie's boyfriend was a drinker and she joined in. She failed her sophomore year, losing not only her classmates but also her identity as an athlete. Her parents, completely disgusted with their middle child and convinced she would be a bad influence on her younger sister, told her that she would have to leave home as soon as she turned eighteen.

Then her sister's marriage broke up, and "the perfect daughter" returned home with a baby. "It sucked, it really did."

Overwhelmed by her memories, Debbie begins to cry. We have walked all the way to the Charles River. I ask if she might want to stop and get something to eat. Through tears, she laughs at me. "Don't you know that using food to take away bad feelings is how you get fat?" she says. Mindlessly, I answer that it's better than drinking and then try to grab the words back. But Debbie is ahead of me. "Yeah," she agrees, "it is better than drinking, but you don't *have* to do either of them, if you get well."

Debbie dropped out of high school at sixteen. She had two abortions that year and started to have suicidal fantasies. Her parents, perhaps shocked by how extreme Debbie's situation had become and sobered by their older daughter's divorce, encouraged Debbie to get some help. Within a year, she began seeing a counselor. She went to AA meetings and took a part-time job at the "Y," helping the coaches with the younger children. She loved working with the girls who were self-conscious about their athletic abilities. "I would spot the fat, clumsy ones right away. I just couldn't wait to get them into it."

Since that time, Debbie has received her GED, moved out of her parents' house and in with her (now divorced) aunt, and has started working toward an associate's degree in sports medicine. She still works at the "Y" and, on occasion, she still attends AA meetings. She is a crusader against drugs and alcohol and has "gone on the school circuit" to tell youngsters how easy it is to get into trouble.

And sex? Debbie holds on to her belief that boys, men too, are not interested in a girl unless she is sexually accommodating. She points out that even good guys will try to hit on you when they know they really shouldn't. I ask what she means. She offers as an example that one of the alcohol counselors at the teen center had tried to "hit on her" for sex. *While she was going to her appointments at the center, a male coun-*

selor had tried to date her? Debbie smiles at my surprise. Dating, she tells me is a polite way of putting it. And did she tell anyone? Debbie told the other girls to avoid him, but they had all known about him already. It happens, she tells me, it's everywhere. But what about the girls who don't know how to handle a grown man who is an authority figure and wants to exploit them? Debbie says it the hard way this time, "They get fucked every which way, what do you think?"

Later that day, I ask Debbie about sex for pleasure. She says she has not yet had much sexual pleasure and that, with help, she has decided to try to avoid having a boyfriend for a while. "But," she tells me, "if you want a boyfriend, and who doesn't, you give it to him because, if you don't, someone else will."

Usually when I shared Debbie's story with groups of other women and girls, they seemed to know it by heart. Debbie, a white girl from a two-parent, semi-employed family, was as familiar as the face in a mirror to other girls, white girls, girls of color, girls who had grown up on welfare. But when I related Debbie's experience to the High School Group that included TaShawna and Brenda, I got mixed reactions.

TaShawna was impatient with Debbie's acquiescence to sex when "she didn't even get off." This time, Brenda agreed with her. "Not me, no, I wouldn't be sleeping with a guy if I didn't like it, what's with that?" "Those parents teach their girls to please," TaShawna said, "and then you end up with this weak girl who can't say no."

Noel considered the issue to be more complicated. "Lots of girls we know give in to the pressure when they convince themselves they 'just loooove that man.' They say, 'Oh, oh, it's so great, now he's *my man*.' But it's a lie and we're telling it to ourselves." An out-of-the-closet virgin, at seventeen, Noel says that she will "make love" when she is good and ready and that the man has to be a "hero," a man whom she can trust and believe in. Her friends tell her "good luck," but Noel, who has a voracious appetite for romance novels and writes about a world without racism or bullies, is holding fast. Ever provocative, she adds, "And I don't care if he is Black, white, or red as blood, it's his insides I care about."

TaShawna finds this pretty disgusting. "You'd do it with a white man?" she snorts. Reminded that there are white people in the conversation, TaShawna faces them directly. "I don't mean offense, it's just that I think no self-respecting Black woman would." Her friends challenge her. "You're really prejudiced, you know. You say it's just your personal feeling, but it's prejudice." Brenda intervenes on TaShawna's behalf. "Hey, you know what my father would do to me if he thought I was dating a Black kid? He'd kill us both."

It is Noel who has the last word. "So, since when do we have to believe everything that our parents do?"

SEXUAL ABUSE: "GIRLS WHO ARE CRAVING"

Another theme lurking in teen dialogue about their sexual world was the belief that sexual abuse is commonplace. These adolescent girls believed that predatory male behavior was all around and that vigilance, first on the part of parents and then by girls themselves, was critical. They saw incest and childhood sexual abuse, though more rare than date rape, as the most damaging to girls. Sexual abuse, they said, produces "rag doll girls" or "craving girls," girls who are particularly vulnerable. One-time attacks or rapes were regarded as a constant danger for girls. These assaults were seen as sometimes avoidable and sometimes not. "You know where to walk and where not to walk," a fifteen-year-old told us. "But even still, my home-girl got jumped just by some guys in a van. Now, what's she supposed to do, stay locked inside?"

In the Girls Project, seventeen girls (almost 7 percent of the group) responded that they had "had sex" before the age of thirteen; twelve indicated they had experienced sex before the age of twelve. This is very likely an under-representation because the question which elicited this information asked about "the first time you had sex" and not about sexual abuse. In a follow-up focus group, several girls advised that they would have answered this question only about voluntary sex, not about incest or forced sexual contact. In the fifty Life-History interviews, 14 percent reported being raped as children. The perpetrators of sexual abuse whom women and girls faced were largely men who had easy access to them and who chose to exploit them. These men included a (white Irish) father who was an alcoholic, a (Latino) father who molested three of his daughters, an (African American) grandfather who baby-sat for his daughter's little girl. Also included were a (Latino) uncle, a (Haitian) brother-in-law, and two (one white and one African American) boyfriends of girls' mothers. Outside the family, abusers often turned out to be men who were in positions of authority over women and girls, including a minister, a (male) welfare official, a van driver who drove children to a special-needs program, the son of a baby-sitter, the building manager in a federal housing project, a foster father in the home where a girl was placed by the state, a vocational education teacher for teen welfare recipients, and a drug rehabilitation counselor.

Girls and women did report stranger assaults, as well. One eleven-year-old was gang-raped by men who came to the house where she was baby-sitting. A nine-year-old was raped on her way home from school. Another was raped in the hall of the apartment building when she went out to get her cat. One sixteen-year-old was raped on a dirt road in Alabama. And the list goes on.

When this grim information was presented to groups of women and girls, the response was quiet assent. It happens, they would respond, it happens all the time, to girls and to women everywhere, that is anywhere predatory men can get away with it. And are these girls, who live in low-income communities, any more at risk than other girls?

Some debate whether this question can be fairly answered. An activist on human rights recently challenged me to consider the social construction of child abuse. When middle-class people hurt their children, she argued, the cleanup crew is a cadre of well-paid doctors and therapists. Their cleanup work goes into privately held records of family pathology. "The middle class can white-wash their sins to the grave," she told me. When I shared this woman's comments with others, many agreed that this bias exists. One young woman pointed out that, when a wealthy businessman from a Boston suburb recently was accused of killing and eviscerating his wife, a newspaper quoted a neighbor as saying: "'We never thought this would happen here.'" This young woman found the comment insulting: "Like here in Dorchester [a low-income Boston neighborhood], you'd expect it. Like [low-income] men cut up women all the time?"

The opinion that "family dysfunction" is publicly overstated in low-income America and kept secret where people are more privileged was a common one. Yet many of the low-income women and girls in this study consider their streets, schools, and other public places to be unsafe. "We have stores on every corner where you can buy a gun," wrote one fifteen-year-old. "If they care about [violence], why don't they just shut them down?" And another advised, "If you stopped the sale of guns and drugs and maybe even liquor, lots of the violence would stop." Some teens pointed out that the tide of violence flows both ways. They pointed to adult behavior, particularly police behavior, as harassing and often brutal.

Does an environment of violence provoke personal violence? Most of these girls and women thought there must be a connection and had the sense that violence is endemic. The young women in several groups of high school juniors and seniors blamed the "machismo" cultural expectations of males—the standards of "being a real man"—as the chief culprit. "Like, if you see your father doing it [abusing women] and you see brothers doing it, it's like, this is how to be a man." When I presented the results of a small survey on the issue of domestic abuse, these girls were not surprised. In interviews with twenty-four high school students, girls were offered a list of couple-conflict situations and asked under which, if any, of the circumstances, would "most boyfriends become violent with their partners." While some of the answers differed, *every girl interviewed* believed that most boys would hit, "if treated disrespectfully by his girlfriend, in front of his male peers." Public face, it seems, is considered to be the key component in young men's pride. Even boyfriends who were considered to be thoughtful were not expected to tolerate what could be interpreted as disrespect in public.

Yet these girls and others drew a real distinction between sexually predatory and violent male behavior and the attitudes of *their* boyfriend and brothers. When this paradox was brought to their attention, they chewed on it for a while. And then a girl spoke up for them, "There's a lot a sickos out there and you always have to be looking out for them. But there's a lot of guys just *trying* to look bad and 'hang in the hood' you know . . . it's hard to know." One sixteen-year-old explained the danger of rape this way: "We always know that there's guys out there going to try to jump you. It's part of the world, you know. It's just part of your life."

Among these and other discussants, there seemed to be an acceptance that sexual abuse is prevalent, even universal. While not passive in their acceptance, they regarded the existence of sexual abuse as part of the world. Child sexual abuse was regarded as particularly traumatic. "It changes everything, how she acts and talks and dresses." One eighteen-year-old offered the reflection that most "really promiscuous girls are always sexually abused girls. They didn't get that way by themselves, anyone knows that."

Melanie, Dorchester, 1992

"I thought his love would see us through."

In 1992, Melanie is a twenty-three-year-old Irish Catholic woman from a working-class neighborhood in Boston. Her father left her

mother when she was very young, but not before Melanie had witnessed terrible abuse. Her father would beat Melanie's mother "senseless," and Melanie witnessed him rape her mother more than once.
"Can you imagine seeing that?" she asked me. "Can you imagine how
a kid feels seeing that?" Melanie calls hers a "sad family." She lived
with her mother and one younger sister in five different apartments, often moving on when they could not cover the rent.

Melanie recalls feeling the need to soothe her depressed mother
from the time she was very young. "I was like the mother sometimes,
like I had to make *her* feel better, but she didn't take care of me."
Melanie's mother was not able to protect her daughter, nor even to hear
Melanie when she tried to explain the sexual abuse that was going on
in the neighbor's day care where she was left while her mother worked.
The neighbor's adolescent son would come home and be left in charge
of the several—"I really don't know how many of us"—little girls.
Melanie remembers that he not only molested her, "but the other girls
as well." She says she still wants to vomit whenever she smells maca-
roni and cheese because "that's what she fed us almost every day."

Melanie's mother claims that she did not have the slightest notion
that her five-year-old was being sexually abused, but Melanie is unforgiving. "Like, you don't even go over there and check up, or when I told
her I didn't want to go there, she didn't do anything?" Melanie believes
the experience of abuse and her mother's ongoing need for emotional
support drove her to some extreme places. But she adds, "My mother
was weak and abused and had no help. She did not expect to manage
a family on her own."

Melanie remembers her family often went on welfare and she recalls shame that was very public. "We were the 'wellies,' the kids at
school called us that. It's like they always knew the wellie kids, we were
shabby. I hated them."

And Melanie grew into a truculent girl. She fought other children
at school who mocked her for her poverty. She was labeled an "act-

out." "What bullshit," she says. "I was desperate." Melanie cannot re-call a time when someone took a real interest in her, or encouraged or empathized with her. What she does recall is that, as she developed phys-ically, she received sexual attention and she welcomed it. As she sees it, she did not have the tools she needed to protect herself or to find people who would care for her. When she was seventeen, she went drinking with "some friends" and, after an altercation with them, took off for home on her own. She was cornered by a group of young men and gang raped. Melanie does not want to talk about the assault. Instead, we talk about how she had felt that night. She felt, she says, that once again she had been abandoned by people who should have helped her.

Melanie received counseling through a rape crisis service. To her surprise, the counselor discouraged her desire to take the assailants, who were arrested that night, to court. "I felt like they were saying, 'just let them get away with it.'" Later she realized the counselor was say-ing something else. The middle-aged Italian woman, who had herself been assaulted, explained to Melanie that she would not win the case. Given her personal sexual history and her drinking behavior that night, "my chances of getting any justice were shit." Melanie heard some-thing else too, from this woman who counseled her. She heard some-one who thought that Melanie was worth something, worth more than winning a court case or pursuing justice at her own expense. Melanie believes this woman opened the door to the idea that there could be help for her.

At eighteen, Melanie fell in love with twenty-five-year-old William. He was the son of a family friend and was staying in their apartment until he could manage to get his own place. Despite her mother's cau-tions, Melanie was blind to any criticism about William. She believed that they could build a long-term relationship, that his love was what she had been waiting for, that "his love would carry us through any-thing." It did not.

After moving out of her mother's home and moving in with William, Melanie discovered she was pregnant. She explains that they planned to marry but that William seemed reluctant to move ahead with the wedding, and she did not want to push him. Two years later, Melanie was living in a homeless shelter. She had not yet completed her high school diploma, she was estranged from her mother, and she had a year-old baby girl. Melanie can analyze her own behavior very well. "I had no self-esteem. I didn't get the support I needed as a kid and I wanted to believe that I was loved."

She doesn't suggest that she has resolved all of her problems, but she is trying. Melanie returned to the counselor at the crisis center who gave her a referral to another, longer-term mental health program. After completing her high school degree, she entered a community college and has become active in various campus issues, particularly in the school's "Take Back the Night" campaign, which works to make the campus safe for women students. She is proud of her B average and of the apartment which, she points out, is always spotless. The child-care center where she received a publicly subsidized placement for three-year-old Lucinda is staffed by women who have taken the time to compliment Melanie's patience and care in raising her daughter.

Yet Melanie's battles are not over. "I know I have a battle with my self-esteem. I know I have a bad image of myself and that I need to feel better to do better. But I don't feel good about myself most of the time." She refers to herself as "ugly, fat, like my boyfriend used to say 'a pig.'" And she still craves the love of a man. The first day that we spoke, in her sunny apartment, she showed me a man's bracelet which she was planning to give to someone whom she had just begun dating. She wondered if it was appropriate and if it would be appreciated. The look in her eyes was asking about herself.

The day I say goodbye to Melanie after our third meeting she tells me that she has put the bracelet away. She will wait awhile, she says, before bestowing gifts upon this new man. She smiles at me while saying this and I smile back. "I could see the look in your eyes when I opened the box," she says. "You were like smiling at me, but I could see you didn't think I should give it to him." No, I hadn't thought so. Melanie nods and says, "I should wait until I know more."

BOYFRIENDS

Far more dominant in girl talk than conversation about sexual accommodation or abuse was talk about boyfriends. They framed their sexual decisions largely in connection to boyfriends whom they were keen on finding and fearful of losing. The contradictions buried in these views challenged those of us conducting the girls' focus groups to dig down deeper into the discussion. We asked about it in many ways. But the heart of the question we were asking was, "*Why is it so important that you have a boyfriend?*" It was a disingenuous question, not at all neutral for us. We held fast to a host of attitudes; we felt a sense of danger; we anticipated losses looking into lovely proud faces. We had fears for our own daughters, girls who looked just like these before us.

The girls critiqued this question before they answered it. One seventeen-year-old came right back at us. "When you were a teen, didn't *you* want a boyfriend more than anything?" There were many eyes on us looking for the truth, and exchanging weak glances, we beat an awkward retreat. Later, when we reviewed this exchange in a focus group of grown women, the influences that shaped the interplay seemed obvious. Women have a strong desire to "warn off" girls, to convince them to put more attention on their educational future and less on their romantic attachments. But, as several women pointed out, it is difficult to persuade these young women of a future independent of developing a relationship with a man, having children, and caring for a family because they see so little alternative. As a forty-eight-year-old grandmother mused, "You can talk and talk till you turn blue but the question is, what do they *see* . . . do they see another life? 'Cause if they don't, save your breath."

The drive to acquire a boyfriend seems universal among heterosexual adolescent girls. The adolescent girls in this study, however, must also be considered against the backdrop of their real lives. Real life for most of these girls, as discussed, includes complex and time-consuming obligations of family caretaking while they are still very young. Their lives are largely built around going to school and working at home, where they are caught up in child care and other family needs. Coupled with their parents' need for them to fill essential roles at home is parental fear about the dangers facing these girls outside the home—all of which seems to most girls to collude to "keep me locked up." As they enter adolescence, in a culture which revels in sexual and romantic pairings, another feasible and worthy role emerges, that of being someone's girlfriend. The counterforces which might help offset the drive to pair up with a boyfriend are not apparent to most of these girls. They simply do not "see another life." The older women who discussed the "real life" these girls experience believe that alternatives are not apparent because they do not, in fact, exist for girls in poor America.

Jaylona, Roxbury, 1992

"I found my way back."

Jaylona and I meet in Franklin Park in the Roxbury section of Boston. It is a beautiful Frederick Olmsted park with a zoo, a golf course, and acres of woods. Jaylona's mother, Althea, had laughed when she heard that we were going to use Franklin Park as our meeting place. "You'd better put rope around that girl," she told me, "'cause she'll be all off in those woods looking for a sick squirrel or something in two minutes." Jaylona had laughed with her mother. This was an old family joke. Sitting beside me now on the park bench, she says, "From the time I was a little girl, I would always be going out into the woods, the park . . . I would be looking for animals because I love them. I feel good when I'm with them. I would bring home pigeons and squirrels and the like.

I just loved to hold those little animals. I knew how they felt really."

Jaylona's father left her mother when "I was just little." She never knew him. Althea, who had baby Justin ("Sweet Pea") when Jaylona was seven, always had one or two jobs and was constantly busy keeping her family afloat. Jaylona admired her mother's determination and her energy, but she felt left alone much of her childhood. Althea commuted to her secretarial job in a high school in another part of Boston three days each week. Justin was left with an aunt who lived right across the street from the school where Althea worked. But Jaylona, who attended an elementary school near their home, returned in the early afternoon to an empty apartment. "I would come home from school and be by myself for hours," Jaylona says. "I was supposed to stay inside and wait, but I would go to the park and play and look for animals. Ma didn't know it but I would sometimes fall asleep in the woods."

One fall evening, Althea discovered Jaylona was not in the apartment when she arrived home from work. She went to the neighbors and then out to the streets around their building. With growing fear, and carrying her baby son, she went into the vast park to look for Jaylona. She ran across the golf course, calling and calling. She went into the woods, sobbing for Jaylona. When she reached the zoo, the park workers came out to ask what was wrong, and hearing Althea's description of her missing daughter, they said, "Oh, that little girl is here almost every day, hanging around the animal pens." Only that day they'd seen Jaylona with a man who was buying a hot dog for her. Althea tells me later that when the park workers said Jaylona had been with a stranger, "I saw her dead, in my mind I saw her dead, and me nowhere near to help her."

The police were called. They found eight-year-old Jaylona on the other side of the park, wandering down a street. The man had taken her to an apartment, sexually molested her, and then dropped her off near the park.

"I don't remember much about it," Jaylona says quietly. "I remember my mother picking me up like I was Sweet Pea, and she was crying and shaking. I remember all the commotion and all . . . but I was kind of sleepwalking."

Jaylona believes that she has overcome the events of that day, but she says that she "never lets down her guard" around men and now, the mother of a little girl, she trusts no one else to watch her daughter except her mother. Jaylona believes that "lots of girls get molested . . . a lot more than you think. It's like, if they don't have someone *right there*, watching out for them, those perverts will find them." Jaylona believes that "perverts" look for girls who are unprotected, who are alone, girls who "you can just tell from looking at them that they've got no back up, no one is watching out for them."

Despite loneliness and that bad night, Jaylona recounts a pretty good childhood, overall. In elementary school, she was a good student. She loved science and math, and she laughs when she recalls how the teachers were surprised that, as she puts it, "some skinny Black girl from Roxbury" could excel in math. She loved to draw too, always pictures of animals. But by middle school, Jaylona's attitude began to change.

Jaylona has more than one theory about why this change occurred. She had been very comfortable in her grammar school, but she hated the new middle school. She found herself at odds with some of her teachers who "hardly spoke to you except to yell." She did not have a close group of friends, and her interests, still largely devoted to the outdoors, were kept hidden from her classmates. She found that to be integrated into this school, she had to prove that she was tough and ready to fight. Yet her mother hated this kind of behavior and became increasingly critical of her pubescent daughter.

Jaylona also resented "all the baby-sitting I had to do for Justin. I felt like saying, 'You had this child, not me, so why do I have to watch him after school?'" Althea, always anxious about Jaylona's safety since the day she was molested, insisted that Jaylona come straight home from school, and stay in to watch over her brother. By that time, Althea was working full-time as a secretary and also pursuing an associate's degree in special education. She was gone most of the time.

Jaylona explains, "It's not like I didn't love my brother and all, but I felt trapped. I guess everything got bad then. My friends were pushing at me, my mother was always criticizing me, and I hated school. I started to do bad, you know . . . after always doing good." How, I ask, were her friends "pushing at her"?

By the end of middle school, Jaylona tells me, the girls were "all off into boys" and the boys were getting "rude and crude." In thinking back now, at the age of twenty-one, she realizes much of this behavior was just for show. But at the time, she felt as though, to fit in, she had to assume a real interest in sex and in being sexy and acting "like I was already doing it."

In analyzing these pressures, Jaylona thinks that things could be made different for girls. There should be open conversation at home and in schools, she tells me, with parents, peers, and with older teen leaders, whom "kids will listen to." She thinks that many girls and boys get started in sexual behavior because "there's pressure and ignorance and all the adults are too busy to see what's going on . . . or they lock you up which just causes rebellion."

Jaylona pretended that she was sexually active when hanging with her new girlfriends, many of whom she was to discover later were also pretending. Sometimes the pretense came close to reality. "If guys from school, or just from around, know your mom's out there working all the time and you're home alone with a baby brother or sister . . . well sometimes they just come on over. They travel in packs, you know . . . like dogs out there getting hungry." Jaylona suddenly winces. "You know, I could have been gang banged and I had friends who were."

Jaylona entered high school but not one of Boston's better "exam" schools. "I kind of blame my mother for not making me get into Latin School . . . but I was being disrespectful and kind of wild. And Justin's father was coming around, and he was drinking and Ma was in the courts about that. And Justin was having some trouble."

Early in her freshman year, Jaylona met Marquee who was eighteen at the time. She gave birth to their daughter, Martinique, the week after she finished her sophomore year. "I can only say to you that I was in love with that man. And I stayed in love with him for years."

Marquee, as Jaylona describes him, was a gorgeous, friendly, popular boy who lavished attention on Jaylona. He "didn't push on me to have sex for months." And what's more, "He came to meet my mother. He was respectful. He went to church, you know what I am saying? He was a good man . . . even with all that happened." And what did happen?

Jaylona explains Marquee's descent from grace as though she is reciting a legend, an old brutal tale which gets told too many times, in America.

She recalls, "When we realized I was pregnant, we were both like . . . now what . . . now what do we do. We started to get some money together to have an abortion, but it made us both cry to think of it. Like I think a girl's got to make up her own mind, but to me this was killing a part of us."

Althea quickly recognized her daughter's pregnancy and told her she must terminate. Filled with rage and remorse, Althea took her bitter feelings out on Marquee. "She was ready to kill him," Jaylona says. "*She was, like she was after that man . . . you know the one who messed with me* . . . it was like she was after him again." Marquee, who had been put out of his own overcrowded family felt, "like we had all turned against him."

Jaylona, torn on all sides and sick at the pain Marquee was feeling, told him that she would "have his baby, no matter what." That was the moment, she says, when she and Marquee were closer than at any other time, before or after. It was "like a star bursting." Jaylona says she "went ahead for him," but also knowing that, "in the end it was going to be me . . . and my mother who . . . had to do the doing."

Jaylona gave birth to her daughter and lived with her mother. Althea told Jaylona that she would "have to move out the day Martinique turned two years old." And so Jaylona applied for housing under public housing regulations. The only apartment which would become available within two years was in South Boston's McCormack housing development, notorious for being staunchly all white. "When my mother heard me tell her cousin I was going to move over to the McCormack development, she hit the roof. She said, 'You're not taking my baby over to that place where those people will stone you as soon as look at your Black face.' And you know I knew her instincts had come back to her."

And Marquee, the boy whom Jaylona spoke of as bursting stars, what became of him? Jaylona watched Marquee gradually succumb to pressures and to peers who had long given up on school and long-term commitments. He held out for awhile, supported by his love for Jaylona and then for his baby daughter, but after he graduated from high school, he found none but dead-end jobs and he "played the trade." "He got bent over," Jaylona says, "he got thin with the pipe, he stayed with people who I was scared of." Marquee died before his daughter turned four years old. Saddened by her memories, Jaylona suddenly ends our talk. I press her to let me walk her home. Silently, we return to the apartment she shares with her mother and daughter.

Althea is looking out for us, her face beside Martinique's round one pressed up against the window. Jaylona looks up at her daughter and says, "It's his face, you know?"

Jaylona was one of many young women interviewed who had faced extreme experiences in her relationship with a beloved boyfriend who was trying to manage a dangerous world. While "rude and crude" male behavior, and even male cruelty, was regarded as prevalent among boys who are vying for their manhood, true boyfriends were lovingly described or painfully missed. Cherished boyfriends who faced extreme obstacles moved girls' hearts and prompted sacrifices by girls in spite of their knowledge that hardship would follow.

Because boyfriends were so dear, losing them, or being "dumped," was a source of terrible pain and humiliation. "You try to do anything to make him stay, say anything, but he goes anyway," said one sixteen-year-old. "You hold on . . . hold onto anything. It's like going over the edge, and you know it, you grab onto anything, a twig, just to hold on," said another. This panic which a girl feels as she recognizes the signs of a boy in flight was identified by some girls as the prelude to a pregnancy. "You think that having his baby will make it different . . . but it's not." Sometimes a girl described being left by a boyfriend who had been the source of family conflict, the catalyst for her rebellion against too much responsibility at home. Parents, fearful for their daughter's safety and the advent of a pregnancy, may have forbidden the association or may have harshly criticized the boy's character. If girls become increasingly estranged from family relationships in the course of developing loyalty to their boyfriends, they often feel rage and an overpowering sense of loss when they are abandoned by those boys and left alone to raise a child.

TaShawna, Brenda, Elana, Tara, Noel, and Felicia: High School Study, March 1994

Liliana asks, "So do the guys you like . . . like a girl more for her intelligence or her personality or her looks?"

The adolescent girls wait a minute, and then Noel, teller of hard truths, speaks up. "We know you want us to say her brains and all that. But that's not what it is. Most boys don't want a smart girlfriend who has too much to say . . . that's not what makes him feel like a man."

"So what makes him a man?" Liliana prods. TaShawna has a well-known lecture on this subject, and she offers it again now. "He has to go out there and get him some, and get him some more. And not the uuuugly women, the pretty ones and the new ones. He thinks he's *all that* and tells his friends. But, you know, when she comes walking down the street after that, he's a man and she's a slut." And why do girls go along with this? Felicia, generally reticent in conversation about sex, answers this time. "It's the way of the world. It's always been that way. And it's not going to change neither."

Tara has been more silent than usual this day. Now aware of her pregnancy and her determination to keep the baby, Tara's girls'-group friends are cautious with her. They know that Enrie, her boyfriend, has been having second thoughts after his first flush of joy at the idea of fatherhood. He is working two jobs and will graduate from high school in a month, as will Tara. The girls know that he has been meeting with military recruiters and talking about leaving the area. For most of the year, Enrie has been meeting Tara after the girls' group ends to accompany her home before heading out to his evening job. But lately he has been working more hours and so she goes home on the train alone.

On this cold March day, as the girls separate, they are more subdued than usual, as if all of them know that they are bearing witness to Tara's inexorable journey into single motherhood. Quiet Felicia, who nervously glances away from Tara, knows it. And also brave TaShawna, who will "godmother that baby" because she will be much needed. Elana, sweet and vulnerable, won't consider the pain and says she just can't wait to hold the first child born of this group. Brenda is angry. She is the first to condemn Enrie, but only privately because she knows this criticism will hurt Tara's pride. And Noel, who has long looked up to Tara for her strength and maturity, still can't believe that this is happening.

Tara tells the girls she is going on ahead to pick up something for her mother. Big in the middle now, she moves in the slow, deliberate pace of a pregnant woman. The girls watch her retreating back, aware that she wants to be alone, aware of the future that is rushing toward her.

Girls, Love, and Choices in Low-Income America

Girls' reflections on love and sexuality were filled with both longing and with trepidation, with desire and cynicism. Through a complex interplay of feelings, the desire to establish a boyfriend relationship was a dominating theme. And, as many girls and women concluded, the boyfriend theme makes sense. This is a theme which—as many of the girls and women who interpreted this data concluded—makes sense. When one grows up burdened with family work, with caring for children, and facing the unending complications of low-income family life, a boyfriend may appear to be a ticket to some other place.

But they know this won't be a holiday. Knowledge of the obstacles promotes tension and cynicism about love and sexuality. The majority of girls did not express confidence that they would be the leaders in their sexual lives, but felt instead that they would be largely reacting to others and would always be negotiating the more powerful male sexuality. Most girls identified and condemned sexual abuse, particularly the sexual abuse of children, and other assaults on girls as threats inherent to a dangerous male world. They acknowledged that the lines between sexual accommodation as leading to a lasting relationship, on the one hand, and sexual accommodation as simply being abused, on the other, were lines vaguely drawn. However, while many girls seemed savvy, even cynical, about the vicissitudes of entering into the world of men and sexual relationships, still the pull seemed inexorable. Often, they spoke wistfully of male partners, those here, those gone, and those not yet arrived.

New scholarship on women's and girls' psychology has diverged from earlier analyses of human development as genderless and paved the way for sociological analyses which insist upon the power of gender in human development.[1] That research, conducted largely with middle-class and white females, reveals pubescence and adolescence as a time of particular vulnerability. The challenge to hold onto self, to one's own expression, amid the contradictory forces which surround girls-becoming-women is considerable.[2] These new approaches to the study of female adolescence reveal culturally condoned pressures on young women to conform and to silence the self, pressures which may lead to loss of self-esteem and vulnerability, to depression, to eating disorders and other self-destructive behavior.[3] Leaving childhood and entering adolescence, it turns out, is a time when "ordinary courage" may be needed by girls just to hold onto one's self, one's voice and heart in the face of cultural "silencing."[4]

Girls "coming up" in low-income America speak of some similar dilemmas as they leave the relative clarity of childhood and are pressed into new, often conflicting roles. The girls in this study eloquently spoke of competing forces: voices in their heads which reiterated prudent lessons opposed voices all around them that spoke of romance and sex.[5] And they spoke of seeking approbation, the desire to be attractive and chosen despite the knowledge of the risks involved. They pointed to forces which seem to demand "early sexualization" or the pressure to go "straight from dolls to sex," a youth-culture backdrop often recognized and sometimes resisted.[6]

But these girls and women also brought other forces to the table as they went about interpreting the context of their lives. They pointed to the importance of class, or of being members of a family or community *known* as low-income, when they contrasted themselves with suburban youth, often depicted as privileged and "babied." Privileged youth largely was seen as having "very little to whine about," as having less work to do, less pressure to perform, and much more access to good education and therefore a future. It was hard for these low-income girls to envision those suburban girls as sisters in some kind of perilous gender passage. Many low-income girls, both girls of color and white, distinguished themselves from "suburban" girls (and boys, for that matter) as tougher, braver, bolder, and more capable of "dealing" (coping with hardship and losses).

The young women who participated in these discussions also considered racial and ethnic identities, sometimes mixed into a class perspective, to be forces that are as powerful and present as gender in shaping their lives. Girls of color clearly articulated a racial or ethnic context for at least some of their ways of navigating the adolescent passage. Young Latinas described living in the intersection of a culture which tells them to stay "inside," housebound, and a neighborhood culture which insistently calls them out. They spoke almost simultaneously of the strength of a Puerto Rican identity and their deep frustration at the traditional role of women, "the ways of my grandmother," in Latino families.[7]

African American girls were the most likely to articulate and claim a strong and independent image of womanhood, expressing impatience with an image of female weakness and fearfulness.[8] Yet, numerous Black girls, particularly African American, spoke of Black men as "endangered," as facing acute perils in America, and they seemed to regard this dilemma as relevant in their relationship choices. Young men—their brothers, friends, and boyfriends—were under pressure to "be a man" in a world, they explained, and sexual conquests were part of realizing that effort.[9] While some young women brushed off this idea—"I say just kick that to the curb"—others acknowledged it held power over them.

Racial, ethnic, and class-laden identity are not simply collateral at-

tributes to these women and girls, they are central forces in understanding who you are as a woman in this world. The demands of "being wrapped too tight,"[10] of being hyper-competent girls who are expected to meet heavy challenges without bending, was a source of pride
and of resentment. As one hearty, white seventeen-year-old said, "Ain't
no Barbie dolls living around here." At the same time, she also thought
there was little room for playfulness. While women and girls bemoaned
the weight of responsibility, still some pointed out that such assumed
competence may lessen conflicts which are felt by adolescent women
who are focused only on gaining approval for their femininity. Less absorbed with an idealized body-form and weight than some research reports on middle-class girls,[11] many of the low-income girls in this study,
particularly African American and Irish American, reveled in their
physical strength and forceful character.

I was to hear some version of certain opinions, countless times:
"Black women know they have to be strong and so they are"; "Puerto
Rican women know what it is to be a woman, how to put family first";
"Everyone looks up to the mother, she's the one who makes the family"; "People know not to mess with me and my sister 'cause we'll break
your ass." Pride in race, ethnic origin, and community and tough-girl
identity was not only described, but also seemed to be in full presence
in the clear voices and straight-ahead glances of these girls as they
looked full in my face and openly critiqued each other and me.

Girls living in that confluence of gender, race, cultural, and economic pressures may learn lessons of holding onto self early on, lessons
taught by elders who know about the need to withstand. Such early
lessons, nested deep in family life, may serve to protect some girls to a
certain degree against the silencing which affects middle-class girls.

Yet this may also be the social, economic, and cultural context in
which the quest for a boyfriend is particularly urgent. While "girl culture" and the search for romance is ubiquitous, low-income girls, for
all their diversity, may find this route the only tangible pathway to

move on from daughters' lives.[12] As they stretch toward womanhood, deal with the day-to-day, and negotiate the sexual pressures around them, "hooking up" with a boyfriend may seem the best alternative.[13] To most girls in this study, boyfriends seemed to be more than people. They were described as the next part of life. They had been central in the passage of women before them and were seen as the nexus of obtaining a new role and social status. Older women could try to warn them off, parents could try to lock them up. But these girls' lives were largely split between the family work which would never get done and going to schools which would not send them on to college. Pairing up with a young man seemed the one clear path to move into a new role.

CHAPTER THREE

Choice and Motherhood in Poor America

"If you're one of these girls sitting there in the projects, why not? What are you waiting for anyway? You look for a boyfriend 'cause you need somebody and then you get pregnant. Nothing's coming . . . you have a baby to love."
— EIGHTEEN-YEAR-OLD DANIELLE, 1994 GIRLS PROJECT STUDY

Growing up female in poor America is always hard, as women tell it, but there is much joy too. These girls' early lives are filled with family work and grownup troubles, but also with girlish pleasures. Although adolescence seems to be dominated by social and sexual pressures and the quest for a boyfriend, these girls also expressed pride and confidence in their early competence. They described tedious domestic labor, but also recalled family celebrations, the birth of a baby, the coveted attention of an older sibling, and times of family harmony. Kitchen-table wisdom, wicked humor, and huge family meals were lived alongside evictions, domestic eruptions, and transient parental despair. These early years seem to be a gritty mixture, of hard times and losses and times of peace, rooted in relationships with people infused by love and loyalty.

The period of early motherhood, on the other hand, for most poor women marks the beginning of protracted hard times. The compelling mixture of hardship and optimistic effort that often characterizes their descriptions of girlhood is replaced by aching accounts of raising children without help. For most, early motherhood is a time of great change and the beginning of overwhelming troubles.

Most women's accounts of early motherhood begin with the stunning realization of pregnancy, so often unanticipated. The discovery is met with shock, and some fear, and yet a certain joy as well, particularly if a young woman is in a close relationship with the father of her child. Yet, inexorably it seems, things quickly begin to unravel as the families try to sort it all out. Girls are sometimes rejected or feel the brunt of their parents' anger and disappointment. And boyfriend relationships usually undergo transformation as pride and pleasure give way to the intensity of the impending responsibility.

"Going Through with It"

Oddly enough, even though pregnancy seems fated in the lives of so many of these young women, many said they felt a shiver of surprise when they realized that "it" had happened. The majority of juniors who participated in the High School Study in Boston high schools believed that "most girls" know about birth control, particularly about condoms. Access to contraception was more of a problem, they said, but they also reported that there are places to go and people who will help you if you pursue it. Yet the respondents claimed that they and most of their girlfriends don't use birth control "all the time." They do try, they said, but "sometimes you don't have it, sometimes you don't think about keeping it on you, and sometimes guys don't want it around. And you know too, sometimes they just don't work . . . like things do tear, you know?"

Clearly, many of these young women are bound for unintended or "mixed-feelings" pregnancies, which precipitate an emotional and moral hurricane. They remembered fearfully anticipating their family's response, reflecting upon their religious beliefs, and anxiously informing their boyfriends of the pregnancy. They recalled lying awake and imagining the baby. They spoke of abortion, the idea of choice, and the image of becoming a mother. They spoke about school and graduating, about "walking with my class."

It is in the midst of all of these feelings and pressures that most of these girls choose motherhood. Here, for example, from the 1993 High

School Study is fifteen-year-old Danielle: "I'm not saying that you all should have a baby . . . or that abortion is wrong for you. 'Cause I think you have to decide, it's *you* that's got to face it. But for me, abortion's wrong, I couldn't do it." She speaks for many in these interviews, focus groups, and girls' group discussions. Most girls believed that the decision to have an abortion must be left to the young woman who is pregnant, not her boyfriend, her mother or father, nor the state. But 75 percent of the girls surveyed in the Girls Project claimed that they would continue a pregnancy rather than have an abortion.

In most cases this was not a smug position. Many of the adolescent girls who held these prochoice but personally antiabortion beliefs were at the same time troubled by the familiar phenomenon of pregnancy as a result of sexual abuse. They also found challenging an even more familiar situation, one in which an additional child would clearly hurt the status of the family and result in additional deprivation for the children already born. Some acknowledged that many young women *will* choose to abort when facing either of those situations, even though they would suffer with the choice. All of the young women interviewed rejected out-of-hand the notion of placing a baby for adoption ("give my child away, never" and "I would never sleep not knowing what happened to it") unless the adoptive mother was their own mother, or a close female relative. Most, having watched their own mothers or other women take over as primary parent for a daughter who had refused to abort but cannot care for the baby, considered this a selfish choice. "It's *your* baby, right? So *you* raise it," eighteen-year-old Arlette insisted. But most discussants agreed that some young women are not equipped to raise children.

Most of these adolescent girls did not speak of a fetus as differing from a baby. Most had seen or heard detailed descriptions of anti-abortion films and believed that the act of abortion was terrible for the mother and painful for the fetus. While *few* girls considered abortion a murderous act and most were fairly sympathetic to peers who agonized their way to the choice to abort, still three-quarters of all the girls surveyed and two-thirds of sexually experienced teens stated unequivocally they would "keep the child" should they discover they were pregnant.

Felicia, TaShawna, Tara, Verona, Sarah, Alfonsa, and Shevron: Interpretive Focus Group, 1994

"It's not like you plan on it or anything, but condoms don't always work, and sometimes your boyfriend won't use it 'cause he says it feels better not. So like he's going to pull out . . . only . . ." Felicia's sentence wanders down to nothing.

The other girls wait politely because Felicia is not a big talker and she had stuck her neck out a bit with this revelation.

But TaShawna can hold on only so long. "But *come on,* you know what's up with that. That's like 'welcome to getting pregnant,' it's like 'here come the baby.'" TaShawna wants to say something more emphatic but many eyes are on her, warning her to be careful. Tara and TaShawna are closer than before, but on edge now that Tara is almost due. Tara is very sensitive to criticism. She says quietly, "It happens and you can't just judge girls who get pregnant. They're just the same only it happened."

When asked, these and other adolescent girls expressed the belief that "kids everywhere are having sex," that adolescents are sexually active everywhere—in middle-class communities, in small towns, and in wealthy suburbs—and national data largely bear out this perspective. "Why do teens in city neighborhoods, like in housing developments, seem to have *more babies?*" we asked. Their responses indicated that they saw vast differences between themselves and these other populations of teen girls.

"Girls in the suburbs just get things fixed for them," Tara says. "Because if they don't, well there goes college." Her point was taken by several others. They see suburban girls as having opportunities which would be lost should they proceed with a pregnancy. They are girls who choose to go ahead with a pregnancy or to abort in the context of alternatives. The issue of suburb versus city, clearly a class euphemism, sometimes substituted for race terminology as well. Seventeen-year-old African American Verona explains the race edge this way: "I don't want to speak offensively, but white girls, suburban people, don't feel the same way. They get pregnant, they run to the abortion clinic the next day. They don't think about the baby." Sarah, who is white, as well as some of the girls of color, object to this simple analysis, but Sarah adds, "You're right though, my mother would speed to the clinic as soon as I told her." Yet she was not alone, and it was not white-only territory.

Alfonsa identifies her mother as the major proponent for abortion when her older sister became pregnant. She explains the hard decision as one which, in the end, was better for everyone. "My sister already had a child and she had just started at (a local community college). She was doing really well then, and another baby would have wiped us out." The girls agree that this belief that motherhood will stunt a girl's chances, *if she has any*, is the motive for many abortions. Never seen as an easy or casual matter, these girls discuss abortion as wrenching at the heart of family.

And what about the baby's father? "All you do is say 'preg' and that man is gone," Shevron asserts to general agreement. Yet this sentiment conflicts with other opinions expressed in this and other discussions: "A man likes to have his girlfriend get pregnant," one sixteen-year-old told us, "because he's more the man." Others claimed that a man will come back to his "babymomma" because she has that essential claim on him. Whether the father can actually provide much help or even if he has moved on in his romantic ties, "when you give him a call to say you've got a problem with the child, he pushes everything aside and comes to you."

Does this create pressure on the father's current romantic partner to produce a child as well, to have that critical link which seems to transcend romance? Yes, the girls respond. Several report having known men who periodically disappear to visit their children. They agree that this creates worry that the former partner will "reel him back in again."

This belief that having a baby with a man creates a powerful tie and a life-long link is shared by adult women as well. "Let's face it," said Nemesis, a woman in her mid-thirties, during her Life-History interview, "when you get with a man, and he's being with your kids by another man, well having a baby brings everybody together. That baby belongs to everyone, holds everyone together."

But back in the girls' group, the idea of having a baby to accommodate or keep a man is under fire. All agree that this is risky and places too much on the baby. Shevron hits the table. "It's wild and disrespectful to have a baby because you want to hold onto a man," she says, angrily shaking her head. Tara agrees from her own vantage on all of this. "Boyfriends come and go, but your child is forever," she says with infinite authority.

"What's Coming Anyway?"

These young women's discourse on choice and pregnancy reflected their competence at baby care and their years of experience in running a household. The chores of motherhood did not seem daunting to most of these young women as they often do to youth who have been encouraged to focus primarily on their own lives. Caring for young family members, sorting out family crises, making choices which invariably meant putting self aside, this was their common history. When they became sexually active, ready or not, and began to feel the desire to cement a tenacious bond with a man, motherhood seemed inevitable.

Yet there is another powerful force which shapes their acceptance of that future, and *that is the degree to which these millions of girls in poor America can imagine another life*. Having other options, particularly those leading to a decent job and independent life deter premature parenthood. But what if college, and the possibility of finding a well-employed partner or a decent-paying job seems out of reach and foreign? Love here and now, family ties, and a baby envisioned are real to these young women, real and pressing in on them.

Most of the adolescent girls who discussed these childbearing decisions were well acquainted with women who have had babies early on, and they held few illusions about the demands of child raising. When faced with the monumental decision which pregnancy presents, these young women engaged in the universal weighing of losses and gains. Their discussions revealed that they saw choosing to go ahead with motherhood not as "an easy way out" but as an act of responsibility. And they felt that, despite the hardship, motherhood also represented the potential for great gain. This is not the kind of gain the press might lead middle-class Americans to expect of these girls. Despite the fact that they are often publicly depicted as seeking financial gains through pregnancy, not one of the 250 girls surveyed in the Girls Project, nor any of the 40 others who participated in the Girls Project focus groups, considered welfare benefits a motive for childbearing. That "petty bit of money" gets you nowhere, they told me. Motherhood is valued for the position, the clear and tangible role, it offers. With it, you become the lifeblood of many an extended family. You gain access to the center stage you know best.

One young woman told me the story of her first child's delivery. When she went into labor, she went to the hospital with her two older sisters (their parents were both dead). Though she had a normal pregnancy and the baby's heartbeat had seemed fine through most of the delivery, he died shortly after she gave birth to him. She still doesn't know the cause of his death. "They said something about stress on him, but I don't know why." She remembers being left in her hospital room, but not much else. "My mind was blank." When she went home in a cab the next day, she discovered that her sisters had moved her to a tiny room, a "closet," because she would no longer need the big room which they had set up for her and her baby. "I felt like I had failed even though they were nice to me and all . . . but I had been expecting to have a child with me, to be all special, and I had failed." She delivered her first daughter within a year of her son's death.

In these discussions about early motherhood, I often asked young women and girls, "If you wait to get pregnant, wouldn't that make a big difference? Wouldn't that be much better?" One young girl, perhaps tired of my reiteration, answered, "Wait for what, what's coming anyway?" Her companions watched me and waited for my answer.

Chantal: Facing a Tough Choice

Chantal stopped me in the busy hall of a Boston high school. I had just finished presenting to a group of twelfth-grade African American, white, and Latino girls a summary of the information I had gathered from a study of teens' sexual and reproductive choices. Chantal had been a member of the group. She had not asked questions during my talk, but she had been a very attentive listener. I wasn't at all surprised when she stopped me in the hall.

She wanted to talk. She was interested in discussing her views on teen sex and pregnancy, but not there and not then. I told her I could come back the next day but that I wanted her to commit to meeting me. By 1994, after two years of meeting with teens, I had been stood up many times.

At lunch the next day, Chantal tells me why she approached me. "I don't get a chance to talk about this much. I don't want to with others. It's okay for some, but not me with my personal business." Yet, it is clear that she is not ready to talk to me and so we work our way around the conversation.

"No question need be answered, you can lead the conversation," I repeat my mantra. But Chantal seems to be troubled by something else. Is it a problem that I am white, I ask. Chantal is African American, and some other girls clearly have let me know that they want to "look into a face that's like my own." That can be a problem, Chantal agrees. A lot of white people see girls of color with babies and think "there goes another lazy girl who wants that check." But that isn't the problem to-day, she says, because "you wouldn't be here asking us like you are if you had those ignorant attitudes."

For Chantal, the problem is my age. I am probably too old to re-member, to remember how it feels to be young, to be facing the things she is facing. And besides, times have changed. "You have a teenage daughter of your own, you said. I bet you're watching her . . . trying to keep her in, *telling her* she's messing up." I admit to a rush of relief knowing my older daughter was not about to appear and join Chantal in this line of questioning. Yes, I tell her, I do that, but I try to listen too because she has a lot to say about her life, her rights, her choices.

Chantal mutters, "That's right. People want to know about us, talk to us. Don't all go judging us, saying this and that. We can tell you how it is out here, now, if you listen." That's why I'm here, I tell her, this time looking into her eyes. And so she begins to talk.

Chantal is pregnant, she tells me. She is only "nine weeks gone" and she is trying to decide what to do about it. Chantal wants to know my opinion about abortion, about the obligation to reproduce, about a woman's morality. The pizza I've just eaten sits in my stomach like a sack of stones. I tell Chantal the truth, that I believe it is up to each woman to decide for herself, that I don't believe a woman is bad or good based on how she resolves this moment in her life. Chantal seems to respect this answer, but finds little to guide her in it. So we sit for awhile, and then I ask Chantal if we can go back to some time before she was pregnant, to remember what she imagined about her life.

Chantal's mother, Maxine, was fourteen years old when she gave birth to her first child, Chantal, a tiny premature baby whom the doctors were sure would not survive. "I was way underweight, 'cause my ma didn't even know she was pregnant when she had me. She told my grandmother she was having a terrible belly ache and then there I was."

She spent two weeks in the pediatric intensive care unit fighting "like a little rabbit," her grandmother told her, fighting to breathe, fighting the tubes and the gloved hands that touched her. Chantal's grandmother, Anthea, believes it was Chantal's fighting spirit that brought her through. Even though she was furious that her youngest daughter had gotten pregnant so young, Anthea raised Chantal. "I called her 'Momma' and I called my mother 'Maxi.'"

Chantal is very clear that her mother was not at all prepared for motherhood. She remembers Maxine going out "to play bingo" throughout her childhood and leaving Chantal with her grandmother or with other family members, anyone "she could grab and stick us to." Maxine had another baby when Chantal was three and then another after that. Chantal spent much of her earliest years tending babies. "My mother had this step-up stool at the sink so I could climb up and get diapers down and change my brother. I was five but really small still."

At night, Chantal would get up to care for the babies if they awoke. She did this rather than go to her mother's bed to wake her because "I didn't want to go and find she was gone. That scared me so much that I would just pick up the baby myself, so I wouldn't know."

When social workers from child welfare services threatened to take the babies away because they were neglected, Anthea took over. "But she told my ma, any more and they go to the orphanage." Chantal distinctly remembers moving into her grandmother's house and going to sleep in a little room with her brother and sister sharing a crib next to her. It was crowded and hot, but she was so glad to know that there would be a grownup there, if she woke up during the night or if "my babies," as she calls her siblings, needed anything. She knew that her grandmother would not leave them alone.

At the age of twenty-one, with some counseling and after becoming drug-free, Maxine began to take better care of her children. She pulled free of the life that had drawn her away from her family. She returned to high school and entered a training program to become a nurse's aide. Chantal's younger brother and sister reconciled with their mother and moved back in with her, but Chantal could not accept Maxine. Now, at eighteen, Chantal says she thinks the feeling was mutual. "I couldn't treat her like a real mother after she had been that way. I wouldn't mind her like she wanted. I didn't respect her."

Chantal believes that her mother felt guilty about her behavior and that receiving "forgiveness" from her two younger children was a source of redemption, but Chantal refused to give her mother that peace. Chantal lived between her grandmother's and her mother's apartment, moving back and forth throughout grammar and middle schools. Eventually the conflict with her mother became so fierce that she stopped seeing her altogether.

Despite the difficulties which Chantal faced, she recalls happiness in her early girlhood. Chantal has a wonderful relationship with her grandmother and her younger siblings. Both she and her mother seem to have kept their conflict separate from the younger children, who "really have three mothers, if you count me, then my mother, and then my grandmother."

Chantal was also a very successful student. Under her grandmother's tutelage she worked hard, doing her homework at the kitchen table and reading out loud to her grandmother every evening. She regularly attended church, read the Bible to her grandmother on Sunday evenings, and was active in a church youth group. In middle school, Chantal had an English teacher, Mrs. Peterson, who praised her writing and the creativity of her ideas. She encouraged Chantal to read and gave her books by several young writers and African American women writers. Chantal read one of her own short stories "on stage" during middle school graduation exercises. She recalls looking out to the crowd and wondering if her voice would work. She thought of her grandmother's kitchen table and then read out, loud and clear, pretending she was speaking to her grandmother alone.

Alongside these happy memories Chantal recalls a persistent fear of boys. "I was always scared of boys in school. I didn't want to end up like my mother." It was more than a fear of ending up pregnant at so young an age. Chantal had watched her mother's boyfriend beat up her mother and this terrified her. Was this man her father, I ask. "No, he was my babies' father," Chantal says. I stop her. Which babies are we talking about? Chantal laughs at my confusion and then snorts with disgust at the notion that this man had fathered her pregnancy. She says she calls her siblings "her babies" because "I raised them more than anyone else." The look of hard pride in Chantal's eyes tells of an epic conflict with her mother.

As a result of having witnessed Maxi's beatings, Chantal avoided boys. Throughout her schooling her socializing was largely confined to one very close girlfriend. However, at the start of her senior year of high school, she met and fell in love with a young man who ran a local retail store. Chantal describes him as very sweet, kind to her, and not at all pushy or "being like a dog."

I ask Chantal what she had imagined her life would be like before she met this man. She had talked at length about what she wanted to avoid. She knew the kind of person she didn't want to be. She loathed her mother's "lack of self-respect," her choice to be with a man who abused her. "I would never put up with that," Chantal told me. And she liked how her grandmother was respected in their church and in her local neighborhood. Anthea is "kind of old-fashioned," Chantal carefully admits, and she really doesn't know much about the world. But Anthea has pride.

And what would make *her* proud of herself? Chantal sits up straight and speaks sharply. *She is already proud of herself.* She is graduating from high school, she has all but raised two siblings, she takes no abuse from men, and she did not get pregnant until she was "older." Chantal never drank or drugged, she hates that behavior. Her voice told me that she was full of righteous pride which only a blind person could miss.

Will the baby's father be there for you, I ask Chantal, if you decide to have the baby? No, she says, but that is not a big part of this decision. He does not want Chantal to have an abortion, he doesn't believe in them. But he is already married and has two children with his wife. He is a nice man, she says, but she had never imagined a life with him because "I am not a fool about that."

"I will be alone if I have this baby," Chantal says, staring out the window. She does not want to burden her grandmother with another obligation and she hates the idea of welfare. And her future? Chantal suggests that I am confusing her future with her decision whether or not to have a baby. Whether or not she goes through with her pregnancy, she plans to become a teacher someday, to teach writing to children. "That sort of thing takes many years," she tells me. "It's not like you finish high school and go to college and then become a teacher or something ... I mean, that's just not realistic." She will continue to work part time in the local community center and take courses when she can. "You don't go waiting for everything," she tells me. "It's not coming to you. Maybe someday you'll have something more. Maybe not."

Postscript on Chantal

She chose to have her baby, and in 1995 she gave premature birth to a girl who has some neurological problems and is blind in one eye. The baby's chances of survival were slim, but Chantal "moved into that hospital" and provided most of Crystal's care. She reports the nursing staff "were the nicest ladies I have ever met, like sisters to me" and they helped her through. She also received counseling for the first time in her life and has been dealing with more than "just" her immediate crisis. To her surprise, her mother Maxine has become a chief source of support and is extremely attached to her fragile granddaughter. "She's really trying to make up for when I was a baby and I need her *now*."

Shareese, Rosa, Theresa, and Shannon: Interpretive Focus Group, January 1994

"That baby is going to be with you for life," Theresa says and then quietly contemplates the idea. "It is a companion for life, you know what I mean? When you decide to go through with it, it's for life." Theresa has had an abortion and she still turns the decision over in her mind. She regrets getting pregnant, and still believes she could not have supported a child nor raised one properly at the time when she was pregnant. "I was just not mature enough," she has told me in private. She also knew that, if she had the baby, she would have had to give up a four-year scholarship at a local university, one guaranteed to her and her classmates if they maintain good grades which Theresa has done. Her mother convinced her to keep the pregnancy secret for the week that they discussed it. Theresa's aunt was informed, and she told her niece that she, too, had been pregnant before her marriage and had had an abortion. "She told me it was the hardest decision in her life, she's like religious, you know, but she believes that in the end, it was right." Theresa believes that she made the right decision as well, but she admits that she came "just that close" to going the other way.

The other girls in the group don't know that Theresa has had an abortion, although perhaps they suspect it. She comes on strong when the abortion question comes up.

"Some girls who have an abortion just get pregnant again a few months later," Shareese points out. "They didn't figure out what they were doing the first time, so they just do it again."

"I think they just want attention," Shannon adds, "and it's a pretty stupid way of getting it. They think they will hold onto their man . . .

that's the main reason. And then they think, 'I will do this differently, better than other girls, I will love my baby.'"

"But it can just be an accident too, you know," Theresa says, and they all agree. "A girl's got to figure it out herself. It's the last choice, but sometimes it's the choice you got to make."

"Yeah, but most girls don't go that way and you know it," Shannon says. "Most girls just go ahead on and have the baby." Everyone nods in agreement.

Shareese adds, "A lot of mothers had their children young because there was no reason not to. So why should you wait? Who's coming?"

"Lonely Days": Arlette Again, Roxbury, 1993

When I walk around Roxbury with Arlette in the summer of 1993, she speaks of being "thrown out" of her family when she told them of her pregnancy. She is not alone in this experience. Several other adolescents (and grown women recalling their teen years) spoke of parents' fury and rejection at the pregnancy announcement. Of girls who were surveyed in the Girls Project, 15 percent of the 250 indicated that their parents would exile them if they were to come home pregnant. And it was interesting to note that young women who lived in families with fathers present were more likely to believe they would be banished if impregnated than those who came from mother-only households.

Arlette was told to leave the night she admitted to her mother that she was "carrying a baby." Her mother, always obedient to her husband's wishes and beliefs, had immediately gone to her husband and shared the information. Arlette knew that her mother would tell her father, but she could not keep the secret a day longer. Arlette's father came to her bed and told her to get up and get out. Arlette tries not to recall details of that terrible night, her mother and younger siblings crying, her father yelling how she had shamed him, and then there she was, literally, standing on the doorstep with a paper bag of clothes and her book bag for school the next day. Her mother had called her uncle on the phone, and he came by an hour later and picked Arlette up. He and her aunt put Arlette up for a week and then arranged for her to live in the local Catholic home for pregnant teens. Altogether, she missed only five days of school during her pregnancy.

Arlette was able to get some little help from other relatives during this period and, unbeknownst to her father, all of her siblings visited her. But for the most part she was all alone and so she went on welfare. Does this kind of rejection often happen? I ask Arlette. Sometimes, she says, especially in religious families where the parents are ashamed of what people will think of them. But Arlette believes some parents stand by their daughters, even when they "do like I did." Arlette believes her mother loves her father more than "all of us together" and would sacrifice her children to his wishes. Yet she also describes her mother's undertaking elaborate ruses to ensure that food, small amounts of money, and visits from kin reach her banished daughter. From the underground, her mother has stayed in touch.

But Arlette has suffered from lonely days and nights. Proud head held high, Arlette does not like to admit pain. But one afternoon I watched round tears slide down her impassive face, and only when she saw me wiping my eyes did she stop pretending not to hurt.

After the birth of a first child, many young women describe finding themselves living in extreme isolation. Their earlier lives, often overcrowded with people, noise, and family activities, had made many of these girls long for some privacy and solitude. But having a baby alone without resources was described as purgatory. It was a time when all vestiges of childhood were left behind, when anxiety and loneliness prevailed. Sometimes, as with Arlette, parents cast a girl out. Sometimes the conflict which arises between an adolescent mother and her parents becomes intolerable for everyone, and the new mother and child are the ones to go. This is the period when most young women talk about the loss of youthful dreams and notions of having someone who will stand by you. They speak of searing solitude, of days and nights trapped in shabby rooms with a needy baby. They recall not hearing a single kind word come to them for weeks on end and somehow trying to pass on some little joy to babies.

Paulina, Waltham, 1991: "Trying to Make Everything Go Away"

Paulina tells me to call her Polly as we settle into a deep old sofa in her living room. The walls are covered with children's pictures. Bins of Legos and building blocks overflow onto the floor where Polly's identical twin sons are constructing something grand. They are almost four. I met Polly at a child-care center which both our children attend.

Seven years ago, Polly had just entered a training program to learn a trade in construction when she realized she was pregnant. Her oldest son was born when she was seventeen. Polly dropped out of high school and out of her parents' life, at least for several years. She had lived on welfare and some employment, under the table, for a while, but the mean, perilous life in a rundown housing development in Chelsea, just outside of Boston, finally became unbearable. Polly wanted to change her life, so she began attending high school classes in the evenings, trading off child-care duties with her cousin, who went to work during the day. Both young mothers were seeking a way to find work that paid better than the minimum-wage jobs that, "keep you poorer than welfare does." The realization that she was carrying "my son's younger brother or sister," as she puts it, came as "big shock really . . . I know how stupid that sounds but I was being careful and all." She spent a month going back and forth, trying to decide whether or not to have an abortion. Her relationship with her boyfriend (the father of all three boys) had deteriorated when she began to pursue school and a trade. Always morose and longing for his native El Salvador, Polly's boyfriend was delighted she was pregnant again. Thinking back, it has occurred to Polly that he "used the old stick a pin in the rubber trick . . . so it seemed like he was wearing protection but there's that little hole big enough to let a baby in." In the end, she decided to keep the baby (who turned out to be twins) but to break up with the man.

Polly thinks of this time as the most miserable in her life, which had hardly been a cakewalk from the start. Her working-class, "Greek, and just plain white" family was dominated by her volatile father and his "vicious" mother. They considered Polly a "misfit" because she dated "a colored guy," and they were not reconciled to "an illegitimate" child in the family. They were barely speaking to her, and when they did, they made it clear there would be no contributions to help her out. "They were like, 'You made your bed . . .'" She didn't bother to tell them that she was pregnant again.

Polly's cousin, who was also a single white mother of children of color, had been a soul mate for Polly when she first left home pregnant. They had offered each other comfort and baby-sitting help and had talked "a lot about having kids who aren't white and dealing with people's attitudes about that." But halfway through Polly's second pregnancy, her cousin made the decision to move to Florida to live with the father of her two children. Polly was glad for her cousin, but the anxiety of being truly alone nearly choked her. Then, she had two babies instead of one.

"I was alone in a two-room apartment with my three babies. I spent my days figuring out how to get to the grocery store on foot or using a shopping cart I had stashed in the back, stuffing three kids in it. I washed diapers in the bath tub and hung them on a line in the hall. The windows were so loose that the wind blew through, and I couldn't keep the apartment warm. My kids were sick all the time. I finally got a half-day nursery school slot for Petey, but I had to pack up my babies to walk him over there, and they [the Welfare Department] had cut the clothing allowance so they didn't have winter clothes. Petey would tell me, 'I'm not cold, Mama, I'm not cold,' to try to get to go to the center when he was turning blue and the babies had ear infections." Polly found herself wishing she had never had the children and then hating herself for such failure. At twenty-one, she wished her life would end. Then, she started drinking. "At first, I would wait until the kids were asleep, but then I found that I was hurrying them to bed . . . I wanted that bottle more than anything 'cause . . . well, you know, it makes everything go away." Polly would sometimes cram all three children into her bed where she kept the bottle under the blanket. She would "sing lullabies and drink and sing and drink."

Quick Notes

"*I cried myself to sleep every night. I felt my misery creeping into my baby but I couldn't stop. I was all alone and I had nothing, nobody. It was his little smile in the morning when I turned over and saw him, that was the only sunshine in my life for years.*"
　　—Tabitha, 1992, on being a single mother on welfare

"*I would watch her struggle with all the tubes and all. Be fighting just to breathe in a breath. I would breathe with her saying, 'Come on baby, you got to live, 'cause it's just you and me and I'm waiting on you.'*"
　　—Chantal, 1995, in the neonatal intensive care unit

"*I hope he stays . . . but you can't just count on that. Not if you are paying attention. My mother did it on her own 'cause she had to and I will too . . . if I have to. But I am scared. I am not ashamed to admit it . . . I am scared.*"
　　—Eighteen-year-old Bernadette, 1994, anticipating
　　　　　　what will follow her baby's birth

Talking It Over

The young women who discussed the experience of early motherhood, and who are themselves still very close to this time in their lives, focused on their attachments to men and babies and on their conflicts with their own birth families. They identified "sitting in the projects" and the conviction that "nothing's coming anyway" as factors which influence their own and their peers' reproductive decisions, but they talk for the most part about love, about their longing for it, as leading to early pregnancy.

Older women who discussed early motherhood, however, took a more caustic view of all this "love stuff." Five older women (late twenties to mid-forties) who reviewed all the data on adolescents in an Interpretive Focus Group focused on girls' whole lives, not just on their sexual and reproductive behavior.

A forty-something Puerto Rican woman in this group considered one major influence to be the way women are raised. "There is nothing more sacred than being a mother. It's kind of an ultimate role . . . for Hispanic women anyway, maybe for all women really. So it's this really sacred thing and then, what else is there really? What did your mother do? She was a wife and mother . . . maybe not even a married wife, if you know what I mean." Everyone did.

A younger African American woman said that "Black people" also hold motherhood as sacred, but, "we, I think, don't get so into the wife thing the way Hispanic women do. We kind of assume we are on our own. And we don't see it [motherhood] as this end. I raise my children as I have been growing up, we grow up together. But I never thought that I was supposed to be all done with my growing before I had a baby."

Another, older African American woman asked her, "But don't you think if we thought that waiting made sense, to us, we would? I don't think we'd wait until we are in the late thirties or forties like some of these women with big careers do, 'cause that makes no kind of sense to me. But I think what that girl said about 'waiting for what, what's coming' says it right there. We can't be waiting for the men, and *no one's* coming around recruiting *us* to college."

In pulling apart the pieces, these women repeatedly raised the issues of education and opportunity. They pointed out that, "all girls, white, Black, brown get into the *maaaan thing*." And they agreed that girls in the middle class are having sex like everybody else is because "those boys out there are after the same game as any boys are anywhere." But they also suggested that this activity is less likely to lead to premature childbearing, leaving school, and ending up on welfare, *if there is somewhere else you truly believe you are going.*

Their comments reminded me of Renata, an African American woman in her thirties, whom I'd interviewed a couple of years before. "You're more careful when you got something on in life, you pick a man more carefully, you dump him quicker, and you don't go having babies like a fool."

The older African American woman recalled that education was always emphasized in her life and asserted that she has always pursued it. Her two children, now in their twenties are also pursuing ongoing education. But she adds, "It's not like I thought that I would leave high school and go straight through college. *I mean, how many* [of their classmates] *when you graduated did that?* [The other four women answered "none."] You do a little [schooling] here and then a little more and maybe you have to deal with other business for a while and then maybe you get back to it a couple years later."

A white woman in her thirties remarked, "My family never thought college made any sense. My brothers are both firefighters and I was supposed to be a firefighter's wife . . . only I didn't like firefighters." The group laughed. She went on, "When I got pregnant I thought, well, I can probably make him marry me but why? I won't be happy. It would just make everyone else feel better." And what did she want to do with her own life? "Like I said, I didn't have a picture besides being a wife and mother. I found my picture later on, and I did it *with* my son. He helped me understand that I wanted more."

These women believe that when young women choose to go through with pregnancies, the choice may be in some part about sex and love, about cultural and family tradition, but above all it is about having few alternative roles: "Like all that stuff you said about girls working at home and doing for the family and babies and doing for the boyfriends . . . *You've got to give them something else to have . . . to a picture of . . . of themselves.*"

And welfare? Is this a big draw for girls to have babies early on?

The younger African American woman in the group is critical of teens having babies. She sees girls of fifteen and fourteen pushing baby strollers around downtown Boston, showing off their babies like "little doll babies." Whenever she sees this she says, "I hope that there is some grandmother back behind this girl and I pray for that baby." But it is not about welfare, she says, not really. "I mean, sure, girls think, well . . . if my family kicks me out and the boy is gone . . . 'cause you know he can't afford a baby . . . well there's always welfare. I heard that sometimes. But *that's not why that child is there with that baby.* She's there because she had no notion of anything else . . . what is she supposed to see in her life?" The white woman in the group repeated, to everyone's agreement, "We have got to give her another picture of herself, like I had to find."

And what about girls who have no backup, who don't have that mother or grandmother to see them and their babies through? What about the young women like Tabitha and Pauline and thousands of others who find themselves all alone and on welfare. Most of the women just shook their heads. They are in for bad times, it was agreed, and worse now than before. "White rock" and more guns, desperate men and less public services have made poor motherhood a jungle. And a lot of women get "warped" by it, get "changed and sick." The white woman said, "That's why the foster care is full to overflow. And those babies have already been to hell."

Paulina Continued: "I Came That Close to Never Coming Back"

As Polly describes it, she was on a descent into alcoholism and despair. One night, after putting her children to bed while drinking, she did not notice that one of the twins was so ill with fever that he was having a seizure. It was Peter, then four, who yelled and screamed at his mother until, despite her inebriation, she noticed that one baby was barely breathing. The nightmare emergency trip to the hospital brought the Department of Social Services into the picture, and Polly temporarily lost custody of the three boys.

Polly tells me, "You want to talk about hating yourself, you have no idea how bad a woman can hate herself. I hated myself so bad, I just wanted to cut myself or burn myself down right down. No one hated me as much as I did." Polly, without custody of her children lost welfare, her apartment, and "my mind for about a year." After several months of life on the street, which she did not wish to discuss, Polly turned to a detoxification center and was accepted into a residential program for alcoholic women. She saw a social worker and was in a peer counseling group of women who had also lost their children because of drinking. Polly believes that she would not have become an alcoholic if she had not become so isolated and depressed, but "you aren't allowed to blame it on anyone but yourself . . . so OK, I said it was all me and I was going to get better." She visited with her children as she remained sober. She took classes, completed her high school diploma, and returned to her pursuit of a job in the trades. Now, four years later she is an apprentice in a construction trade and can make "let's just say somewhere in the mid-thirties."

Her life is transformed now, she says, not easy with three kids and a lot of loneliness, but transformed. She has a five-room apartment in a Boston "triple decker." Her children's father, who is now married to someone else, is "on decent terms" with Polly. He makes only sporadic child support payments but does come by and see the boys. Polly has been reconciled with her mother, and her father has "just started to thaw a little." They are now giving the boys "really pisser" birthday and Christmas presents, and they have a Sunday dinner together every so often. All of this seems pretty good, but the best is before us, constructing a building out of blocks. Two beautiful boys, who are so absorbed in their project they have allowed us an astonishing hour and a half of quiet talk. And Peter? His last report card was "all A's and B's," and he is, according to his mother, the best, if an overly anxious, kid in the world.

I ask Polly, does it all come out right in the end? As I knew she would, she rejects that notion. "I was so close to never coming back. I was beaten out on the street and other stuff I don't even want to mention," she says in a cold voice. Some women who have been down that low, but survived, believe that God intervened. Others believe some little moment of fortune, or some small inner voice, or an "angel" is all that stood between them and absolute defeat. Polly believes that today, just at this moment, some child is lost to foster care and some mother will "go down the tubes."

Some Don't Make It Out: The Story of Simara

In October of 1992, I am sitting in the lobby of a neighborhood health center, waiting with Arlette, whose baby is in for a checkup. We are on the tail end of a prodigious list of patients. It is clearly going to be a long afternoon. Before two minutes have passed, Arlette nudges me, gesturing broadly with eyes and shoulders, signals which I am dull about receiving. Exasperated, she jerks her head vigorously to the corner of the room, raising protests from Damika, whose sleeping head rests on her mother's shoulder. I turn to see a seated white woman who has turned her chair to face the wall. I can see tears leaking down her trembling chin. I turn back to Arlette and we sit, both of us tense, both of us balancing the desire to reach out with the desire to pretend we have not noticed. As I begin studiously examining my hands, I feel Arlette's eyes boring into me, demanding that I do more than just sit here. I muttered something fairly unfriendly as I passed by her chair on my way over to the corner, but she just sniffed hard with satisfaction.

I am not ready to hear the pain I am sure will come pouring out of this woman, nor ready for rage which sometimes comes when you break the pretense that you haven't noticed suffering. But thirty-four-year-old Linda is not weeping for herself and she is glad to talk. In the hour and half that follows, she tells me the profoundly American story of a cast-off girl who does not gain adult attention until she becomes pregnant.

Linda, a social worker, met Simara when the girl was fourteen and about to deliver her first baby. Linda, no pushover, says that wild Hispanic Simara "broke right into my heart that day." She has been following Simara for four subsequent years.

Simara's life was filled with horrors, the worst kind that prey on lost girls, the girls I had heard called rag-doll girls, craving girls. Orphaned early through sickness and abandonment, Simara's crisis-ridden extended family was far too distracted to stop her passage into foster care. Simara was sexually abused before she was six, left in the streets at night by age eight, and at the age of ten was kidnapped by a group of grown men who "used her as a sex plaything." Simara received intensive social work intervention only after so much harm had been done to her that "it makes hardened social workers like me cry up a storm for her," Linda told me.

Simara spent two fairly quiet years in a very structured foster-care home, headed by a caring and experienced Puerto Rican woman, who seemed to handle Simara well. But when this woman's own daughter became ill and needed help with three young children, Simara had to go. She went to the street. "Simara ran after that, you know, a runner. You can't keep them if they don't want to stay. She had one menstrual period before she got pregnant."

It was at that point that Linda met and became so attached to the fourteen-year-old. Linda describes her as bright, often full of humor, but "inappropriate" with males. Simara also becomes disengaged at times, "spacing out on you right in the middle of doing something. She's pretty disordered." When Simara went into the hospital to deliver her tiny premature son, Linda, knowing she would lose him immediately, brought a pile of teddy bears into Simara's room. Simara had agreed to give the baby up, had acknowledged that she had no idea how she would care for him. Linda recalls sitting with Simara then, an eighty-five pound sick little girl with breasts full of milk and empty eyes.

"How do you go about telling a child who nobody ever took care of, that she needs to understand she can't take care of her baby, that *he* deserves a good home?" Simara still totes one of Linda's teddy bears around with her wherever she goes. And here they are again, waiting for the next baby to come from Simara's broken life, her third at age eighteen. Linda accompanies her to the doctor and tries to make arrangements, knowing that Simara is going back to the street. "At least she's saying, this is the last one, which she has never said before."

I ask several girls why Simara keeps having babies. I ask because I have been asked this same question so many times.

"She's just crazy," Arlette tells me. "She's lost her mind."

"She's got no sense about nothing, a girl like that. Everybody used her and abused her, so now she's doing it to herself," commented Brenda who hates accounts in which the girls sound pathetic.

But Linda says it a little differently. Linda thinks that Simara is having sex and having babies as a way of forcing people to *see* her, so she can't be overlooked all the time. "I think she is screaming 'Look, here I am, you may hate me, you may pretend I'm nothing, but you *have* to see me when I do this." Simara, Linda and I agreed, is that distorted but popular picture of young girls in poor America. Statistically, she is a tiny minority. Only 2 percent of parenting teens are under the age of fifteen, but they are often the most abused and their number is growing as more children are abandoned and foster care systems unravel. Most of the young women who bear children early in America have not endured the atrocities that Simara suffered. But the story is becoming more common, Linda warns, "it's where we are heading."

Linda and many others who work right down in the heart of the matter regard the Simaras of this nation as a product of American social policy. No one helped Simara's mother before she had babies in chaos, and no one intervened in time for Simara. And how will it be for them, for the daughters and sons of Simara? Linda says to me almost angrily, "*Oh please . . .* I am not even going to think about that."

Beyond Teen Pregnancy: Talking about Girls' Lives

Premature childbearing or teen pregnancy was viewed as part of life by the low-income women and girls who participated in this research. They supported potential ways of avoiding adolescent motherhood, but both older women looking back on early motherhood and young women speaking from their current experience regarded an early and hard motherhood as the most likely path of women in low-income America. Significantly, they seldom used the terminology "teen pregnancy," a term I abandoned years ago because using it seemed to put me outside the real conversation. I learned that both women and girls avoided segregating the issue of early motherhood from the other issues and pressures in female lives. Whether women were remembering the flow of their own girlhoods or girls were analyzing the plight of friends and sisters, these people considered childbearing as complex, as involving all kinds of influences and pressures. Above all, what marked their analysis was a consideration of girls' whole lives, not merely their sexual behavior. And thus they took into consideration the pressures of home life, of family duties, and of troubled parents. They folded in the forces of early sexualization, peer pressure, and male sexual demands. They echoed the words of other girls, "so why should they wait?" In fact, in doing so, participants reiterated much of what is documented by teen fertility researchers.

Historical population data traces a steady increase in adolescent premarital sexual activity over the course of the last four decades.[1] Some research documents modest differences in early sexual activity and somewhat greater differences in birth-control use between lower- and higher-income teens.[2] Overall, in the United States today, a large proportion of adolescent girls and boys become sexually active, have imperfect birth-control use, and thus have accidental pregnancies. The popular explanation for pregnant teens, who are more often low-income, is simple irresponsibility. But the low-income women and girls who participated in this study interpreted the data another way.

They suggested that what *most* distinguishes the behavior of low-income young women from that of higher-income or suburban teens is that, once pregnant, they are far less likely to have abortions.[3] And these discussants argued *this* choice is deeply embedded in family history, culture, religion, boyfriend relationships, *and above all* in the "picture" low-income girls have of themselves. They suggested, in other words, that what teens bring into their anxious ruminations about becoming sexually active *or* pregnant in the inner city of Boston is very much what they do everywhere else. But the outcome is different because so too are the essential pulls in their lives.

Early pregnancy was never discussed as one uniform circumstance. Girls who had babies under the age of fifteen or sixteen, like Simara, were largely regarded as unprotected girls, girls who have been abused.[4] Some girls were viewed as trading sexual accommodation for attention, any attention, and thus were regarded as having low self-esteem, a popular idea in the discourse on teen parenting.[5] But most discussants expressed the belief that, as most girls are seeking boyfriend relationships, many become sexually active in the context of establishing a relationship. The majority of discussants affirmed that having a boyfriend meant having sexual intercourse. And their discussions pointed out that some young women and young men are awkward in their courtings and pairings and are hesitant to make requests for condom use. They assumed that some young men will say they don't want to wear one because there are social forces pushing them to behave that way.[6] Discussants also said that, while many girls try to wait until they know all is well, and most try to be consistent and safe, "things happen." They acknowledged some girls will let the "accidents" happen because they foolishly and desperately think they can keep a young man from slipping away. So when girls do conceive, there are many reasons why most will bear children.

But all of these steps in courtship, sexual intimacy and pregnancy were cast against the bigger world of girls' lives and against the notion of having choice. They argued that the way families raise daughters, and how girls come to know their role and place in the world when there is no tangible path to college and career, affected how girls understand the notion of choice. Choice was not a simple yes or no to sex, pregnancy, or an abortion. I heard complex, interactive variables woven into an analysis that accepted the power of a girl's place, her identity, and the longings of all young people.

Much of the interpretation these women and girls offer is validated in relevant scholarship, particularly qualitative and ethnographic research on teen parenting. Constance Willard Williams has examined girls' life experiences in low-income, specifically African American families, and describes them as "socialized to motherhood," as being raised into competent women who regard motherhood as a responsible and attainable role.[7] Consistent with this analysis of adolescent childbearing, Arline T. Geronimus has argued that an entrenched lack of economic resources may pave the way for early motherhood, as a "rational reproductive strategy."[8] And Kristin Luker has explored the "epidemic of teen pregnancy" as politically contrived, a public policy lightning rod which belies the facts.[9]

The social roles pressed upon daughters in low-income families may collude with external economic conditions to exaggerate their focus upon managing family life. Child welfare efforts toward "family preservation," creatively posed as "kinship care" strategies (and particularly explored in the survival of African American families in America)[10] may in fact be institutionalized practice which burdens women and daughters in those families who take on responsibility for the additional children.[11] The cost of foster care for the children of poor America is, theoretically, a public cost borne grudgingly by the society as a whole. But more often it is women and girls in poor America who put aside their own lives to offer the social glue, the daily attention and care needed to support this nation's economic orphans.

Many discussants pointed to influences which can serve to direct young women away from the worn pathway to early motherhood. Above all, education was viewed as vital to girls finding another course. This common sense is confirmed in research which indicates that high educational aspirations are associated with delayed childbearing, and conversely, that girls who have little academic success are likely to bear children after leaving school. Family attachment to education is an additional influential factor. A mother's pursuit of education appears to influence her daughter's childbearing behavior, perhaps by offering a girl another image of a woman's way to grow up.[12] But a larger influence is the world in which girls reside.

Listening to the lives of low-income women and girls, one quickly understands that older adolescents (whose childbearing constitutes

more than 70 percent of teen fertility)[13] largely are regarded as grown
women in their world. They work as women do and may have done
so since they were ten years old. They handle adult troubles and face
trials and losses from which their families may attempt but fail to
shield them. Many mothers admitted that they believed they had no
choice but to wean their girls early of any childlike ways. Where there
is no special support, no money, nor adequate educational prepara-
tion for college and career, the role of mother is simply the next tough
part of life.

Some social critics have theorized that economic deprivation creates a condition in which early childbearing is adaptation.[14] Young
women, who have no access to college, career ladders, and other en-
tries into the dominant society and economy clearly face little loss in
childbearing while adolescent. Further, many adolescents believe that,
as young mothers, they have a greater "call" on their family circle, either immediate or extended. Thus, childbearing while still young may
offer the greatest security in an environment which holds no promise
of future opportunity. Perhaps the most important observation which
has been made, based upon a nationwide study conducted over several
decades, is that poor women face continued socioeconomic problems
whether or not they have babies as teens.[15] This observation resonated
in the everyday dialogue of women and girls. "Wait for what . . . what
is coming?" they asked. According to the experts, very little. Such research offers precisely what women and girls themselves have insisted
repeatedly in analyzing the course of girls' lives. The pull of female roles
in families and in society, as well as boyfriends' pressures, *can* be resisted, but only if there are tangible alternatives.

Losses and Loathing in the Welfare Years

"You go to welfare when you got no place else, it's the worst, the last stop."

—RENATA, 1990 LIFE-HISTORY STUDY

W hat follows early childbearing for most young women in poor America are the welfare years, the years of being caught in the confines and culture of welfare institutions. Teenage mothers in low-income America often can find help in no other quarter. Usually their birth families are very low on resources. Stretched thin by competing needs and out of patience with a daughter who threatens to increase those needs by bringing a baby home, birth families sometimes force out a pregnant girl. Or sometimes the same tensions cause family conflicts to so escalate high that a girl chooses to leave home. While these studies indicate that many birth families offered some help to pregnant daughters, and some assimilated the next generation into the family circle, two-thirds of all the women interviewed who had borne babies when they were under the age of twenty were living separately from their families within two years of those births.

Most of these young mothers found little support from their boyfriends. The interviews indicated that boyfriends (and, in two cases, husbands) were largely missing within two years of the children's births, as well. Luscious, now thirty-four, remarked, "It's like, as my belly got bigger and bigger, he started to really realize what was coming, and the bigger I got, the less he came over." While the birth of a baby might temporarily draw young parents together, their unity was often short-lived. These women observed that even young men who had committed to help raise a child became increasingly ill at ease with the impending birth and then the reality of a newborn. Several young women sympathetically described ways in which their brothers had reacted to a girlfriend's pregnancy. If a boy has nothing to give, they said, that is, nothing beyond his affection, then he starts to feel bad, to feel "less a man." When the boy's girlfriend, who is frightened by her situation, starts needing more and more from him, she often begins criticizing him, his friends, and his lifestyle. She wants him suddenly to transform himself into a supporting man, with an income and a real understanding of fatherhood. She wants him to reassure her again and again of his love because she is so scared. In other words, as explained by an older sister of a brother who left his girlfriend and daughter behind, she does everything a woman can do to drive a young man away. The majority of women in these interviews reported being estranged from the father of their child by the baby's first birthday.

So, for many of these low-income mothers, two significant sources of financial and emotional support—the family and the father of the child—very quickly disappeared. Those losses were evident in the way these women talked about this period of their lives. More than anything, they spoke of little erosions which finally wear you down into someone you don't want to be. They spoke of chronic exhaustion. They spoke of having no car, no warm coats, no baby clothes, no functioning laundry in the building, no elevator and many stairs, no heat sometimes, no Pampers, no tampons, of long lines at clinics, and of being able to go only to stores which accept food stamps, and, above all, of having no one to "offer a kind word." They spoke of being scared, angry, and alone both inside and outside.

Given all of this, it should come as no surprise that most of these women, and by their accounts, also their mothers, sisters, and others, spent several years on welfare while raising young children. The statistics for the Life-History Study are very similar to national data. More than half of these families spent less than five years on welfare, about 20 percent spent less than a year. But some, particularly those who had more than one child and had not yet completed high school, were likely to be on welfare for much longer.

When I asked women about the popular idea that there is a "welfare culture," they were emphatic that this was so. They said it is a culture in which incoherence rules, where the game changes weekly, where paperwork disappears, and the same forms must be filled out again and again, but no one can say why. They said it is a culture of listless caseworkers who cite rules and regulations but cannot explain them. They recalled appointments abruptly canceled and rescheduled without notice or regard to any other obligations a woman might have. They described a culture of mandates, a snarl of housing, job training, Aid for Families with Dependent Children (AFDC), Medicaid, and other regulations which sometimes contradict each other. And if you look straight into the eyes of the public official, these women claimed, there is a certain wink there, a silent acknowledgment that, no, there is no map to guide you because there is no intent that you should find your way. Occasionally someone *will* advise you, they said. Occasionally, an empathetic welfare worker will suggest how to navigate a particularly chaotic passage, but mostly they stare back at you without response or affect. All of it "stinks of stigma," said Veronica, a single mother of two in her mid-thirties who used welfare intermittently while her children were little.

And, you may even meet a caseworker who will harass you or try to take advantage of you because they can get away with it, because *no one is watching their behavior*. Above all, women remembered long, long waits which might lead to nothing at all. Being kept waiting can teach you that your time is without value, that your own effort and efficiency is not expected or noticed.

"It's not about making sense," said Veronica. "It's supposed to make you feel helpless, make you feel you are trash."

Nemesis, also in her thirties, said, "They see you as a commodity, one that no one wants. They hold you in contempt so you'd better do the same back."

And Luscious said, "There's this smell I have only smelled in that place, for me it is the smell of shame."

All of this, I was told, can have a corrosive effect upon a young mother. The welfare years were a time of regulatory purgatory. These were years of loneliness and deprivation, years of coping with a tangle of contradictory regulations. And beyond all that, this was a time of stigma, of being cast as "low-lifes," the female underclass. The combined hardship and isolation, and the thousands of ways in which they experienced welfare stigma, caused many women to lose heart and then to lose caution. Some became ill with depression. Some reached out for a man just to fill the loneliness, even when they knew better. Some grabbed onto alcohol and drugs to numb everything painful, numbing themselves as well to the pain their children endured. A few hurt their children. Young women on welfare, the grown women said, are "an easy hit." They get stunned from all sides, and from inside too. Poverty, loneliness, and shame can destroy a woman's "second sight," they said, her common sense and caution about men, her devotion to her children, her decent friendships, her "businesslike" behavior, her belief in herself.

"It's like you are all alone in the world and you know maybe it's not a good idea, and maybe you know he's not all that good, but you're all alone. And then next thing you know, you're in it and it may be years before you get yourself out again."

—*Nell*

I interviewed Nell in 1992, early in this study, and as the years passed her words seemed prophetic. Of the fifty women interviewed between 1990 and 1998 for the Life-History Study, more than half had experienced abuse, violence and/or sexual abuse, from partners over the course of their child-raising years. Violence included burnings, beatings, knifings, marital rapes, and forced prostitution. Twelve women were involved in substance abuse, their own addictions (three women) or that of men whom they turned to and lived with despite their addiction. "I really didn't have no other place to go," I was told. This was a time, the women recalled, when their children endured three or four, sometimes seven or ten years of life in a place where anxiety and deprivation reigned. A place where access to food, a roof, a winter coat and shoes, a heated home, a quiet night's sleep, a visit to the doctor's office, was not a child's right. For millions of American children, Black, white and Latino children, there is no such thing during these years as bodily safety, nothing is secure. And in most cases their chief advocate is an isolated and vulnerable young mother who is struggling with more than she can manage.

Facing Welfare History Together: Terry and Rona, Roxbury, 1991

Terry and Rona are both in their thirties when we meet at a multi-service program in the Roxbury section of Boston. Both are single mothers of two children and have been on and off welfare during their years of child raising. They suggest that we talk all together, rather than set up several individual interviews because "we already know each other's business." They are very good at drawing each other out, and I find myself sitting back for much of the two interviews, listening to them reconstruct their separate but shared history.

Until her father's death when she was finishing elementary school, Rona lived with her parents and six siblings in a working-class community that she remembers for its flower boxes, large school playgrounds, and well-known neighbors. After her father died, Rona's mother moved with her seven children into an aging public housing development and began working double shifts as a kitchen aide in a local hospital.

Rona says her mother made the wrong decision when she tried to avoid public assistance by working so many hours. Her mother wanted to avoid "going on the dole" at any cost, but Rona thinks that she should have stayed at home with her "pack of kids." In the housing development, Rona's brothers began to "run with a group of criminals," and two of her sisters "started messing with boys when they were still babies."

Terry interrupts to point out that Rona's mother was "just trying to do right by her kids," trying to keep food on the table and a roof over their heads. "You can't really put her down for that," Terry says in a voice that tries to guide Rona away from bitterness. But Rona remembers that she and her siblings were dealing with every kind of danger and temptation, with no adult guidance. She was suffering, she says, and her mother should have noticed and stayed home. Yes, Terry agrees, but Rona's mother was just trying, "like you and I have been trying and we don't always do everything right." Rona looks down. "I did nothing right," she mutters. Terry intervenes forcefully this time, "Now, don't start that, Rona, you know that's gonna bring you down."

By the time that Rona was eighteen years old she was living alone in a small, "nasty" apartment with a two-year-old daughter. The father of her child was still "coming around" once in a while but offered very little help. She spent a year living in a "drug-filled" building, scared and isolated. She seldom left the tiny apartment and she started daydreaming about suicide. "I think I might have done it only there was little Nicole following me around. She was already worrying about me." Terry pats Rona's arm in sympathy.

When there was a shooting death right next door, Rona fled her apartment for the next one she could find. On moving day she met Kabrel, the father of her son. "There I was, a baby hanging off my arm and this man came along," she says ruefully. Rona was carrying boxes up the three flights of stairs with Nicole clinging to her pants when Kabrel appeared. "He seemed like an angel to me. He scooped up

Nicole and a box of my stuff and carried them up. He helped me with all my stuff." Kabrel, the angel on the stairs, turned out to be something very different. He sent Rona to the hospital several times with lacerations and broken bones, violently abusing her even when she was pregnant with his son. When he started whipping Nicole with a cord, Rona packed up her two babies and nothing else and fled to a battered women's shelter. Eight years later, she is still trying to patch together some security, a chance to raise her children in safety.

Rona believes that her loneliness, poverty, and despair nearly extinguished her ability to fight against abuse. She was so reduced that she allowed her daughter, at least for a time, to be abused, until finally she found the strength to get out. "Where I came from," she tells Terry and me, "was poor and so I stayed poor, stayed with others who are poor. And that can make a woman lose her second sense, you know, her sense about her self. She gets used to being with a man who abuses her, she gets used to abuse. And then, don't you know, she teaches her daughter to do the same . . . what else does the child know?"

Terry quietly listens while Rona explains how she came to tolerate abuse. She takes a deep breath when Rona falls silent, waiting a few moments before letting loose with her own story. A fast talker, she tells a story that is similar to Rona's in some ways. Like Rona, Terry became detached from her birth family at an early age. Terry's mother remarried when Terry was fifteen, and her stepfather increasingly behaved toward her "not like a father should." She recalls feeling as though her mother was both jealous of the inappropriate attention her stepfather gave her and also worried about it, torn between treating her adolescent daughter as someone to protect or as a competitor. Convinced that her stepfather was sexually harassing her, and that her mother wanted her to leave, Terry began staying out late, "messing around with drugs and alcohol," and doing very poorly in school. Her mother sent her to live with her father's mother for the summer. Her father's family was cold to Terry, critical and disrespectful, and Terry felt they wanted nothing to do with her. She took off in the middle of that summer and didn't return to her mother's house until her stepfather moved out eight years later, "when my ma realized he was starting up with my little sister." Rona shakes her head in sympathy.

Terry spent the next ten years of her life living by her wits, waiting on tables, and doing drugs. When she realized she was pregnant, she tried to curb her addictions. The idea that the baby might arrive sick and addicted appalled her. "I had sunk down pretty low by then," she tells us. "I had sold myself on the street, I was living with a man who beat the hell out of me if I didn't come home with enough cash for his habit." Rona puts her hand on Terry's arm and asks, "Do you really need to tell about all that stuff again? I can never sleep at night after hearing about it," she explains to me. Terry admits that she used talking it out, over and over again, as part of her therapy. "But, I'm getting past it," she says. "I don't have to do that now." I feel a shiver of relief, which Rona notices. "You're a wimp, too," she says with a grin.

While she was pregnant, Terry gave up smoking and drinking and managed a drastic reduction in her drug addiction. Going into delivery, she feared that her baby daughter would have some traces of cocaine in her, despite Terry's effort to avoid the drug. But the baby, astonishingly, was over six pounds, healthy, and "she immediately wanted to suck, like right away, which the nurses told me was a good sign."

Terry still hadn't left her abusive partner, even though he beat her into premature labor and "tore my stitches after I got home." The catalyst for that break came one year later, when child protective services threatened to take Amelia away. Terry went on AFDC and tried hard to care for Amelia. "Yeah, it was very depressing," she says, "but after what I had been through, I was glad it [welfare] was there. I had nowhere else to go." She plunged into every kind of therapeutic group she could join and now goes to battered women's peer-support meetings on Monday, Narcotics Anonymous on Tuesdays and Thursdays, and serves food at the neighborhood shelter on Fridays. "That's a night I stay really busy," she says with enthusiasm. She attends more support group meetings on the weekends. Everywhere she's gone, Terry says, she's taken Amelia with her, "first in a basket, then in a stroller, and now holding her hand." Terry believes that she needed help as a girl, as a teen, and as a young mother. She claims fears and addiction as her own demons, but she believes also that "I could have been helped before. I mean, once I got help, I ran to it, you know? I could have been helped years before that."

We sit quietly for a few minutes after Terry finishes talking, each of us looking off somewhere, beyond the park benches and trees in bloom and the narrow Boston streets that surround the small square park. It is a beautiful spring day.

I ask Terry and Rona how it is for teens and young women now who have children and no help. Terry, the "motor mouth," takes off. She believes the heart of the battle is education. And she believes that education is reserved for the middle-class. Instead of being educated, she asserts, the lower classes are trained. "We do training programs, like 'sit up, dress right, be good,' but not education. We don't educate girls, to go to college, to think about *being somebody* in the world and not just being with some man."

Currently, Terry and Rona are both attending college. Terry says the experience is "like a light bulb went off, like I *see it* now." "They" don't want others to get this perspective, Terry says heatedly, to recognize that there is no justice in the American system of education, in the labor market, in welfare policy. Rona, who has been listening to her friend and nodding in agreement, gently puts her hand over Terry's mouth. Terry, looking sheepish, subsides into silence. After a pause Rona says, "That's why Black people have been about education from the beginning. That's why they never wanted us to read. When you read, you know, and after, you know, that's when you *do*."

Terry bursts out laughing and turns to me. "See, she tells it in one sentence and me I go on and on." Then, she's off and talking again. Lots of white and Hispanic women need an education too, she reminds us. "Poor is poor, it's not a color," she says with conviction. Rona nods in agreement.

The Early Years Were the Hardest: Tania, Dorchester, 1990

Tania calls me to say that she has heard I am looking for women to interview, women who, as she puts it, "have done hard time on welfare." She'd like to participate. I meet her, an African American woman in her mid-thirties, her two adolescent sons, and two young "god-children" in a large park.

I can see that Tania is surprised when I arrive carrying my youngest daughter, who is only a few months old. Not surprised that I bring a child, of course, considering that she has two in tow, but surprised that my daughter is so young. Tania and I are both well into our thirties, and in her carefully phrased opinion, we are a "little too tired for giving milk." Still, she is charmed by Clara's sloppy baby grins. Tania's two little god-daughters, Jasmine and Tayisha, sit beside me, gently trading Clara back and forth, singing to her and discussing her attributes.

Tania comes from a family of twelve children. Her mother left her father in the South and migrated to Boston with their seven children, Tania among them. With her second marriage, Tania's mother gave birth to the five younger children.

"We were pretty poor," Tania remembers, "but in most ways we didn't know it." Finding a place to live and keeping food on the table was very hard with so many children. Her large family lived through a gutting fire, several evictions, and serious illnesses. Tania and her siblings had a difficult time keeping up in school. "We were from the backwoods of the South, and we had that 'country' accent, and we wore shabby clothes. But my sisters and me were best friends, and most of the time I didn't feel bad." Tania and her sister, who was only one year older, stuck close together, worked hard to keep up, and found support from a wonderful teacher, Miss Jones, who went out of her way to help her students. "When my sister asked to be held back so we could be in the same class, Miss Jones went along with it. But when we asked her to hold us back again so we could stay in her class, she said no. We would have stayed there forever, she was so nice to us."

Tayisha, the older of the two little girls, interrupts Tania. "'Scuse me," she says with a solemn expression, "but this baby needs her other blanket 'cause we think she's going to catch cold." One little girl holds Clara's fingers, the other is touching her nose. "It's the best way to tell if a baby is cold," they tell me. I smile at Tania as I fish out Clara's other blanket and hand it over to the girls. Tania watches them with pride, as they tenderly wrap my daughter in the second blanket.

There was seldom enough food or shoes or beds to go around in Tania's childhood home. Miss Jones came by the apartment one time to speak with Tania's mother. She asked permission to give the girls each a new dress and sneakers. Tania smoothes out her skirt and turns her face away, recalling this astonishing kindness twenty-five years later. "I didn't know so many white people then, you know," she says, turning back to me. "But she helped me know that they can act like us, they can have strong feelings."

Tania's older siblings left home, some with hope in their hearts, and some came back beaten down. Before the babies of this family were all grown, more babies came home in the arms of dispirited young parents. "There weren't any jobs for people who sounded like us," she says. "The older boys had very little education."

Tania's mother was always the center of the family. Throughout her life, she relentlessly worked to "keep us having hope to believe that we could get to be somebody. We worshiped her." Tania explains that she was never a follower but, like her mother, a leader. Only *she* had no intention of having all those children. Tania and her sister worked hard to catch up in school, and pretty soon they were "pulling A's and B's."

But her grades never led Tania to think she would go to college. Instead, she entered a trade school in Boston, one of the first of five females who ever attended the school. It was strange, she says, to be among so many boys all the time, but having lots of brothers and not being "a sissy" helped her out. Her sister, who also entered the school, "got into some men troubles and dropped out." But Tania finished the program, the only girl in her class to do so. She is still very proud to recall this achievement, not so much because of the skills she gained, which as it turned out did her little good, but because she saw it through.

Tania met Peter, the Jamaican father of her children, when he was attending a community college near Tania's trade school. Peter's family was not charmed by his growing relationship with an African American woman. She explains, "You know racism isn't only the way of white people, we all have our own ways too. The people from the islands look down on Black people here, like, you've been here all this while, why haven't you done better?"

Tania had a baby when she was nineteen. While Tania's mother "never ran out of love for us," she was, nonetheless, completely overwhelmed by the poverty which had swept into another generation of her family. After Tania's son was born, she faced the welfare office alone for the first time. "My mother finally convinced me to go 'cause she knew that I would put it off forever, and Peter's parents would make sure there was food for the baby but I could starve to death. So she dragged me down, and they started their questions and more questions . . . they wanted to know where my moles are." Their questions, she recalls, were that intimate. "They thought nothing of me as a person, a good student and someone who didn't hang out or get high. I just needed some help because I had a baby and we had no money. But they treated me like a garbage can."

Tania had just gone back to work when she realized she was again pregnant. She had been relying on Peter's family to care for her two-year-old son, but when they heard another baby was on the way, they

told Tania she would have to go. Peter, who had increasingly regarded
Tania as an obstacle to his future prospects, became cold and abusive.
One night, after hours of fighting with Peter, she went into preterm labor. Peter moved to California while she was still in the hospital. Tania
moved into a one-bedroom apartment in a public housing complex
with Tyler, her eldest, and her newborn baby and went back on welfare.

"I went into a deep depression," Tania says. "Maybe I thought that
Peter would love me again, the way he had when I was carrying Tyler.
Then I knew it was hopeless, that he thought he could never get ahead
with me and another baby just meant more burden. I lay in bed for five
months crying. I wouldn't contact anyone, not even my family. My son
watched me cry all day long." Tania's sister, mother, and mother-in-law
helped out when they could, but Tania felt truly alone. She remembers
the time as the worst part of her life, caring for a newborn and a distressed three-year-old in a tiny place that steamed in the summer and
froze in the winter.

When Marcus, her second son, turned two, Tania says, "I got over
that man and I realized it was all up to me. I had two beautiful boys
and my own determination, and that's all that kept me from falling
apart. But remember, I spent months in bed crying, wheezing with
asthma that I never got before or since. Tyler still calls them my 'crying
times.'"

Descriptions of deep depression, like this, were often a part of these
women's accounts of their welfare years. What they describe is not only
sadness associated with losses which tend to mount up during this period, but the slow-moving, sick-at-heart depression which can transform a person. Tania had a lot of company, I discovered over the years.
Polly, for example, told me, "I longed for night because then I could
drink and get numb." The anesthesia of alcohol would disguise despair
for Polly for awhile, but she still cries when she thinks of her children
watching her drink at night. Rona recalled, more than anything, the

worried face of her little daughter who "tried to make little jokes for me so's I'd maybe laugh that day—'I be funny for you, Momma,' she'd say." Tania too feels guilty about the misery her sons were born into. She understands how she arrived at such a depressing place, but she won't forgive herself for the suffering of her children. She is still shocked at the woman she became, if only for a few years. "Those were important years," she says, grieving aloud. "They were the first years of my sons' lives."

Quick Notes

"He would hold my head as I cried. I would tell him, 'It's OK baby, go to sleep. Mama's OK.' But he stopped sleeping well. It was like he knew I was thinking of ending it all."

—Tania, 1990

"I would cry all the way to the welfare office and my daughter would cry with me. Once inside, I never cried, never smiled, never said nothing I didn't have to. And you know, I think she saw that too 'cause she would go all quiet with me. . . . How did I feel? Like a stone. We were two stones, a big one and a little one."

—Renata, 1992

"I lost control, I went crazy that night. I took the pillow and I covered her face [she pushes off her sister's comforting hand from her arm]. YES, I DID, I DID . . . Then I took it off and then I did it again. Then I said to myself, 'Jackie, you're killing Kenata, your baby, you're killing her.' I ran to the phone and I called DSS [state child protective service] and I reported myself."

—Jackie, 1990

"I hear someone keening in the hallway, a high-pitched crazy sound. Carmen and I stop short in our conversation and quickly walk out into the hall of this busy child-care center where we see Elba, her

arms around a struggling woman. Elba is speaking a rapid stream of
Spanish to the wailing woman, rubbing her arms, and Carmen, hear-
ing what she says, seems to collapse. She tells me that Theresa, the
woman who weeps, is learning of her sister's death, a sister who has
three small children. This sister has been depressed for several years
and wasn't able to endure some recent misfortunes. She recently lost
her husband and also had to face the new welfare policy in Massachu-
setts, which takes no prisoners. She'd been notified that she was being
cut off of AFDC and had to find a community service job or employ-
ment. This woman, Theresa's younger sister, had committed suicide the
evening before.

"It is a sickening blow that everybody seems to feel, a feeling of loss
that moves throughout the building. Adults and even children seem
subdued by the news, speaking quietly of people they know who are so
similar to this young mother, people close at hand, some here right now.

"Over the weeks that follow her sister's death, Theresa tries to fig-
ure out how she might keep her sister's children, bring them into her
own family. But she has three children of her own and a marriage al-
ready strained, so her sister's children go into foster care. I watch from
afar over the next few months, not about to say more than the simple
words of condolence because I do not know Theresa. I see her walk-
ing the halls more slowly now. She doesn't look you in the eye. Her face
seems frozen."

                                        —In Jamaica Plain, 1996

There's No One Else to Blame: MaryBeth, Boston, 1993

I meet MaryBeth while conducting a research project in a community-
based family program in the South End of Boston in 1993. MB, as she
is called, is a social worker, focused on children of young mothers on
welfare. She spends her days referring mothers to the frayed web of services which still exist at that time. She tries to place children in low-cost

child-care programs. She encourages battered women to go to shelter-ing programs. She gets tough with drinking and drug-taking parents. She watches hardship pour in the office door from nine in the morning until late at night. MB sees the very worst of what goes on when par-ents despair in America, and above all MB watches the children. She is very discouraged on the day we meet for an interview.

"You see kids come in [to the child care center] and you know they are crazed. They've come from a no-sleep night in a crowded apart-ment and you already know that family is in crisis, the mother is hold-ing on by a thread. And these kids are supposed to sit still and say 'bye-bye' to mommy [as she goes out to handle housing, welfare, and job training problems] and they really don't know if she is going to make it back."

MB has seen babies lose weight and lose heart. She has watched de-pression set in, a particularly savage process in tiny children, stunting little bodies and young minds. And she has seen rage too, toddlers try-ing to beat on babies and babies bruised and "who the hell knows how it happened." MB is full of vitality and outrage, but also vulnerable, and she is unable to stop her tears as she recalls the faces she has seen. As she speaks she grows more and more angry, expressing contempt for inadequate mothers, absent fathers, family madness. Mothers par-ticularly anger MB because, well, who else is there? And those moth-ers who scream at their kids, scream curses at them, who hit them. MB is barely controlling her fury as the old stories come spilling out.

I ask MB if she is a mother and she nods hard, yes, of three young children. She works and she gets tired, but she doesn't lose control. She has a husband who agrees with her that hitting children is wrong. They had to explain this "no corporal punishment" to MB's mother, who watches her grandchildren some afternoons. Even with her master's de-gree in social work, her husband's salary as a postal worker, and her mother's ready availability, MB and her husband must struggle to stay in a place that is safe and has decent schools, and to stay positive. Gently, I prod MB with a question. How would it have been if she had had those babies young, alone, with no man, no mother, no safety, no respect, and lots of troubles? MB, no fool, sees where this line of reflection leads. She does not know how she would cope with what these mothers face, she says, "but I get to the point where I can't take it and there is no one else to blame." I ask whether it is easier, and cheaper too, to blame parents. Maybe that's how we wash our hands of the pain. MB looks out of the window of her crowded little office. "Maybe I'm just at the end of my rope, you know. Burnt to a crisp. Maybe you can only do this for just so long," she says wearily.

ABUSE AMONG THE REGULATORS

In the course of listening to many accounts of women dealing with the welfare system, I came upon an experience for which I had no immediate terminology. This experience rose out of women's accounts of abuse, almost always committed by men, but not boyfriends, husbands, nor even strangers. I have termed this experience "abuse among the regulators." It is an abusive dynamic set within a distinct relationship, the relationship between one who has power and is male, and one who does not and is female. It occurred between a woman who approaches public institutions because she is poor and a man who is the institutional official. It happened between a woman who is in public housing and the building manager who repairs her apartment. It tainted the relationship between a woman and her male caseworker at the welfare office; between a woman in a mandated job training program and her instructor, who will pass or fail her; and between a woman and her drug counselor, who will say she is staying sober or she is not. It even emerged between a mother and the driver of a van who took her children to a publicly funded children's program each afternoon.

Over the years women mentioned counselors, caseworkers, building managers, and other men with particular power conferred upon them by public offices who had used their position to sexually exploit and abuse the women. These stories of "regulatory abusers" caught me off guard. More than two-thirds of the Life-History interviews were complete before I recognized a pattern in these casually described experiences. When I began to ask systematically about this harassment and exploitation, the data which emerged was as profound to me as it was unremarkable to many of the women I questioned. Most men, they counseled me, attempt to extract sex from women over whom they have power, as long as they can get away with it. It was the way of the world. *"I mean, come on Lisa, where have you been?"* Close by, I thought to myself, close enough to have seen this before.

Twenty-four-year-old Janet entered a job training program through the welfare office. While she loved the outdoors and wanted to do something active, she was sent to a computer training class. The vocational instructor found her attractive.

"He wasn't bad at first, you know, compliments and all that, but I knew what was coming." Janet needed to maintain her welfare and subsidized child-care status through successful progress in the program. "You know, I put him off with a little of this and that, I kind of went along with some of the rubbing and all that. He started to hit on some of the other girls, I kept out of sight." But did she tell anyone? "Tell who, what for?" Janet asked me disinterestedly.

Maria, twenty-eight, was propositioned by a landlord in her publicly subsidized apartment. He told her he would fix the windows and other basic repairs "for sex." Her cousin's husband made the repairs instead, in exchange for child care which Maria provided. But sometimes she would let this landlord fondle her to get him to do the most basic kinds of upkeep. The worst was when her son would see it occur. Her son knew that she hated this landlord and yet there he was, stroking Mommy's arm.

Rona, who is almost thirty, says that the building manager in her apartment complex told her he would give her a better unit if she "delivered." Despite holes in the walls and the decay around her, she chose to stay put.

Tabitha, who is in her twenties, had a welfare worker who was a source of torment to her. She was called in for frequent "case reviews," a process which reassessed her eligibility for aid. At those meetings, "all he would ask about was my sex life, like, had I had any after my son was born? He wanted details and details of what my boyfriend did, what I did, how it felt, like that." Tabitha's aunt eventually confronted this welfare voyeur, but he remained in his job and Tabitha was passed on to another caseworker.

Tracy, in her early thirties, was referred to a drug rehabilitation program as part of a process to reclaim custody of her daughter. If she did not "pass" the program, she would lose parental rights. Her counselor in the drug program told Tracy that sex was required to pass. "Look, to the world I was nothing but a coke-whore. Now I had not had any kind of substance for months and I was trying my best. He made it simple, I was to give him what he wanted or he would report me out bad. Who would believe me anyway, come on. There was nothing I wouldn't do to get my daughter back . . . nothing."

Dianne was in her late twenties when a fire destroyed her apartment, and she and her children had to live in a "welfare motel" for several months. It was a place where the conditions were never monitored, Dianne says, where children are shut up and "mothers are bouncing off the walls." They lived in one small room, with a cacophony of sounds day and night; screaming, crying, sometimes a sad voice singing. According to Dianne, men would come to the motel at night looking for sex. She would hear truck drivers drive into the parking lot at night and they would start banging on the doors. "You know, we're homeless, on welfare, we're whores right?" One night she saw two men dragging a young girl out of her room, she was screaming for help. "I ran down to the guy at the front desk and yelled at him to call the police. He told me to shut up or he'd say I was a troublemaker. I found out they gave him money to look away." Dianne stares out of the stained glass window of the church where we meet that day. "God knows what happened to that poor girl."

When I asked other women and adolescent girls if they knew of these kinds of incidents, many just shrugged. It happens, they told me again and again. It happens all the time when girls are out there, with no one to help out, and no one who's going to believe you. Some people can withstand it, hold out, they explained, and some may have too much at stake. Or they just don't have the strength left. And then, "they kind of believe you ask for it anyway." It's part of the welfare culture, they explained to me.

There has been some work, local to Massachusetts, undertaken to expose and analyze the "lawlessness" of welfare institutions. Vickie Steinitz has considered welfare reform in the context of international standards of human rights violations, and she argues that there is a "dismal picture of abuses and injustices by the state on vulnerable women who are struggling to provide for themselves and their children under very difficult circumstances."[1] An overt effort to reduce the number of families who receive assistance, accelerated in those states which boast harsh welfare-reform policy, provides a cultural backdrop for all kinds of "lawless" behavior. Such a culture may give rise to a lack of restraint among officials in their treatment of women, the essential condition in which sexual abuse thrives.[2]

I often found it difficult to get responses from women when I first asked them to analyze this data on regulatory abuse, even from women who reported such incidents had occurred in their own lives. This difficulty perhaps reflects the common social habit of silence about experiences of abuse. Yet I also found it was relatively easy to break the silence if I suggested that the abuses I had uncovered were

unusual—if I suggested they were trivial or invalid. Suddenly, I was offered more evidence, more stories, more suggestions of where to look
for such abuses. A woman from El Salvador, for example, suggested
we look at what happens to women who cross the border from Mex-
ico into the states. A young white woman referred to "getting messed
with" when a girl has cop trouble, that some police will take sexual
advantage of a woman. Or guess what happens to girls in foster care,
queried another, one who had been there. Or women with prison
records looking for work, or women who are homeless, or girls in
youth services programs run by men, or even, nowadays, women who
have to do mandatory community-service work with men bosses.
What do you think happens, they asked, to a woman who is here ille-
gally when the boss she works for under-the-table wants more than his
kitchen cleaned. Or when the landlord comes for the rent and you
don't have it all. And so on.

Numerous women offered suggestions about where to go, who to
watch, and how to recognize what they would then matter-of-factly
sum up as "just the way it is." "This is not something a woman wants
to speak about, you know, it brings shame," I was told. Most women
reflected this kind of hard acceptance, and very few asserted that the
shame should be placed elsewhere. Some did, however. A few older
women suggested there is a collective history of women and girls in
poor America and that this history includes degradation through sexual harassment and abuse. Several African American women regarded
welfare abuse as the latter-day version of slavery culture. Women
slaves, they said, "had no rights, just like welfare." A few women who
have become involved in women's rights work suggested that wherever
power is particularly unbalanced, there is covert license to abuse those
with the least of it, "and who's got less power than some girl on welfare?"[3]

BREAKING THE RULES

In their stories of their welfare years, women not only detailed ways in which the system worked to increase their troubles—the long waits, senseless regulations, incompetent officials, and shaming environment—and the sexually abusive violations of authority by some male regulators, they also described to me ways that they have learned to resist inhumane rules. There are, they said, as many ways to break the rules as there are impossible circumstances to live under.

My cousin bakes cakes for parties, one woman told me. My sister has helped teach English to family members, said a Puerto Rican woman. I heard about cleaners, caterers, school-lunch monitors, and hairdressers, all part-time and all off the books. How much money does this come to, I asked. It comes to a pair sneakers for my children when they go back to school, something which makes them feel a little better about another year. It comes to a "coming-out dress" for my fifteen-year-old, said another, the only party she has ever had. It comes to a large Christmas dinner for my family, my grandparents and aunts and uncles who have fed me and mine too many times to recall. And what about what we read in the paper, I made myself ask. Like what about buying drugs, drink, handing money over to boyfriends to use for what not. Sure, some women do that, I was told, some who are addicted to substances and to a man. But most women search the underground for ways to make some cash because the income of welfare is not enough to care for the people you love, not nearly.

I came to think of this as an "outlaw" analysis, a stepping outside of laws which no one can abide. It can be shaky ground, older women acknowledged, because while you do your business to survive, you must hold onto a sense of right and wrong, and teach that to your children. Sometimes, some people can lose their bearings and then they turn into people they don't want to be. It can be hard to hold onto your own ethical code, after years of hardship and no exit.

These "outlaw" strategies seemed to contradict what many women had told me, that you acquiesce to regulatory authority whenever possible, saving up your strength and anger. They had counseled passing through the various agencies unnoticed and impassive, just as Renata had described it, *being stones*. But I learned that complex strategies are required, and that you choose those best suited to the struggle. Sometimes when the rules contradict each other and pile up in incomprehensible ways, it becomes necessary to subvert them, to go around them. Sometimes when welfare officials tell you, this is all the money you have to eat and pay bills, and you know *and that official knows as well as you do* that one cannot survive on that amount, well something must be done. And then a duel begins, one which necessitates prevarication, duplicity, playacting, risk taking. It *is* risky. It is an old conflict which adjusts and evolves with the turn of many screws. To stay healthy in this culture, one must hold on tight to what you know, to the way you have been brought along, to what is necessary to deal with this world.

I asked people who sit on the other side of the desk—social workers in community health centers, staff in jobs programs for low-income women, day-care center teachers who serve families under certain income levels if they had an analysis of this same gambit. These points of reference stretch well beyond the core welfare program, AFDC, but they are closely allied. Some people bluntly agreed, the rules do not add up. Whether they were sympathetic or not, they saw that duplicity, creative accounting, and vague, unaccountable answers to regulatory questions were an adaptive survival technique.

Luscious, Boston, 1993

> *"We all be creative with our accounts you know, just like the man."*

Luscious was born in Boston twenty years ago, the fifth of six children. Her family comes from Jamaica. When Luscious was five, her mother had a stroke which left her unable to speak clearly or walk without a cane. Neither the baby of the family nor yet old enough to negotiate her own place in the scramble that followed her mother's illness, Luscious felt lost.

Luscious recalls other experiences which shaped her childhood. Her family was a religious one, but Luscious remembers rejecting religion at the age of six: "If God could do like he did to my mother, then we have nothing to talk about." She remembers her father's mother as someone who seemed to recognize that Luscious was adrift and so "became my guardian angel." She also recalls with great tenderness one girlfriend who remained very close throughout her girlhood, "like a sister, you know, like you take her side no matter what." She speaks of having been raped as a young girl by several men who came into a house where she was baby-sitting one night. Luscious believes that the owner of the house, a member of her church, had told these men—one was his brother—that she was all alone. Her family never filed charges against the men. They were so shocked and shamed by the incident that they did not want it to become public.

"But my granny did something back to them," Luscious adds. What was that? She carefully eyes me and then, in an authoritative tone that is surely a perfect replication of her grandmother's voice, says it can't be discussed. After a moment, I move on to a different subject, but Luscious interrupts with a whisper: "They all got pretty sick, really sick. My grandmother knows about spirits."

Luscious had a baby at the age of seventeen, a few months after she graduated from high school. Her child's father left for the army two months before the baby was born. Like Polly and Arlette, Luscious was ejected from the family before she became a mother, but *she* landed in the arms of her granny. "I knew she would be there for me so it wasn't as bad as it would have been . . . but without my guardian angel, who knows what would have happened to me?"

Her grandmother's affection was a great support to Luscious, especially when she found that dealing with the welfare office was an exercise in humiliation. She had agreed with her child's father, given his family's kindness and periodic financial help, not to reveal his name to welfare officials. Her "in-laws" were very supportive of Luscious and provided child care which was dependable and safe. "If I'd of told on Lennie," Luscious says, "he would have been in trouble and then it would have ruined everything." Her grandmother disliked the lie but advised her to stick with it. This meant saying that "I didn't know who the father was . . . like I was so loose I didn't know who I'd had sex with." This deceit was antithetical to everything Luscious had been raised to believe and value. It meant accepting the most disrespectful label a woman can have.

Luscious said the walk to the welfare office was like a long march. "I would cry all the way there and all the way back." They required identifications, birth certificates, information about her parents' status and income. When she told them that her parents "don't have anything to do with me," they told her "too bad, call them up and get the information." Finally, her grandmother went to the welfare office and made the caseworker call Luscious's father. When he harangued his daughter as a whore and the caseworker as the devil's assistant, they were finally persuaded that Luscious would receive no help from that quarter. She says that she never received any hopeful encouragement or guidance from welfare officials, that the whole exchange was based upon the idea "that I was some loose girl, that I wanted to be some single mother with nothing but their dirty money. I wish bad things on them," she tells me in a low voice.

And how does a woman survive on welfare, I ask Luscious. She tells me what women have told me for twenty years, ever since I first listened to them talking in the Charlestown candy factory. No one survives on welfare alone, even if you live with your grandmother. Everybody has other sources: supports, trades, barters. Sometimes you get

hooked up with questionable people when you make your underground deals. Like drugs? I ask Luscious, because that is what I am
asked so often. Maybe, she says, but anything you do off-the-books
means you have crossed the line. You are into the cheater territory. If
you're on welfare and your grandmother is teaching you to give counsel to people to rid spirits which plague them, and you charge for this
service, you're cheating. If you provide child care for a fee for friends
who are working several nights a week, and you don't report the income, you are a lawbreaker. "Or like, if you use your nephew's Medicaid card [for your own child] 'cause you don't have one yet, 'cause
they won't process your papers until you get some paper, but no one
can tell you how or where to do it . . . well . . . that's cheating."

One social worker whom I asked about welfare survival strategies,
Anne, offered this analysis. The culture of requisite prevarication, she
said, is part of a backdrop which gives rise to the whole "dysfunctional affect" which labels so many poor women. This affect, she explained, is the kind of no-response, shutdown behavior that is typical
of many women on welfare. Like stones, I offered, and she approved
of the image.

Anne recalled for me a story from when she was a younger and
deeply engaged social worker. She worked with a young white woman
for over an hour; cajoling, encouraging, and informing her about what
was needed to get her son into a special-needs program and receive the
benefits involved. Eventually, she all but filled out the forms for the
blank-faced, friendly young woman who shoved them into her bag and
said, "OK, bye now." Anne, convinced the woman was retarded, wondered if the lethargic three-year-old who was drinking coke out of a
baby bottle would ever have a chance.

After work, Anne went out for pizza. While waiting in line, she listened in on an animated conversation between some young women,

and turning to look, she recognized the "slow" client from earlier in the day. The young woman was bouncing her baby on her lap and laughing with two friends, talking about the preschool program her son would attend. "She was saying something like, 'If you act *really* dumb, they figure you really need the help and they *see* those forms are in proper order.'" The woman's baby was now drinking milk with a straw.

I asked Anne if she felt angry about the charade. Anne was a "little pissed off," she says, but really more embarrassed. She pushed herself, though, to consider what was at stake for this woman who had used what tools she had to cope with a situation in which she had no say. Anne thinks this woman handled the situation pretty well. "I mean, if you think about it, she wanted that kid in that program. She knew that *I'd get all the answers* straight and that I'd think he needed it with that kind of mom. What's at stake for her? If her kid gets in the school, so what if I think she's an idiot. He did real good in the special program too," she adds softly.

Over the years, Anne says, she began to collaborate with her clients, first in an obtuse way but finally, systematically. "I tell them when to say 'I don't know,' what to ask for, and how to get the most out of it. I use my body language. Like when they answer something wrong—*maybe honestly*, but wrong to get the service—I kind of wince or make a face, and they get it. I mean they're not dumb, you know, they're poor."

And what does that make you? I ask Anne. She looks me in the eye when she answers, "A social worker."

Anne believes that, if you do social work, you eventually have to make a choice. You can learn to see the worst in people, and then to identify deeply with the institutional mandates which express social stigma. Or you begin to see the world standing in another woman's shoes. If you do, you start to think differently about what is right. You start to think, if I was there and that was my baby, what *wouldn't I do* to get over the blockades. When you start to think in this way, she says, your whole perspective starts to change and then you may find you do things differently.

When I opened the subject of breaking the rules with a group of "welfare survivors," various voices conveyed the same message: breaking the rules is necessary because the rules are destructive to your family. "We all be creative with our accounts," Luscious explained to me. "You know, just like the man." When I asked her to elaborate, she smiled and shrugged, but egged on by others she explained that other folks, educated wealthy people, are all the time creative in their accounts. She thinks that if it is good for them, well maybe it is OK for a woman trying to survive in low-income America.

Nemesis offered another name for this creative accounting. She called it civil disobedience, disobeying rules that treat you and your children as having no value. Haven't women *always* disobeyed such rules and wouldn't any righteous mother do so, she challenged the other women. The law is not always right, she said, and then it is right to disobey. Nemesis came to this understanding through the teachings of her mother and other family members and has since had it confirmed in college courses. She told the group that Black people have historically refused to collaborate with laws which diminished them, that made them collaborate in their own oppression. The other women in the group were a little startled by Nemesis's view, but also intrigued.

Veronica could not agree more. "You're a welfare cheat, right? If you just do the things anyone would do to keep your kids OK," she said. *"They make you into what they can get you for."* There is method to all this, she said. The welfare system corners you into postures which require outlaw behavior just to survive, but then you are labeled as criminal. Luscious concurred: "I say this [snaps her fingers] to the law. You're breaking the law by making sure you and your kids don't starve on the street—well, that's not *my* law."

These women see the welfare system as somebody else's law, rules that work for others, but not for the women and children who live in the world of poor America. And so, if you believe you have the right to survive and that your children have the right to grow up and have a place in the world, you start to see and do things differently. You break their rules.

WAYS OF KNOWING THE WELFARE CULTURE

The women who spoke with me about their welfare years reflected the broad range of that experience. Some stayed on welfare for only a short time, some for four or five years, and some had been using AFDC to "get by" for over a decade. They were diverse in other significant ways: racially and ethnically diverse, very young to middle-aged, Boston-born or from the South or from islands far away. Some had left welfare and poverty behind, some had not. Their level of education was correlated to their economic status: some had graduated from a post-secondary school (most often from community colleges), a few older women were in graduate programs, and others were still working on their high school diplomas. All but two young women had employment histories, and most of the participants over twenty-five had years of paid work behind them. Even so, all of the fifty Life-History participants experienced significant setbacks over the course of their child-raising years. These were setbacks which, in twelve cases, returned an employed woman and her children from relative stability to extreme hardship once again. Some younger women, listening to these frightening histories of moving forward and falling back down, shivered. "It is enough to freeze your blood," one told me.

These women spoke of a welfare culture from knowledge buried deep inside. But it was not their culture they described. Rather, they spoke of an institutional culture which has gradually crept outside the welfare office and insinuated itself into public schools, health centers, job programs, housing offices, and all the other places where poor women go out and deal with the day-to-day. They spoke of relatives, neighbors, close friends, and communities which had dealt with the insidious impact of welfare.

These women recalled the wrenching beginnings of going down to the welfare office for the first time, all alone with a baby. They knew the games that go on, the overt regulatory games and the nasty covert ones. They knew about bravado, speaking up loud and proud, at least for a while. And they knew about the daily erosions that can eventually strip your courage as the months pass by. These women spoke of sexual and physical abuse, mental illness, withdrawing into numbness, addictions, the haunting terror of losing children, and the worst feeling of all, that maybe you *should* lose them because you are such trash. Some spoke in teeth-clenched tones, others fought tears from spilling, and a few became absolutely silent.

I heard this as welfare knowledge in your face, insider knowledge which comes from lived experience. It is about a welfare culture which is imposed upon people, not one of their making, one which is despised. But I also heard within these groups of women who have "been there" echoes of the popular beliefs outsiders have about welfare. These women would blame other mothers for the bad name they all must bear. I heard numerous women say, "There are some out there who don't deserve it, who don't care for their babies and give all their money to their boyfriends. Or take drugs and neglect their kids." When I asked these women if they knew anyone intimately who behaved this way, many acknowledged that they did not. Yet they accepted the idea of these "low-life" mothers as prevalent, based on neighborhood talk, newspaper and TV accounts, or the occasional sighting of women who look so shabby and seem to have no pride. Some people who had struggled with poverty and the welfare system sounded remarkably punitive, their remarks were very similar to conservative welfare rhetoric. But only a few women suggested that this behavior was evident in their own families, and when they did, it was with deep disgust. Most often, a sister, mother, or cousin whose history was shared was carefully examined in the context of that woman's own complicated trials. Sometimes she was described as rising to meet them and other times as falling down.

As most research on women and poverty suggests, the welfare system is loathed by the people who have to live with it.[4] Almost every woman involved in this research described intricate plans to get away from welfare and to attain a better life for herself and her children. But again and again, the lack of tangible ways to gain control of one's life—the inability to obtain needed schooling for employment, to get safe child care, to meet the daily demands of hard family life—would obstruct even the smallest steps taken to break out of welfare.[5]

Equally difficult as these practical impediments were other powerful obstacles to moving ahead. Women spoke of trying to stifle rage and shame, of trying to face isolation, abuse, and stigma—work which left many of them exhausted and numb. "Trying to take care of babies in this condition is hard, you know? Hard to give them what they need, hard to know you cannot make it all better. Makes a woman weak, sometimes." Keeping certain kinds of madness at bay is a part of the work of women on welfare.

The emotional well-being of women raising children in low-income America has received attention in the mental health professions, yet this issue is largely absent from the broad welfare debate. Some scholarship that explores the relationship between women's mental health and their experiences of poverty focuses on the limitations of clinicians who cannot grasp the dynamics of life in poor America.[6] Deborah Belle and her colleagues, who examined depression in poor women, point to causes not only in the external pressures upon families but also in the power of stigma against women receiving public aid. Their work suggests that not only do poor women have many more upheavals than experienced by individuals in the general population, but that they must also contend with the chronic stress of poverty, requiring constant adjustment. These demands are ultimately more eroding than episodic troubles.[7] Further, the routine lack of control over one's own life that is experienced by women on welfare, the inadequate or mistaken information rampant in welfare systems, and a universal awareness of the welfare stigma have been documented as contributing to depression and mental illness. One can imagine that such stigma would be hard to ignore. "Women on welfare have been variously characterized as lazy, cheating, promiscuous, dependent, freeloaders, and daughters of mothers of equally poor character."[8]

And as these researchers point out, such conditions can give rise to depression, feelings of hopelessness, and even suicidal behavior. Sixty-six percent of the women in one study experienced a high rate of depressive symptoms, were currently emotionally distressed, and expressed anxiety about the stigma they face,[9] findings which repeatedly emerged in my own work. In a more recent study, it was found that continued receipt of welfare over time had an undermining effect upon women's self-esteem, contradicting "prevalent stereotypes of women who readily receive a welfare check."[10]

"Why do they hate me so much, just for getting on welfare?" one woman asked researchers Ann Withorn and Diane Dijon.[11] Why is she such a despised person, she wanted to know, just as Ellen interrogated me, why is this the way our nation treats poor mothers? Withorn goes on to describe the lives of women who spoke to her as being a "series of small Sophie's Choices, a painful, bitter, humiliating juggling act." It is not only material hardship which places women in poor America in such a marginal position. It is the absolute awareness these millions of women *and their children* have that the dominant society regards their hardships to be a reflection of their inferiority.

Many of the discussants recognized strong connections between domestic violence, poverty, and the welfare culture. Some participants considered the acute vulnerability of poor single-motherhood as the cause of some women's acceptance of abuse from men in their lives. They pointed to the exaggerated sense of hopelessness which many bat-

tered women feel when their options for leaving are profoundly limited
by poverty and welfare rules. They listed the material obstructions to
escaping abuse: no car, no money, no credit card, no place to go but
shelters which were often full and sometimes scary. This connection
has been validated by recent studies.[12] Leaving any domestic partner-
ship is hard, but it is particularly difficult when leaving is as perilous as
staying.

The experiences of living with institutionalized welfare culture cut
deep and leave indelible effects. The people who know about the welfare culture are not just individuals who have lived it, but also their
families and other kin. In time, whole neighborhoods and communities assimilate such treatment as part of the world of poor America. It
becomes class knowledge.

As I learned over the years, the effects of the welfare experience are
sometimes a self-loathing which can cause madness of sorts very particular to women under unmitigated stress and stigma. This is one of
the ways of knowing the welfare culture. But sometimes these conditions, instead, cause people to turn their gaze outward and then to reframe the terms which govern their lives. Along with others who have
undertaken qualitative research with people on welfare, I found that
the welfare years are a time when young mothers reframe the terms by
breaking the rules to survive and to ensure their children survive.[13] If
you add up even minimal family costs, and then count the dollars that
welfare offers, the conclusion is irrefutable. No one keeps a household
intact nor children safe by relying solely on welfare, even with the an-
cillary supports available. This is known almost everywhere in welfare
systems, in the offices and hallways where allowances and benefits are
meted out and received. The impact of this structurally contrived paradox is that low-income parents caring for children must construct alternative ways of making ends meet. And of course, they do.

CHAPTER FIVE

Moving On: "Don't Call Me Out of Name"

"Don't call me out of name, 'cause I won't answer you. Don't call me welfare mother, 'cause that's not who I am. I will turn my face away. . . . Don't call me out of name."

—ODESSA, THIRTY-TWO, SPEAKING AT A PUBLIC FORUM ON WELFARE, 1993

The previous women's accounts universally described the welfare years as the hardest time of their lives. Early motherhood for these low-income mothers was spent in isolation, with partners gone and missed and families often estranged and overburdened. There seemed to be no place to turn for help except welfare institutions which did not reduce poverty and were described as treating women "like trash." There was an eerie similarity to the individual descriptions of the welfare period, one which always seem to include reference to lack of physical safety and to chronic emotional distress. Yet, I noticed that some women marked this time as a period in their lives which seemed to gradually change as they moved into their late twenties and thirties.

Older women recalled their progress as stages unfolding. Looking back to young motherhood, they recognized gaining a tentative foothold, despite many troubles, as they reached their late twenties and early thirties. Babies grew old enough to sleep through the night, they stopped using diapers, gave up milk bottles, and began to walk on their own. Some children went to preschool and then grammar school. Adolescent boyfriend relationships were long over, and in most cases women told me "good riddance." Old dreams got buried under countless daily chores, most wounds gradually mended, and many young mothers were convinced they were done with having babies.

Some women spoke of this changing time as the beginning of a discovery, when the hazy picture of self gradually gained definition. They spoke of developing new ideas and of slowly gaining a new perspective. They started to examine the disparate forces which sometimes had coaxed and sometimes had catapulted them to the place they had landed. Then, with the relief of a little less chaos and children a little less vulnerable, as Renata mused, "I guess I just started considering my own life."

Of the fifty women who participated in the Life-History Study, thirty were over twenty-eight years old. Of those, twenty-five women had, from their own point of view, "made a lot of positive changes over the years," and all of them were eager to discuss just what this progress meant. Numerous women were clear and hard-minded about what had helped them move forward and what had stood in their way. They distinguished between the "me, myself" inside work they had taken on and the forces at play in the outside world. I presented this information from the life histories to women in Interpretive Focus Groups and in informal discussion groups in varied neighborhood settings. In these meetings, we picked apart the stories about "moving on," and despite the great variation in personality, family life, race, culture, age, and religion represented in these life histories, certain unifying themes came through.

In many cases, seeking a change to the misery of the welfare years meant ending unhealthy relationships. This was a big part of the inside "me, myself" work which many women described. Sometimes it meant moving to another neighborhood and changing friends or leaving a boyfriend. Sometimes it meant disconnecting from one's own family, whose troubles threatened to take everyone down. But more often it meant reuniting with helpful kin who had been out of the picture. Seeking out relatives, restoring valued rituals, and joining in family gatherings were often ways these women built new and healthier relation-

ships. Over the passing years, most of the young mothers found themselves more focused on the traditions of their early lives and the ways
of their mothers. Time and trouble had sometimes brought home to
these women how much their own parents had struggled, not always
successfully. Even very young women began to consider another perspective as they grew accustomed to being mothers themselves. Nineteen-year-old Chantal, who had raged at her mother's failings, admitted that she gratefully accepted her mother's help with her gravely ill
daughter. She told me, "I can see how sometimes it gets to be too much,
and my mother was just a child when she had me, nothing but a baby
herself."

Another common theme which maturing women raised was greater
concern about self-preservation. They became more discriminating in
their choices about people, about their own health and safety, and to
the degree possible, about the neighborhood in which they would raise
their children. They seemed to regard themselves as more precious as
they gained momentum in their role as mothers and heads of households. Dominating most women's discussion was a concern for the
well-being of developing children. They saw their children as needing
more than strong arms and vigilant eyes to see them through the day.
These children were going to school, making social networks of their
own, asking questions, and seeking to make sense of their position in
the world. In most cases, they went to their mothers for the explana-
tions.

One critical obligation in child raising is explaining place, assisting
children in understanding how they fit into the scheme of American society. It is about who "your people," your family and your ancestors,
are. It is about what your people believe in and how they worship. It is
also about how others regard you, the categories in which you are
placed even before you say one word. In America, of course, it is about
your race, ethnicity, nation of origin, color, and even how long ago your

people landed on American shores. In the child-raising stories told by scores of women, the need to explain "place" in a stratified society was a given. At least a dozen different women have told me about that moment when a child looked them in the eye and asked, "Momma, are we poor people?" When I recall meeting these women and hearing their stories, I am always swept into that instant. I imagine the question coming to me and hope that, in their place, I could offer their dignified and honest answers. Again and again, mothers told children to "stand up, and be proud" of themselves, to set out with dreams. "Do you feel poor?" Renata asked her children. "Do you see a poor woman in front of you?" Deborah asked hers. "We are rich in love," Nemesis's mother had told her four daughters. And Tania reflected, "I have got to think *I* can make it if my son is going to."

Another common, if more muted, theme in their descriptions of this time of change was a letting go of the early effort to find or hold onto male partners. Black women, white women, and also some Latinas expressed the idea that the dream of a good and lasting relationship with a man was a thing of the past. Sometimes this was couched in terms of great loss and compromise, while at other times it was described as a great relief to give up "that foolishness." Most women suggested that if a fine man came along, suitable as a partner and a father, well . . . that would be different. But the focus on relationships with male partners seem to be fading for many women who were still quite young.

All of these changes were a part of what women considered to be the strengthening work they had done inside of themselves—shifts in attitudes, relationships, expectations, and priorities—in order to move away from the welfare years. But these women reminded me that there is another critical ingredient in changing one's life. Every single interview and group discussion enunciated clearly and with detail that you cannot move on, overcome problems, and seize onto new dreams if you cannot get some real opportunity and practical help, not rhetoric but tangible, adequate support. Some of the women whom I have spoken with over the years have found these critical resources and others are still looking.

"What helped? Well just getting a real chance, with people who know what it takes to get out . . . most people have no idea."
—*Tabitha, 1993*

Several of the women interviewed in the Life-History Study reported that during the 1980s and early 1990s they had found special child-development programs which worked for *both children and parents*. During this same period, some had entered subsidized career-development programs, which included child care and social support. Some women had found help through a local human service program which offered a job with career development opportunities. Three women with substance abuse problems had gone into residential treatment with their children, and two had emerged drug-free, with a high school diploma. Some women had used the job-training resources available (in the 1980s and early 1990s) through the Massachusetts welfare office to make some gains. Three women had begun working in their own children's Head Start programs and had made their way up, slowly, to better jobs, receiving subsidized education along the way. A few women had gained a chance through a relative, close family friend, or mentor figure who had reached out and invested some significant time and resources in a young mother.

Another source of outside help to some women was mental health counseling. In a few cases, this help was mandated, but more often it was sought voluntarily. Mental health services are hard to come by for people without money, and many women who had sustained trauma, losses, and abuse never received individual counseling. Most of those who did receive this kind of support believe that it made a difference, even those who admitted that, "I don't like telling some nosy person my business." Numerous women found that spending time talking about old pain, recalling troubles which haunted their childhood, and considering the connections between "what went on then and what goes on now" made them stronger. Particularly important to consider is that they thought that counseling helped them raise their children more thoughtfully because it helped them recognize how they wanted to change some damaging family patterns. Tania, who was seeing a mental health counselor named Margaret, told me: "I don't want to pass it on, it can stop here. Like Margaret says, I can stop it here."

The Life-History Study also included a small minority of women who did not report these kinds of positive changes occurring. These were women who had not yet been able to move on beyond the despair of the welfare years. Instead they continued, crisis after crisis, to see themselves as trapped in abusive relationships, or continued to be dependent upon drugs or alcohol, or had several children, quickly. This small proportion (two of twenty-five women) resembles the highly publicized image of troubled and demoralized mothers on public assistance. It is noteworthy, however, that the progress of many other women remains largely absent from the public debate.

Given current welfare policy, this is a grave omission. Exquisitely detailed accounts of young women with social problems who are receiving welfare are common public record, featured in the media, and the subject of conservative political rhetoric. But stories of the large majority of women and children who have used public assistance over the last two decades and moved on, graduated from college and graduate schools, entered and excelled in the workplace, become leaders of all kinds, raised strong families, and assisted the development of their communities, remain an unrecorded archive of national history. These women's tales of advancement, hard fought for and triumphantly won, are known in the families and communities where they live, but it is a buried history of some people's strength and pride.

WOMEN MOVING ON: "GETTING SHUT" OF THE WELFARE OFFICE

The majority of participants in all the studies were aching to "get shut" of the welfare world. They struggled against continuing a life made chaotic by poverty, against raising their children in shaky circumstances, and against the anarchy of the public regulatory system. Some of these women seemed frozen by the overwhelming odds they faced; they would describe over and over how complicated and frightening it all seemed. Panic seemed to set in, particularly in the mid-1990s with talk of welfare cutoffs and the growing belief in numerous communities, that children would be routinely taken from jobless women. I was in on a discussion between several women at a health center where one told the others, "I heard the president say it's all ending, he's going to end it all. The lady says I should go to the 'shop stop' [the "One Stop" job center in downtown Boston], but I don't know what she thinks I need to go shopping for." Other women in informal discussions about welfare reform expressed a lack of knowledge about rules and requirements, or one would report what she had been told and invariably it would conflict with what the woman sitting next to her had been told. This lack of sound information, coupled with a growing fear about the safety of children and uncertainty about the future, may foster an increasing underground life in poor America—one where people disappear from official records, ignore inexplicable rules, and reside in places that even well-organized social services cannot reach. This seems to be the grim future that some women currently on public aid see coming, and they don't want to think about it: "I'm just going to wait 'cause I don't know what else to do."

The group of twenty-five older women in the Life-History Study who said they had made "a lot of positive changes over the years" all described their own steps toward breaking away. Some investigated returning to school, pursuing a degree, a diploma, or taking courses. Some looked into a trade or planned steps to a particular career and were still working on their goals. Some women became actively involved in the development of their neighborhoods by participating in tenant and community groups, in safe-street activities, and in church and school programs. All of them pushed hard toward the goals they set, and in doing so most gained skills, experience, and confidence in new roles.

It is important to note that this group of older women, who were taking their first steps toward "moving on" in the 1980s and early 1990s, used home-grown options as the route for moving on with their lives. Most of these women dared to try something new through a trusted ally or a local network. They were guided by a known person or went to work in a familiar place, where standing at the door, they saw someone or recognized some place as known and trusted. This stands in marked contrast to the mandated community service programs which compel women to work, sometimes locally but sometimes pushing them involuntarily out of their communities into the company of strangers.

Quick Notes

"When I was young, I just couldn't wait to get through high school. Ten years later, all I wanted was a chance to go back to school, to go to college. I was scared, yeah, I felt embarrassed. But I saw a light up ahead and I reached for that. That degree meant everything, it meant I was going to be independent. I reached for it."
—Marie, thirty, in her last year of a community college

"I went to this job training thing . . . about health records, like in doctors' offices but I couldn't get a job. So I did another . . . it was office work . . . like filing and all, but that didn't lead to no kind of job. I lost some faith about all this along the way. I did four more . . . maybe

three. Now I'm doing this computer one. We'll see where this goes. Better go somewhere 'cause they're cutting me off, job or no job. But, like she was saying, maybe if they had let me take those kind of [college] courses right at the start, like four years ago when I started all this nonsense, maybe now I would have a real job, you know?"

—Emma, twenty-eight, on job training versus
college education, 1997

"I think a lot of us start getting ready to move on, move up, but you know, you can only do it if someone gives you a chance. I could be good and ready and that doesn't mean there is any place to go."
—Renata, early thirties, on reading a draft of this chapter

At a Community College, 1995

Lena, a white woman in her thirties, tells me she has an explicit goal in speaking with me. "The reason I am here tonight is so that you can spread the word. You might have ways to pass on to other women who have been through what we have . . . getting more education is learning how much *you've* got . . . but it takes guts to try."

Pam, in her twenties and also white, nods. "We're so fragile, you see, we've been put down and we put ourselves down. You keep thinking of all those voices which say, 'You can't do this, you're nothing but a welfare mother.'" Which voices are those? "They're everywhere. Just look in the newspapers, any day. And even in your family you may hear them, from your man, maybe. And some of them are in your own head, doubting you."

Alba, Latina and in her twenties, adds, "Those are the worst ones. If it hadn't been for Mary [the coordinator of the program], I would have given up. If it hadn't been for the group, these other ladies who been through the same thing, the abuse . . . and fear . . . well it was all for one and one for all."

This group is one of ten separate focus groups I met with in diverse

educational and training programs. The women in this group are former and current participants in a transitional program in the community college designed to help women on welfare get the education and
support necessary to seek more education and to find jobs. One of the
main reasons Lena and the others are meeting with me tonight is that
the program is being threatened for removal from the next year's community college budget. They want to tell their side of the story about
"getting welfare mothers to work." I ask them the same question I ask
the other groups: What are the forces which encourage and what are
the obstacles along the way?

Lena says that the first step toward change was her break with her
violent husband. She left suddenly, in the middle of the night, and "ba-
sically camped out" in her mother's house and backyard. She had
known for a long time that she should take her children and run, but
"getting the courage to break away and dealing with welfare" was a
demoralizing struggle. "I had no self-esteem. I was so beaten down."
After she left her husband, she met a woman who was attending the
transitional program at the community college and who encouraged
Lena to apply. To Lena's astonishment, the same woman called her up
months later to make sure that Lena submitted an application to the
program, and so she did, largely to avoid disappointing this concerned
stranger.

Lena applied to the program with little confidence, but shortly after she started attending, her perspective began to change. She began
to think that she could do more, more than her husband had told her
she was capable of, more than the publicity about welfare moms ever
suggested. "I made a pact with my kids," she says. "We will only be
taking steps forward now." Lena completed the transitional program,
and then another which earned her an associate's degree. Now, with a
degree in counseling psychology, she is working with other women
who need help. But she will remind you in the midst of success, that the
early support she received in the community college program, a transi-

tional year with other women who "have been through the same thing" and support from a committed, empathetic leader, was essential to her progress.

Since I met with Lena and the others, the transitional program lost its funding and is no longer available.

Apprentices in a Building Trade, 1996

I am meeting with a group of five women, members of a program specifically designed to apprentice women to the building trades. Much of their talk is about Dottie Travis, coordinator of training programs. They say that Dottie's support has been a major factor in their success. Entering the construction business, a male-dominated environment, calls for a strong character, these women say, a person who "wants to beat the boys playing hoop, not stand on the side and cheer." At the same time, help from someone like Dottie, an understanding woman who "knows how it feels" is seen as critical.

"Having Dottie there," claims Miranda, a white woman in her mid-twenties, "to say she believed in me, to encourage me, to call me up after I had a bad day . . . I think I would have quit but for her." Her fellow apprentices agree. Diana, an African American woman in her mid-thirties, describes how she would handle men on the job, how she would "do the job really well, use my lunch hour to learn to grease the machines," but never make the men feel as though she was out to take their jobs. "Dottie would say, you are one of them, but not one of them," Diana remembers, and help Diana frame a way to manage this contradiction, to be a successful construction worker but not a threat to men on the job.

Diana advises that the trades are "not for everybody." But if you get in it, "you need other women to support you." All of the women nod. "I want to control my own life," says Elaine, a young white woman. "I looked at the kind of money that men make in the trades and thought . . . well, I could get used to that. Why don't they [welfare departments] work to get more girls into these jobs? Jobs where you make forty thousand dollars in a good year, not fifteen?" Elaine and other women in the group emphasize that Dottie helped them think of themselves as worthy of another life, as strong enough to take the jokes and, frequently, the harassment on the job. Dottie would be there, they say, "between me and giving up," until they gained the confidence to persevere.

Dottie and others who are encouraging women to explore nontraditional jobs stress that very few women, regardless of their own personal strength, are able to get into these well-paid and male-dominated trades. The building trade, they say, is not an open labor market but one that is heavily controlled by forces which are not at all supportive of women on welfare entering their domain. But a few women manage to squeeze through. Miranda, one of the few women who has managed to get a foothold, stresses again the importance of getting support from a counselor like Dottie: "I would like to go to high schools and to other places and tell those girls, 'Do you like to win? Can you get your hands dirty? Do you like to see the money and to run your own life? Well, come see Dottie and pick up a hammer.'"

Brenda, Roxbury, 1992

"I'm a loud woman now."

When I meet Brenda, an African American woman in her forties, she is the office manager in part of a large community center in the Roxbury section of Boston. She has been working at the center for almost eight years and previously worked in a local grammar school. Before that, Brenda was on AFDC and lived in a housing development not too far down the road. Her story of a youth devoted to homemaking, family care, and child raising is a common tale of women who have been on welfare.

Shortly after she graduated from high school in the early 1970s, Brenda gave birth to her first child. She was not married then, and never did marry the father of her children. Together, over the next decade, they raised first Taymisha, then Todd, and finally Appolonia. Brenda's husband, as she refers to him, at first worked intermittently in a gas station and then later as an auto mechanic, bringing home wages which supplemented public assistance.

Brenda recalls herself as absolutely dedicated to her husband and three children, whom she describes as well dressed, well fed, and well behaved. "They were churchgoing children, you understand." The family was financially hard-pressed, she says, but they could get by. Brenda spent her days caring for her children, cooking, walking to the stores which offered the best food prices, cleaning her two-bedroom apartment, and being involved in her church. She sang in the choir and helped coordinate various social functions, including a summer camp program for neighborhood children. She also helped two of her sisters with their children in the afternoons, and once a week she cleaned house for her mother who was diabetic and had had most of her toes amputated. When Brenda finishes describing all that she did during those ten years, she smiles and shakes her head. It had seemed important to her then, and in retrospect it all seems just as important now. But it was not until her husband left her and she started to try to manage her family on a shrinking welfare allowance alone that she had to grapple with how little the larger society valued her family role.

There is a soft knock on the door and then a pale young face appears. Directly below, a smaller head pops out of a baby carrier. A young mother who is applying for a child-care slot for her year-old daughter is late with her application and she is very anxious. She speaks in a whisper.

"Brenda I'm sorry, I couldn't get here. My mother said she'd watch Bella but . . . I had to wag her over here . . ."

Brenda nods. "That's why you could use some child care, right? Just give it here."

Kirstin, a twenty-year-old white woman comes quickly into the room and begins to hand over to Brenda what seems to be a dozen-page application. Large happy baby Bella is grinning at Brenda, at me, and particularly at everything on Brenda's desk. She grabs enthusiastically and manages to snatch some flowers in a vase, which tilts precariously toward a pile of Brenda's files. We all three grab at the vase together and of course it heaves off the desk into a broken pool of glass and water. Kirstin, now apologizing frantically, goes down on her knees to pick up the flowers and glass shards, her big baby flopping over and grabbing at the glass with her mother.

Brenda whips around the desk before I can move and gently pulls Kirstin to her feet. Looking into the young woman's teary eyes, she speaks softly and slowly, "It's OK now, Kirstin, it doesn't matter. I don't care about that old jug." Brenda guides Kirstin out the door while I pick up the watery mess. "You remember that?" Brenda asks when she returns. "Running around, trying to get things done, a heavy baby hanging off you, bumping into things, pacifiers falling out, and messy diapers . . ." I do, I say, and Kirstin seems pretty rattled. Brenda nods. "Kirstin has more going on than she can handle right now. She could use some real help."

When Brenda was twenty-seven and adjusting to managing her family with little help, her nine-year-old daughter came home from school with a question. She was working on a family chart in her history class. She asked her mother how to spell welfare recipient. Brenda believes that this was a critical moment for her, a revelatory instant when she realized that all of her work, loving care, and loyalty to the needs of others could be reduced to "welfare recipient," and more, that *her own daughter* was being taught to accept this idea. "If you think about it, I was a welfare cheat on top of a welfare case because I had that money my husband gave me and I never told on that."

Brenda felt humiliated, betrayed, and finally outraged. And there, in that anger, she found fuel for her own personal fire. "I got to speak up all the time. My minister didn't know what had happened to me,"

Brenda says, laughing long and hard as she remembers her minister's confusion. "I had been all meek, with this weak voice, and suddenly, I was singing so loud that I drowned out the choir." Brenda talked to her children, her mother, her sisters, and anyone else she could "snatch up." She talked about the importance of family duty and of respecting women and raising children properly. She was speaking of her own labor and insisting that she be recognized for who she was. One day when she was talking to someone at her children's grammar school, a school administrator overheard Brenda discussing the importance of her community and the families in it. Committed to increasing parental involvement in the school, this man recognized that Brenda would be a valuable addition to the staff. He convinced her to apply for a position in the office. Over the next five years, Brenda worked in the grammar school, gradually increasing her hours and terminating her welfare support. She learned to type well, to serve as a receptionist, to file, and finally to manage a budget. She took computer and accounting courses. When she ventured out and applied for a job at the community center where she now works, she was selected as their top candidate. Brenda still faced a daunting challenge to provide for her growing children. But the victory was delicious. "My children treated me like a queen. My family cooked a victory dinner."

The job, Brenda says, was an achievement, and it also proved feasible. "I could put it together with food stamps, and they gave me health insurance when my Medicaid ran out. I still could get housing help. And plus, they understood that I had to bring my kids by sometimes. They'd do their homework here many afternoons. I had no money for baby-sitters and my mother was too sick to mind them." What if you hadn't had those supports, the insurance, the food stamps, the flexibility about your children? I ask Brenda. Her expressive eyebrows arch high, she shrugs, "Why, I wouldn't have been able to do it now, would I?"

Brenda tells me that, last week, her youngest daughter, Appolonia, came home from school with a prize for a poem, one she had written and dedicated to her mother for being the woman she "admires most in the world." The poem speaks of Brenda's love and kindness as the source of Apollonia's own strength. "That's the same love my mother gave to me," Brenda says, and she reminds me it is the same love and care she gave her older daughter, the one who was learning to write about "the welfare mother, not the heroine."

HEARTS OF IRON

Many of the women in the focus groups which looked at the transitional period after the welfare years described what seemed to them a conspiracy to keep them from achieving their educational or career goals, even as they combated their own fears. This conspiracy was described in different ways, but overall it amounted to society giving these women a powerfully mixed message. We were told, they say, to become "self-sufficient," but every time we turn around something holds us back. Some of the obstacles come from the inside, from the teachings and ways of their families, and others come from the outside world.

We discussed this issue at the community college focus group mentioned earlier. Several of the participants in the transitional program had faced opposition at home. "I really thought that going to class and leaving my sons was selfish," Alba said. "My mother told me it was and so did their father. I kept trying to do everything at home, cook and keep everything all right so it was like I wasn't any different. But when I had to go to class, everyone made me feel bad. The kids cried, my husband told me I was not being a good wife, even my mother shook her head . . ."

Did your family know that the welfare office was pushing you to go to school and that, in the end, things would be better if you got an associate's degree?

"You're not supposed to go out and leave your family," Alba said. "Maybe it's bigger, being Hispanic, but lots of us talked about this."

Her companions jumped in. Tony, an Italian American woman of twenty-seven said, "I ran into the same deal. My boyfriend thought I might be seeing other men at school." ("Yeah that's it too," agreed all the others.) "And even if I wasn't, even if it was just other women, it was that I was out here, I was in a new life." Thoughtfully, one woman suggested that "sometimes men worry more about other women than they do about other men, 'cause they think the other women will change you, give you attitudes." And all the women agreed that they hoped this was true.

Lena had thought a lot about gender pressure, too. "It was really hard for me to deal with leaving my husband and then coming here," she says. But Lena also noticed that the women who were trying to get through school while still trying to maintain a shaky relationship were more likely to give up. "It's one thing to be all alone or with your kids and have to deal. But it's worse if you are with a man and he's about breaking you down."

These focus group discussions reveal that, across the board, these women experienced conflict with male partners when they were engaged in changing their lives. It was true for women in college programs, for women getting their GED degrees and attending English as a Second Language (ESL) courses, for women apprenticed in the building trades and women in state-run jobs programs. In every focus group, several women reported that relationships they had been in at the start of a program underwent a stressful change and didn't last. *Yet when a woman's partner supported her effort, his help made a powerful difference.*

At a focus group of ten women in a Boston college program, Yvette, a Jamaican woman of thirty told me, "My boyfriend was nervous at first. He said, 'It will change you. I won't be good enough for you now.'

I told him, 'Come with me, you can do it too, we can both do it for the kids, together.' And he did. He went back to school, too. Now he jokes to our families, 'We be educated people now.'" Yvette's friends laughed. The story of her efforts to stay with her boyfriend (now they are married) were well known to them. It had been part of her challenge, her daily work to stay in school.

Several women suggested that men get left out of the formula. They said that "the government" tries to make women on welfare take jobs, but they leave the men out of the program. As a result, men feel they are being left behind, becoming irrelevant. This can make a man get depressed, the women said, and it can make him angry. One older woman, Maxine, pointed out that a man who stays home to watch children so his wife can go to school or to a career program may get ridiculed by his friends and will certainly not get any support or credit from the larger society. "He's damned both ways," said Maxine, who has two grown sons. "And maybe he's right," Maxine went on. "Maybe when she gets her degree, she may look at him and say, 'I can leave you now. I don't need you any more.'" When Maxine spun out this thought, some women agreed. Others challenged it. They argued that a lot of women "would have left a long time ago, only they couldn't get away." It's not that education changes her feelings about the man, they said, it is that now she can do what she always needed to do, get away from someone who keeps her down.

This group batted the competing analyses back and forth. Eventually, they came to the conclusion that men must not be left out. That programs for women should have "brother programs" for men. Men need jobs to support their families, just as much as women do. Even so, the group agreed, sympathy for a man shouldn't prevent a woman from breaking with him if he is "jamming her up." If he is threatening her and holding her down, she should get support to leave him.

"We are supposed to solve all of it," Maxine told me later when I met with her alone. "We are to mind the babies, raise the kids, hold onto the man, and make sure he isn't disrespected. And we are to get over our fear, and find clothes to wear, and find someone to watch the children when we go on out there. Only maybe we don't trust anyone else, and maybe the man is acting all foolish, and maybe we don't have clothes. These girls you been talking to have hearts of iron, you know, to get where they are."

Quick Notes

"I tried to do it [find a job] like they said I should. I went here and I went there. I filled out it seemed like a hundred applications. You know I have a high school diploma and I have worked before. I filled out those papers. But do I have a job? No sir, I don't. They are going to cut me off by next fall, and I am raising three children [one of her own and two grandchildren]."

—Antoinette, thirty-eight, 1997

"I went back to school and they gave me a voucher so's my baby could go to the [child-care] center. Then I finished and I got a job at the rec [recreational] center with the children. I typed and filed for them, answered the phone, and what all. It was nice. Then they come tell me I have no more child-care voucher, I had 'transitioned,' that's what they call it. I make too much money. Too much? I can't find any baby-sitter for what I make. After the bus and the baby's food and all, I have nothing left. So back I go, back to the welfare office."

—Andrea, nineteen, 1996

"I have four childrens in four different Metco schools [an option which some parents in the Boston inner city have used to place their children in suburban schools]. Now I been working for five years, so's my husband, and we just getting by. But see, Metco makes you meet with the school four times a year, like they don't think us parents will keep up with our kids unless they make special regulations that we got

to follow, not other folks. Now I couldn't get my kids in the same schools 'cause of their ages—and the two in high school, well they said they had space for one here and one there—so I got to go out to Framingham four times and Natick four times and Newton . . . That's sixteen days of going out on trains or borrowing a car. Sixteen days I got to take off time 'cause you know they not going to stay late and meet you after work. Even splitting it up with their father . . . anyway, needless to say I got fired. It was like, bring them back into the city, which we promised we'd never do after what happened [Michelle's oldest son was almost shot during a street fight outside his old high school] or let them fire you. We may have to go back to the state again, much as we hate it.”

—Michelle, thirty-five, 1996

"It was so perfect. I get into school [University of Massachusetts] so I can get a real job this time, one that's going to take care of me and my daughter. I want to be a child psychologist, and I was psyched about it. So I get in, and then they give me child-care allowance, and then the welfare office calls me and says, 'cause I got this new income, I don't qualify for more than seventy-five dollars a month and half my food stamps is gone. I say, 'What income?' and they say, 'From the university.' I say, 'That's not income, I don't touch any money, that's so my baby can be in child care.' And they say, 'That's income.' So now . . . I don't know, I drop out, or I don't take the child care but then what do I do? This lady, Betty Jane [a community activist], she said we should all pack up our children, all of them. Hundreds of them. And we should take them all down to the office, and you know, call the newspapers. And then say, 'Open up a child-care center, give women education and jobs . . . jobs taking care of these kids.' She's a hot ticket, that Betty Jane.”

—Barbara, twenty-eight, 1993

There is much to juggle as women "transition" from family work and public assistance to school and employment. While facing their own inner fears and their families' reluctance to let them become less home-bound, the bureaucracies they dealt with seem to obstruct rather than assist them. They detailed the housing, health care, schooling, child care, AFDC, and other public regulations which assume "we got nothing to do but answer the same questions a thousand times," as Renata put it.

She described her own effort to juggle the institutional demands. "Here I am," she said, "running between my lunch hour and my child's day care in this job program and the [welfare] folks are like, 'What are you in such a hurry for . . . sit down and wait.' Only I can't wait, I got to get back. 'Well, maybe you don't need day care if you can't be bothered waiting.' I ran back and I was crying and the man [who was teaching the computer course] asks me 'What's up?'" and I told him. He was so nice, he called those folks up and he told them off. But it's a shame you know, 'cause they believed *him*. They told him, 'Those people always got stories to tell,' but you know, I bet most of the stories are true."

Deborah, South Boston, 1996

"Valued for our brains and not just our butts."

Deborah is more than ready for my questions about social policies for women who are raising children alone. With a no-nonsense attitude, she rolls up her sleeves before she begins. "Now make sure your tape recorder's working 'cause you're gonna get some strong words here," she says by way of introduction.

"First of all, we have got to start looking at women as more than breeders . . . be valued for our brains and not just our butts." Deborah, thirty-two and the mother of an eight-year-old girl, Abigail, lives in South Boston. She believes that when she found out her husband, Eddy, was molesting her daughter when the child was three, her world exploded. "My cousin came to my house early one morning. She told me Eddy had messed with her little girl, abused her. She asked me if maybe that was why Abigail was so withdrawn and timid. I felt this punch, to my head . . . I knew it was true." Deborah decided to give her husband a hard lesson. She and her cousin mixed a potion of caustic cleaning fluids in a cup. They went upstairs and poured them on him as he lay asleep. When he leapt out of bed shouting, they went after him with rolling pins. Deborah never saw him again without a lawyer present.

Deborah went to the welfare office five months later. "It was the hardest day of my life," she says. "I was like . . . this isn't something I should ever be . . . a welfare mother. I had an attitude like, this is what Black mothers do, not me. I mean I know how that sounds because, since I been dealing with this . . . I know it's no different for them. But I had that attitude, you know?"

Deborah kept going back to the office, waiting for her first check. She began to show up at meal times at her mother's house, then at her grandmother's, and then at the homes of other family and friends. "I had no food. I actually couldn't feed my daughter." After five weeks, she "pitched a fit" at the welfare office. A guard had to forcibly remove her. But the next week, she received a check.

Deborah says that she tried to use the welfare office as a place to get information to find a way out. She believes that the caseworkers are not trained to help people get off welfare, only to question them, to review paperwork, and to challenge eligibility. Frustrated and shocked by how little information was available for women who wanted to escape that life, and by the caseworkers' attitude, Deborah turned to her community for help. She was intimidated but she went to the local bingo hall, the church, a neighborhood center, a preschool program. And some of her neighbors and neighborhood organizations came through, providing some services for both Deborah and Abigail and assisting Deborah in locating a preschool program which would take Abigail three days each week. During this same year, Deborah's grandmother died of "a brain infection," and her mother, depressed and fragile, moved into Deborah's apartment. Her grandfather, bereft at the loss of his wife of fifty years, took to calling Deborah several times a day "for emotional support."

Deborah says that, while her family became a drain on her, they were also her prime support. With financial help from her grandfather, mother, and AFDC, Deborah was able to manage her family. She also got her daughter and herself into therapy. "There's a lot of alcoholism in our family, and a lot of secrets. I had a lot to work out and I did."

Deborah believes that women need to be raised to believe they are intelligent and capable, and not just sexually attractive. She also believes that the American social support system for poor women "is shit, excuse me but it's the pits." It is, Deborah said, echoing others, designed to impede progress, not support it.

"We need child care in high schools, in job [sites], in apartment buildings. We need classes which teach girls how to survive in the real world, to push girls to think of themselves as survivors. And they need college. *We all need college.* You got to change jobs six times, right, so you don't need to be trained, you need to be educated. And so there needs to be scholarships, lots of them if women are going to be independent and teach their kids the same."

Now a veteran of welfare chaos and an expert on custody battles and child-support laws, Deborah is a confident debater. "Don't tell me there's not enough money *because I am not a fool.* What did we all pay for that savings and loan crap? There's money around, lots of it. We just got to decide who we are going to spend it on, and when *we* start deciding, it will be spent on children first."

Making Our Children Proud

*"When I started, they would stand at the window pressing their faces on
the glass, crying. I left feeling I was a bad mother, I was hurting them.
But I kept on. Now that has changed. The eleven-year-old does for the
seven-year-old, and he does for the four-year-old. They say, 'Our family
is going to school.' Now it's a family affair."*
— Eleanor, twenty-nine, 1995

The most dynamic force in most women's lives was their children. Children were the motivation to try to return to school, to enter job programs, to volunteer at schools, to venture out into an intimidating world. Mothers spoke of wanting to do better for their children, to make a better life for them and to earn their children's pride. But, just as often, they said, "I didn't feel right leaving my children." Sometimes the reason they didn't feel right was well founded.

Ariana, a twenty-four-year-old mother, needed child care for her youngest, a three-month-old son, so that she could attend a job-training course funded through the Massachusetts Welfare Department. She left him with a neighbor who watched five children in exchange for the small child-care payment supplied by the welfare department. She recalls the day when she came home an hour early from her training course because the teacher had become ill. She climbed the stairs to her neighbor's apartment, "hearing crying all the way up."

"I got there and she wasn't there. There was five children lying around in their pissy diapers, crying, hungry, dirty. I waited forty-five minutes before she came back." Ariana dropped out of the job-training program that day, and two other mothers left their jobs after Ariana called to warn them about her neighbor. She wanted to "kill that bitch," but she also blames the way programs are set up by the welfare department. Anger has propelled her out of her seat now. "Do they want us to make it or don't they?" she shouts at me. If "they" do want women to get off of welfare, they have to help provide mothers with safe child care. "No self-respecting woman leaves her child in danger. Not even if they say you have to."

I sit still watching Ariana, and after a moment, she sits down. We look out the window of the old Boston office building. In just a minute, she says quietly, "You see, this is how it gets. This is how I was a lot back then. And it's how they start saying you're whacked, you've lost it. 'Cause you go off . . . it makes you a mad kind of woman."

Many women spoke of this maddening paradox. They spoke of wanting to make progress, wanting to make changes that would benefit themselves and their children, but of facing overwhelming obstacles in finding dependable child care. Women described how husbands, partners, and some other family members (their own mothers tended to be the most reliable) said they would help with baby-sitting, but somehow would not be there when it was time to leave. Or mothers would get child-care help for the hour or two of classes but none at all for homework.

This kind of quiet family sabotage reminded me of what adolescent girls, nearly ten years younger than these mothers, described as occurring when they tried to continue school beyond high school. Family, friends, and lovers would say yes, but they would act no. They would create conditions at home that made doing schoolwork nearly impossible. An odd strategy common to both women and girls as they tried to do their homework was "hiding in the bathroom." Five different women described this subterfuge, in terms of repeatedly flushing the toilet or hiding in the bathroom and "running the tub like I was in the bath." For women, it seemed the bathroom is the only room where a woman can legitimately close the door. "They must have thought I was turning into a clean-nut or something," one woman laughed.

Quick Notes

"I think my kids were sort of taking other people's attitude about this, about me being in the program. But I took to talking to them,

*telling them, 'Hey, I need some support too, you know, I'm a person.'
I think that changed things."*
                              —Marie Theresa, twenty-eight, 1995

*"Mines were fussing and whining when I started too. But gradually,
just like these other ladies, they got to believe in me. Then we started
to do our homework together. We'd hang up our papers all over the
walls. And then my children's grades started to improve and we decided
'nothing under a B in this family.'"*
                              —Hazel, thirty-five, 1995

*"My son was never into school until he watched me do this. He was
in high school but he had no plans for after. Now he is in this community college too. He was, like, 'If you can do it, Ma, I can too.'"*
                              —Althea, thirty-four, 1994

Though children were an impediment to change, they were also a
primary inspiration. Numerous women believed that love of children
was the major resource which fed their resolve to move on. Some family members, some partners, and personal ambitions were also identified as women examined their efforts to change the course of their lives.
But most often women described in detail how children had motivated
them to try something new, despite the fear which the majority of
women felt as they looked out at the world they had to enter. Children,
they said, provided them with the courage to go back to school or try
a new program or job opportunity. And love of children helped many
a mother stick with it when she wanted to quit because "I don't want
to raise a quitter, so I better not be one."

When women discussed the way that children became such an essential part of their own goals, they marveled at each other's stories.
Thirty-two-year-old Eleanor, for example, described her children lin-
ing up at the window to watch her walk away on the two evenings each
week that she went to class. She was convinced that their father put

them up it, just to make her feel guilty. Listening, her student-companions laughed and nodded in painful recognition. Thirty-five-year-old Hazel said, "Nothing makes you doubt yourself more." But, for the most part, they rallied, and now they can find great mirth in their own children's antics. What impressed them most was how so many of them, separately and subtly, turned the tables on their own family's obstructive behavior. Mother became a woman "going places and you'd better catch up."

"*We* were going to school now," said Hazel. "It was the thing we would talk about. We would go to the library together, we learned to use the 'on-line services' [classmates laughed and clapped] together, we checked each other's papers."

Yvette, in her late twenties, added, "My husband and I got to meeting with our children's teachers, like every month . . . when before maybe we'd make the open house, maybe not. We were a learning family."

Naomi, who is twenty-eight, said, "After I got an award here [through a peer-support program at the college] I went right home and made a book of my daughter's report cards. *Now you don't come to my house without going through that book and seeing those A's.*" She explained that never before had she received such support and affirmation for her efforts. She realized how much it meant to her, how much she wanted to continue to achieve, and that her twelve-year-old daughter must feel the same way. Now, they are a mutual admiration society of their very own.

Twenty-nine-year-old Jessica got to the heart of the matter. "Nothing meant more to me than seeing the pride shining out of my son's eyes when I graduated," she said. "He was my witness. He had seen me try and cry, and then keep on trying. He knew I would feed him first and then say I wasn't hungry 'cause there wasn't enough. I tell you if it hadn't been for all the jars of peanut butter and crackers and fruit Adele would keep here ["Always got to be healthy for Adele," another woman muttered], I would have fainted some days. But I made it and he was my witness and when he saw me in my cap and gown he just beamed at me."

When Jessica finished talking we just held on and for few a minutes, no one spoke. She had found words for all of them.

Ronnette, Mattapan, 1996

"I almost gave up."

Ronnette, who is thirty-four when we meet to talk, was the first person in her generation to attend college, and she believes her decision to go both startled and invigorated her family. Her grown siblings debated the wisdom of her choice. They weren't sure that after a decade of jobs and intermittent welfare use, it made sense for then twenty-eight-year-old Ronnette to go back to school. But Ronnette's mother was proud of the endeavor, and she encouraged her other children and grandchildren to take heart through Ronnette's example. Ronnette's father and grandmother, on the other hand, were critical of her choice and her plan to leave her children on their own several afternoons each week. Deeply connected to her family, Ronnette felt that she was going to class with a dozen people arguing in her head. Yet, as time went on, she began to sense that her family was very proud—and the knowledge made her feel wonderful. Her twelve-year-old son and nine-year-old daughter would brag about her. At family reunions, she was called "our college girl."

Midway through her second year, Ronnette's grades went down. She was getting two incomplete grades and she realized that she might fail. Ronnette kept silent about her struggle, ashamed to admit that she might not make it. She became anxious and guilty. She started to skip classes. "I kept everyone out of it but my daughter," Ronnette says. "She knew. I don't know how, but she knew." One day Ronnette's daughter went to the local five-and-dime store and came back to the apartment with a present for her mother. Ronnette unwrapped a small figure of a woman, a graduate in a cap and gown. "I grabbed her," Ronnette says, "and squeezed her so hard she cried out 'Mama you're holding me too tight.' I told her how much I loved her and how I was going to make her proud of me." Ronnette graduated with an associate's degree and is working now to earn her B.A. "I don't panic now when I have some problems, I keep going." What is she planning to do when she finishes? "I want to do career counseling with girls . . . and grown women too. I want to give back what I have gained. *I know how hard it really is.*"

Carmen, Jamaica Plain, 1993

"If you don't have flexibility, you can't work or you can't be a mother."

Carmen is a thirty-four-year-old Puerto Ricanna who meets me to talk in a park near her office. She is the coordinator of an information system in a large human service agency, a job she has held for four years, and previously, she was an office manager. Before that, she was on welfare for almost a decade. Echoing dozens of other women, she says, "I hated welfare. It is degrading . . . the people weren't bad, but the whole thing is degrading."

Carmen's husband was addicted to drugs and had been HIV positive for several years before he died of AIDS a few years ago. Carmen believes it is a miracle that she is not ill, but after having two children while still very young, she insisted that her husband use "protection." "I never thought about AIDS . . . I didn't know anything about that. I was just not going to have any more kids. My marriage was a joke and I couldn't get out with a new baby."

After her husband died, Carmen found out what millions of other women discover when they first go to the welfare office—the numbers don't add up. She realized she would have to augment the welfare payment to support her children, and that meant she would have to lie. "I went to my priest," Carmen tells me. "He said it is a sin to lie. I didn't talk to him anymore."

Carmen started baking cakes for friends and family members to supplement her income. She also took a typing course through a community-development program and then other courses as well. At night, after her children were in bed, she did her homework while the cakes baked. In the morning, she got on the city bus with her children to accompany them to school, then caught a train to deliver her cakes, and finally ran to her afternoon class. "If there hadn't been that after-school program for the kids," she says, "I wouldn't have done it." After class, she had forty-five minutes to get from downtown Boston to her children's elementary school in a distant neighborhood. "I chose that school because they had very good bilingual teachers, and I want my kids to speak *both* languages well, and write them. But if the train was late they would be standing, waiting." The principal of the school, a strident disciplinarian, took to loudly berating Carmen for her irresponsibility in front of her children. This was a shocking breach of basic civility to Carmen. "She'd yell at me, 'What kind of example are you setting for your children?' Then she'd get in her new car and drive on out of there."

Suddenly, Carmen gets up off the park bench. She says that she is sorry but she wants to stop. She has changed her mind and no longer wants to be interviewed. As always, I had begun the interview by saying we could skip questions, or stop the tape recorder, or not use it at all. Several women had rejected the tape recorder or had turned it off. But Carmen is the first person to just get up and say goodbye. I stand up, too, unnerved. Then I pull out the tape cassette and hand it to her. She puts it in her bag, nods at me, and leaves the park. Two days later, Carmen calls me and says she'd like to pick it up again where we left off.

"I just felt angry," Carmen tells me when we meet again. "That woman insulted me in front of my children, and then, wham, I felt angry at you." Yes, I tell Carmen, I had the feeling that maybe I had re-minded her of the principal. She laughs. "You should have seen your face. You were like, 'Uh-oh, this lady is going off.' If I hadn't been so mad, I would have laughed right then." I thank Carmen for telling me the truth and for coming back to talk with me. "Well," she muses, "you weren't the one who had insulted me. I'm not the kind of person who sees the worst in people 'cause of what a few have done."

Carmen tells me how she had been determined to "be her own boss," to get her children into a better school, and to move into another building. Over a ten-year period, she succeeded in all of these goals. But she believes that if welfare programs were enlightened, were more flex-ible and responsive to the varying conditions of families, many people would make their way free of welfare sooner and in much better shape. "If they had let me work, say, part-time, and get some benefits, and say, Medicaid and some after-school program, well, I could have been done with them in three or four years," she says gesturing emphatically with her hands. "And look at me, I was on [welfare] for almost nine years. And that wasn't any good for my children neither."

I ask Carmen why she thinks welfare does not have more flexible, more family-oriented regulations. She thinks that "they" don't believe women who receive public aid are ever capable of anything. And not only "Spanish" women, like herself, but Black women and white women, too, "'cause I have seen them treated just like dirt too. And maybe they think our children aren't worth anything either, so they just make it as mean and small as they can." Carmen pauses for a moment, calming herself. "It is so stupid, you know. I mean look at how many people would do really good and give their kids hope and make things better."

Tania Again, Boston, 1991

Once Tania began to recover from her depression over Peter's deser-tion, she began to think of how she had once thought of herself as an achiever—a person who didn't give up. It had been years since she had graduated from trade school, but Tania felt the school might offer help. She called up a former teacher and asked if he knew of any places she could apply for a job. He did better than that. He accompanied her to an interview in a office run by a woman named Betty who had hired other graduates of the trade school. "That made the difference," Tania says.

Betty, a middle-aged white woman from a working-class community north of Boston, took to the struggling Tania. She "guided me, mentored me," Tania reports, not only by encouraging her but by spending time helping Tania plan her future and plot a way to better-paying jobs. Anytime there was a chance for staff development, "she put my name in first." Betty, a single woman and aunt to "a dozen or so" nieces and nephews, believed that all Tania needed was some serious encouragement. She convinced Tania to take first one college course, then another, and Tania's confidence in her academic abilities grew. "I was a good worker," Tania says, "and I made friends easily. I got close to a few women working there, you know, like a sisterhood. With Betty as the 'mother superior.' We had all of us been through hell and had babies to worry about and we helped each other out."

During this happier period, Tania found it easier to accept her in-laws as part of her sons' lives. While Peter had never given her any child support, his mother and siblings did seem to love her children. "I felt better about myself," Tania remembers. "I'd stopped thinking about him. And my kids loved their grandmother, so why deny them?"

Tania began to focus her interests on human services and finally on child-care services. "My children were my greatest riches, but they were also a big problem when it comes to going to work. I know thousands of other mothers feel the same way. And day care, *not just any old basement with a hundred kids*, but decent day care is something we all desperately need."

Now, years later, Tania has a college degree and is in a senior-level position in a child-care system for low-income children. She also serves as a consultant to various agencies, designing services for single mothers. In 1993 she started graduate classes in early childhood development. Tania also likes to write plays for preschool classes to promote children's interest in the arts.

"Girls need employment skills early," she tells me. "Not bullshit typing courses, but real education for jobs like someone like you can get and, *now, I can get*. They need programs like 'working family programs,' not this thing they call welfare. *It should be talked about as social security for family life*. What is more important?"

And, since it is the question I am so often asked when I take my research back to another audience, I ask Tania, how do we pay for this?

Tania gets up out of her chair and starts to pace. *"We are already paying for it in the streets and prisons and foster care and hospitals.* How about paying for it in child-care centers and colleges and safe housing. Then look at who we turn out to be."

Tania tells me her teenage sons are dreaming big dreams. Tyler loves reading the second-hand atlas and encyclopedia Tania bought for him. He dreams of "being a scientist and discovering the cure for AIDS." Her younger son, Marcus, loves to draw and dance. He talks of acting or "being the president, which is close to the same thing," Tania says with a wink.

Odessa, Boston, 1993

I hear Odessa, a thirty-two-year-old African American woman, speak at a forum on welfare reform. After she completes her address, I ask her about a phrase she used, "Don't call me out of name." I have heard it said many times over the years. I heard a teenager use it when she objected to being called a curse word. I heard an adult say it when rebuking a child for speaking poorly about another person. I heard a woman tell a man that she was being called out of name when he referred to her as a "bitch." But when I heard Odessa speak these words in her address about welfare, I heard more, I heard part of a nation of people speak up.

Odessa tells me that women who have no money and no one to stand up for them get put into a bad position and get misnamed. Sometimes they get called "sluts and whores," she said, "'cause they have babies but no man." Most often they get called "welfare mothers" or "recipients," words which Odessa will no longer acknowledge. For Odessa, these are words which brand people, like racial epithets. And when you let them name you, everyone comes to know you that way, in a sense, you become that.

I believe Odessa speaks up for many people and, particularly, for women who have gone through early motherhood in American poverty and the ways of welfare. With millions alongside her, Odessa emerged by her own strength, through family love, and with the odd luck of finding some support and opportunity. And now, she insists upon naming herself. She turns her face away from words put on her which call her out of name, out of her knowledge, out of herself. Odessa is a learned daughter of a nation's history in which taking away people's names, renaming them, and misnaming them is the everyday practice of the powerful. And Odessa is telling her audience, to their delight, it is a practice that stops with her.

BEYOND WELFARE REFORM: HUMAN DEVELOPMENT IN POOR AMERICA

Increasingly, effort to include the voices of marginalized people into social research has offered greater depth to our understanding, a view from the other side of the interview.[1] In gender research the importance of women's own voices and ways of knowing the world has shifted conventional research methodology as well. Yet most research on the development of women in poor America has been, in fact, research on welfare: who gets on it, who gets off it, who stays on and for how long. Alongside these fascinations is an intense interest paid to the different modes of "moving people off welfare," traditionally seen to be through marriage, and in the last two decades, through single-parent employment. The earlier find-a-husband solution is shaky public policy now, both with the rising rate of divorce (with a historical lack of child-support collection) and the increasing rate of never-married families, throughout society.[2]

William Julius Wilson presents a forceful analysis that the loss of an industrial employment base, which had previously provided African American (as well as other) working-class men (as well as some women) with a family income, greatly affects marital behavior in low-income America. The loss of better-paid, blue-collar jobs reduces the availability of potential husbands (and wives) who could actually support a family on industrial, working-class wages. Those families which, earlier in this century, were building family equity and reproducing middle-class conventions in family life, lost significant economic ground in the latter part of the century. Alongside the economic losses which a gutted blue-collar labor market created, social and family life also began to change.[3]

Such an analysis tends to focus upon the loss of male breadwinners as the critical variable in socially stable family life. The more recent version of father-centered solutions to the troubles experienced by families in poor America sidesteps analysis of economic causes and focuses upon men as family leaders and "promise keepers," or at least as potential ones. This vision promotes father as a solution to family troubles as much for his presence and discipline as for his economic contribution.[4]

Yet fathers have never been taken very seriously in the welfare discourse. Regarded as deadbeat, absent, possibly criminal, and nonworking, low-income men, particularly men of color, have been largely ignored in policy discourse about millions of single-mother families in poor America. It seems the rising trend of families without "male heads" is cause for concern in some sectors of society, but in poor America the issue is ending welfare. With the growing, if largely unspoken, recognition that many men in low-income America do not have access to employment that will solve the need for public aid, the focus of welfare policy became getting mothers into paid employment. At the same time that employing mothers became the absolute mission of welfare policy, the labor of caring for children in low-income families became a nonissue, became nonwork. In sharp contrast to the image of devoted and self-sacrificing middle-class women who "put their careers on hold to stay home with the children," poor women who see their primary role as mothers are referred to as dependent and incompetent.

Over a period of changing economic conditions, welfare mothers were increasingly labeled as "dysfunctional" precisely because they were transformed into nonworkers. Some conservative critics went so far as to suggest that the status of citizenship should be directly tied to employment behavior, at least in the case of poor mothers.[5] By the 1990s, the major welfare policy goal had become how to get welfare mothers into paid work.

Yet, concomitant with the broad acceptance of this domestic mission, numerous researchers and social critics have pointed out that there is a significant difference between ending welfare and reducing poverty.[6] Many women who leave AFDC enter low-wage jobs and remain poor, sometimes losing more than they gain with the loss of child care and other benefits, including health insurance, associated with welfare. As Kathryn Edin puts it, "Welfare use is inextricably bound to opportunities in the labor market. . . . If political will determines that poor, single-parent families should be lifted out of so-called dependency through work, policymakers must determine which jobs at what wages are needed . . . to bring these welfare mothers and their families into the economic mainstream."

Labor economists and social researchers have pointed out that, without integration of people's individual interests and talents and investment in their education—without, that is, development of "human capital"—most jobs available to most women currently on welfare simply will not support a family. So welfare may end, but poverty will not, and the world of poor America will change in ways we cannot yet know.

Early on in my efforts to write this book I found that I was not writing about welfare except as it emerged through girls' and women's explorations and accounts. The research, rather, focused upon the experiences and dynamics which people named and detailed as their diverse processes for surviving in the welfare times and for "moving on." The group of "older" women who offered up their analysis of the transitions do not necessarily represent the majority of women in poor America, nor those on welfare. But they are not alone.[7] The incremental progress which they described—that two steps forward and one-plus step back—and which other women confirmed, is the pattern of most women leaving poverty and, therefore, public assistance. As several studies confirm and these individuals detailed at length, even the best laid strategies and most persistent effort do not guarantee that you have shut that welfare door permanently.[8]

Among many of the older women I met while completing the research for this book, the pursuit of education was a popular choice toward moving forward with their lives.[9] A study of 158 low-income women attending college in New York, revealed that over 60 percent were receiving welfare before they went to college, and only 17 percent after graduation.[10] Whether women were returning to obtain a GED, to take ESL classes, to learn a skill, or to enter college courses, their decision to return to school was experienced as an effort toward a new independence by the women themselves, by their families, and by male partners. As other research explores, this change was not always welcome.[11]

Group discussions suggested that this transition period, when women were making an effort to gain further education, or seek employment, or stretch toward some other nondomestic role, became a kind of testing ground, where you found out who was *really* on your side and who was not. The group of twenty-five older women from the Life-History Study (who believed they had made or were making progress toward a better life) asserted that the welfare system failed this test, hands down, and that a significant number of male partners did as well. Sometimes mothers, siblings, and other kinfolk were also seen as obstructive in the beginning. And many children wailed at the apparent detachment of mother. Most women remarked that, had not it not been for particular programs which offered support and the understanding of other women in those programs, they would not have kept on going. Equally important were the coaches, mentors, and teachers whom these women remembered as providing special help and encouragement. As one woman said, "There ain't no way I would be out here now, on my own, doing like I am doing with nobody's help." The support of women of common experience and the informed kindness and assistance of advocates and teachers were invaluable aids. Once they were on their way, these women often pulled their families, and sometimes it seemed their whole neighborhood, right along with them.

The accounts given by the twenty-five older women in the Life-History Study and by the additional sixty in the Women in Transition Study reveal a pattern of ten to twelve years as the period required for building up strength and seeking new opportunities. This is not so very different from the length of time that it takes to pursue college and graduate level education. But these women used the years to stabilize children, find safe housing, build up healthy social networks, and overcome personal problems, all the while reaching for the courage to pursue a career or employment pathway.

Their knowledge of this tough and stigmatized road, which millions before have gone down and millions travel today, became the essential last part of this book. Embedded in their individual histories and subsequent analyses is a woman's knowledge about the forces outside and inside poor America which hold people down. In the discussion groups, they offered each other counsel, shared strategies, and reminded each other, as Odessa put it so well, not to accept a distorted version of self, never to be called out of name. But I had to wonder at the fortitude of so many in the face of all the hardships they described along with their keen sense of how the larger society judged them. Rooted in brave tales and cold-minded assessments of the world, I recognized the final theme of this book.

CHAPTER SIX

A Common Woman's Resistance

During the course of this research I found that most of the themes which emerged from the data would do so as consecutive periods of women's lives. Thereafter, these themes had the good grace to become book chapters, each building upon those which went before. Just as girls and women guided me through the episodes of their own lives, not as discrete moments but as connected and progressing, so this book unfolded. But early on, I found I was gathering more than sequential data and even more than divergent theory springing from detailed accounts of many lives. Indistinct at first, I began to hear a restless element in the data I had gathered, one which has no patience with a plan or chronology. It came in harsh tones sometimes, the way people speak when they are weary with explaining what should be so obvious. At other times this message came whispered as a secret, as subversive and dangerous. The meaning became more distinct as I gained skill in gathering the data of difference, as I learned to sit in silence, meet eyes that would question me, question my ability to understand more than my own life, test my willingness to cross over.

The theme has to do with life in a social outback, peripheral American territory where the everyday terms of survival are entirely different from those portrayed as a national way of life. It is a theme about growing up straining for elemental needs in a society in which many enjoy wealth and privilege. It is about cultural assumptions of white homogeneity against the reality of racial and ethnic difference. It is the fantasy of soft girlishness against the truth of hard female lives. Above all, the theme is about finding and then holding onto a version of your self which is your own, which has not been forced upon you by others.

In the outback, the need to build a self-definition starts early. I have watched children growing up in poor America bring their worldview with them as they venture beyond their family and neighborhood circles. They bring their cultural heritage, their neighborhood savvy, their ways of coping with anxiety in the face of vital troubles, and their devotion to parents and family, even to those who are in turmoil. As most children do, they present their unguarded selves to a new set of adults who, they have been told, hold knowledge and authority. They meet preschool and kindergarten teachers; school social workers and principals; "lunch mothers" and teacher aides, nurses, and coaches. Sometimes they meet adults who honor and encourage, as well as attempt to modify and socialize them. But often those adults who come from another America simply do not have the awareness or cannot find the courage to cope with a child's complexity or validate a child's truth. These are early lessons taught to millions of low-income children, lessons of learning to hide living contradictions, learning to dissemble and to placate an external adult world. And the lessons continue for a lifetime.

Every day millions of residents of poor America collect abundant data which contradict the notion of a national fellowship. This is empirical data, collected in the form of incident after incident in real lives which are pooled together as people will do with their information. Inexorably the knowledge collected constructs a separate, living history, not well-coordinated nor inscribed in a text. It is a history of stories passed on, legends and advice about surviving intact in a society which does not recognize your hard work, your devotion to family and children, your gargantuan efforts to move on and take others with you. A society which calls you out of name.

I see this clearly now, but I do not claim to grasp the full power and consequence of facing institutionalized denial. But others do; mothers, fathers, grandmothers, and quiet leaders who know they must construct ways to keep children whole, to validate a dichotomous life. It is a different kind of schooling and I have heard the confidence of some graduates. I have heard young people mention a collective "we" or "my people" or "our community" in reference to how life really is, even in reference to how you face ignorant authority. I knew that whenever these terms came into the conversation, a multitude had arrived. "My people see it this way," I have heard it said, or "folks in this neighborhood don't speak about our business" or "in my community we know how to pull together when there's trouble." These speakers come accompanied. They bring with them a history, a vastly complicated history which sometimes reaches back to slavery, sometimes to a colonized Caribbean, or to waged-workers who will never get out of debt, to endless troubles in Ireland, to police raids in Mission Hill in Boston. These are generally not cross-community histories, they tend to remain separated in their own corners, sometimes reactionary in their racial and ethnic lines. But what is shared is the absolute necessity of self-definition, a knowledge passed on by insider voices and by implacable, everyday life.

From the Outback

I used this insight of critical self-definition in sorting through data; accounts of resistance, of creative strategies for survival, even examples of individualized public policy. I found that many women and girls living poor took action of some kind. Often, such actions were privately executed, bent upon getting results and not on making a political statement. These were survivor actions. Yet they were sometimes followed by a consideration of the meaning of breaking with old teachings, with men, the law, one's church, welfare rules, one's own family traditions.

That reflective process might take years as chronic trouble tends to crowd out contemplation. Some will put it off forever, continuously bouncing against one unstable force or another. But I heard numerous ways in which women, adolescents, and even little girls tried to make sense of their place in the world and to hold onto themselves. And of course, such sense, the knowledge which grows out of it, becomes shared. Women will always find words to pass their sense along to others, to siblings, friends, children, grandchildren. It is an outstanding female legacy. Some of that sense, I believe, was passed on to me.

THE OUTSIDE WORLD: SOMETIMES PEOPLE IN AUTHORITY ARE WRONG

"I Refuse to Hear You": Mayisha, Boston, 1994

Taller than I am, very dark skinned, and with dreadlocks hanging below her shoulders, Mayisha looks you in the eyes as she speaks. We are talking in the hallway of a small high school in the city, sitting on chairs we pulled from a classroom.

During her sophomore year, Mayisha was expelled from another public high school and now attends this school for students who have been sidelined for behavioral problems. I ask her to tell me about her school experience. She describes battles with what she views as the unfair and racist administration of her former high school. At that school, Mayisha was sent out of class by two teachers "every day, like even before I had said anything, because they got this attitude about who I was." Mayisha asserts that these two teachers did not treat her with any respect and that they falsely claimed she was rude, unmanageable. She tells me that, at first, she was surprised at how openly hostile these teachers seemed, how they "would yell at me in front of the other students to try to break me down." She responded by not crying, not showing any emotion. It is a source of pride to Mayisha that she could control her reactions this way to what she viewed as their effort to break her. I ask her what, in her behavior, would anger them so. She is vague at first, but eventually she suggests that it may have been her demeanor, her tendency to speak back, her "kind of in your face opinions." Mayisha tells me that she's always been "a loud mouth," not rude or disrespectful, in her opinion, but "I speak my mind, and these two white teachers didn't like that. They had an attitude about me."

When I ask other students about these two teachers, a white man in his fifties and a white woman somewhat younger, they acknowledge that they don't trust the teachers. Several Black students claim they had to steel themselves against these two, and a white student responds that the teachers were "known racists." Mayisha tells me that they were disrespectful, irresponsible, and even cruel. They did "not even bother to learn your name, all year." They ignored your hand when you raised it, except for a few chosen students, usually white kids. And if you said anything that could be construed as a challenge, Mayisha insists, "then you got picked on from then on in."

As she talks it becomes more and more clear that Mayisha sees herself as a kind of crusader against these two people who had authority over her but who, in her opinion, *should not*. This same kind of poisonous conflict seemed to arise for many of the girls and women interviewed for this research. It is the conflict between authority and rightful authority, the sense that you must acquiesce to someone who will treat you badly.

In her former high school, Mayisha was frequently sent out of class to the halls or to speak with the headmaster. He became very frustrated with her, but Mayisha believes that she made a good case for herself, that she gave believable evidence that these two entrenched teachers were not performing well and were prejudiced toward African American and Puerto Rican students. She wanted to bring other students into the principal's office to validate her complaint. One day, full throttle into an exchange with the headmaster, she said that she was going to bring in "someone else, like an advocate or something. I also said something about a petition too 'cause some of us had been thinking about it." In fact, Mayisha was pretty much alone in her struggle. She had not even told her mother about her troubles at school, and soon she felt overwhelmed. "It was getting too much for me, every day was a battle." As Mayisha tired and began to disengage, she set upon this phrase, "I refuse to hear you," as her set response to criticism. She tells me that she had read the phrase in a book somewhere and that she would repeat it, mantra-like, to teachers and the headmaster. She even began to say it at home when her mother, now alerted to her daughter's imminent expulsion, tried to discipline her into behaving. I ask Mayisha what it meant to her, to say that phrase again and again. She tells me that it became a way to stay safe, a way to "keep them out and to keep herself in."

Mayisha is doing much better in the new high school. She likes the classes, she tells me, and her teachers and the (white) headmaster. Her mother now feels that she should have removed her daughter from the other school sooner, and that Mayisha was probably right about those teachers. But when the head of a school and the teachers are all telling you that your child is a troublemaker, her mother told me, it is hard to hear her side of the story.

I hear in Mayisha's account an American tale that can be flipped different ways. It can be told as another account of an undisciplined "out-of-control" inner-city teen. Or it is the story of a Black girl who recognized and resisted, not always delicately, what she viewed as damaging adults and the racist institution which protected them. Hers can be heard as a lonely voice which dared to tell the truth.

Other teenage girls, both young women of color and whites, who listened to Mayisha's story felt immediate sympathy for her. To a girl, they stated that abuse from a certain, fairly small, but brutal cadre of teachers in the Boston public schools was a way of life. They told me that other students alert you to who these teachers are, almost at once, sometimes even before you start going to the school. But there was less of a consensus that Mayisha's troubles were race based. Several students in different group discussions, white and African American and Latino, argued that many white teachers are "so scared of Black kids, especially boys that they *never* discipline them." Others argued that "some teachers hate us, you know, they just hate teens, whether you're white or whatever." But other young women pointed out that, while most of the Boston public school student body "is Black and Hispanic," the teachers are "mostly white Irish." One young woman challenged us all to consider how that can be good for kids, always to see white people as the teachers, as the people "who are supposed to know everything and get to fail you." But even as they criticized teachers, and the system that places, for the most part, white teachers in authority, they also readily blamed subgroups of peers—teens who are disruptive, disinterested, and downright frightening—as largely contributing to a hard, divisive, and unhealthy school environment.

Changing the Terms of Engagement: Margarita, Boston, 1992

Margarita, who calls herself a "welfare survivor," tells me that to overcome the odds stacked against you, you have to be ready to playact. She was nineteen years old and the mother of two children when she went to the welfare office for the first time. She thought out her performance ahead of time and decided on humor as her strategy for facing a numbing bureaucracy.

"I had a three-year-old and a baby and no work experience. Well, I had been volunteering in the church for years, running programs and helping people. And I had taken care of my home with two kids while my man was *busy*," she says with sarcasm, "taking care of his flock. But to that welfare office, I had nothing to offer."

That first time, as during her subsequent visits, Margarita faced a two- to three-hour wait to speak with a caseworker. While waiting, she sang Puerto Rican songs and joked with the other mothers. She marched around "at one point singing 'Oh say can you see,' only I didn't know the words that well, but the other mothers laughed and helped me out with the 'proudly we hail.' I thought it was 'proudly we sell,' which made a lot of sense to me."

The welfare office was glad to finish with Margarita and send the "nutty Spanish girl," as she says, on her way. But Margarita was not embarrassed. The performance had been a conscious tactic: "I didn't want my daughter to remember Mommy with her head all down. She thought we were playing a game and you know . . . she had something with that." Margarita is convinced that the welfare world can know her in only one way, as a supplicant appealing for a handout. She describes their perspective as one which teaches that poor mothers are lazy, that they have babies for money, and that, in the case of Puerto Rican women like her, they shouldn't even be here anyway. Margarita has little interest in educating people with these attitudes, but because she does have to deal with them she tries to out-think them. She tries to change the terms of engagement so that she can hold onto herself.

Margarita tells her children that taking welfare is not something to be ashamed of, that it is "money that comes so we can get by, be together." She tells them they will not always get welfare, but they have a right to help when they need it. And she demonstrated her own ability to be there, in that shabby welfare office for all that time, yet to not be there, at least not on their terms.

Margarita's determination to preserve her dignity and her children's dignity reminds me of Renata. Renata had spoken to me two years earlier of praying for the day when she could slam her case file shut and walk out the welfare office door for the last time. One painful day as they left the welfare office, she told her tearful four-year-old daughter, "The shame isn't ours. It is shameful that we are treated this way. But we are not lowlifes. Even when they treat you like trash, *you've got to know yourself.*"

Raising Resistance: Nemesis and Jasmine, Boston, 1992

Nemesis, who is in her mid-thirties, works in human services and is particularly interested in teen mothers. She will complete her B.A. within the year. She has much to say about her family, particularly about her mother who raised her children alone in New York City. Her father was alcoholic and a batterer, and her mother threw him out when Nemesis was still a preschooler. Her mother had then "gone on the dole," but had quickly rejected this strategy, apparently advising her daughter that one cannot live on that amount of money and that "they think they own you."

Nemesis's mother, who was African American and Mexican, opened a gambling club in her apartment in Harlem and proceeded to run it for a decade. Nemesis recalls how, in the evenings, a baby-sitter would come to the apartment to watch her and her sisters while her mother prepared for the games. All the gamblers were men. Her mother would deal, oversee the drinking and behavior of the guests, and collect a very healthy cut of everyone's winnings each night. She was the bouncer and the mediator. She ruled the games wisely and empathetically, Nemesis says, refusing entrance to any man whose wife or lover called to say he was gambling away the family's rent money.

Nemesis was almost eleven when her mother's apartment was raided by the NYPD. Her mother calmly told the dozen or so police, who seemed to be tearing the apartment to pieces, that she had to arrange for her children's care. She took a box of tissues and mopped up their tears. Then she handed the tissue box to Nemesis, looking her dead in the eyes, and told her that she was responsible for the others and for making sure their faces stayed clean. Nemesis knew full well that there were thousands of dollars inside the tissue box, the family's fortune which her mother "trusted to no bank." When they were led away to stay with relatives, Nemesis tucked the box under her arm, telling no one about it and protecting it until she could return it to her mother's care a week later.

When they were reunited, Nemesis's mother sat her daughters down to tell them about the law and about breaking rules. She spoke of honorable behavior, for women and mothers and particularly, as she saw it, for Black women in America. "My mother said it was wrong to tell lies and to cheat and to break the law. But she said there were bigger wrongs. Having hungry children, being dependent on people who abuse you, are bigger wrongs. She said that you feed your children, first. You belong to nobody. The other comes later."

Nemesis recalls grasping the core, the very heart of her mother's credo, and she seems to want me to understand as well. For Nemesis and her family, it is explicit. There is more than one simple set of rules out there because there is more than one world. Sometimes, when obeying the rules of "their world" means that people you love will be in jeopardy, you obey the ethic of "your world." As I listened to Nemesis, I thought of others who had disobeyed the laws of their land because people's lives were at stake: white outlaw guides, who traveled the underground railroad; gentiles of another country, who stitched the star of David on their arms to become indistinguishable from their persecuted Jewish neighbors. I thought of those who broke laws to demand a living wage, and those who marched, blocked buildings, refused to give up their seats despite the law. Each of those movements were born of common gestures of obscure people, mothers and fathers, even children whose chose life and loved ones over laws.

When Nemesis and I meet later that same week, she tells me about a time when her daughter Jasmine, then seven years old, came home from school and complained, for the third or fourth time, that a "big boy" in her class had bullied and punched her. Nemesis wants me to hear the story because she thinks it will teach me more about a hidden female history. But it is Jasmine, now fifteen, who tells the story. She had been listening unobtrusively from the next room, enjoying the family stories without having to acknowledge it. She wants to be the one who tells this story.

In her class was a boy, she says, also African American, and a big bully. Jasmine knew her mother had previously called the school and talked to the principal about this boy when Jasmine first complained that he had hit her. "When I told my mother that he had punched me again, she got very still. That's when she's dangerous." Yet all her mother did was pat her arm. The next day, however, her mother didn't bother with the telephone. She came to the school.

"I knew it was her when that door swung open and I heard her shoes . . . click, click, click . . . coming down the hall. She came into the classroom, dressed to kill, and she went right by the teacher's desk and grabbed the boy who'd been messing with me. She hauled him out of the classroom *and spoke some words in his ear* and he never did lay a hand on me again."

Jasmine tells me that she and many of her peers believe that some adults with power do not expect intelligence or commitment to learning from low-income students. Worse still, she claims that, *if they do not like you,* some teachers will go out of their way to bully and denigrate low-income students or to ignore it when they are being bullied and denigrated by other students. A lack of equity in the use of power seems a given, but it does not go unnoticed. Adults in authority are expected to be just, but they often disappoint. Some of them have attitudes, and sometimes they just don't understand how life really is. They see the world one way, and you know it is another. For this reason, Jasmine explains, you have to learn when "to stand up and be evil or they think they can get away with disrespecting you." As she speaks, her mother nods in assent.

Creating Your Own Ethic: Veronica, Cambridge, 1991

Veronica and I meet at the Dunkin Donuts shop in Central Square in Cambridge over a period of several weeks. We stake out a corner table which, by 9:30 in the morning, always proves empty. It is a busy coffee bar, not only for local workers but also for locals without work, people at loose ends, it seems to us, as we sit there observing the parade. Veronica, a wonderful storyteller, not only chronicles for me her own life, but also makes me feel like I know her brothers and sisters, her indomitable "Mother Italy," and her children, who sometimes appear at the window of the doughnut shop, hailing their mother.

Veronica was born in Waltham, Massachusetts, a working-class suburb west of Boston. "My people are Italian, you know, the kind who shout instead of talk and give kids bread and butter and candy for breakfast." She describes her mother as a loving, supportive, and generous person who "always took in the strays." Veronica sees her mother as trying to live up to the "selfless woman" model, the Italian mother who cares for everyone and never expects anything but toil and trouble. Yet clearly Veronica's mother was more than that, was inspired by some spirit. "She was always telling us how great we were," Veronica remembers. "She would joke around and be silly and joyful and all that, when my father was the biggest asshole in the world." Veronica's father frequently assaulted his family. He beat his wife, he beat the children. He beat them until one day, "we ganged up on him and bit him and kicked him, and Danny got a knife out and stuck it in his nose." After that, Veronica testified in court to make sure her father did not come back.

Veronica's earlier childhood seems to have been more peaceful, with the domestic violence escalating over the years. She recalls being happy with her mother and siblings and happy hanging around the streets. She was always social, popular with neighbors, full of curiosity, and reading before kindergarten. But when her mother moved the family to a new neighborhood so that her children could attend better schools, Veronica ran into trouble. She recalls that her brothers seemed to find a place for themselves in the new school, joining different sports and "fighting to show they were tough." However, Veronica and her sister, with their "shabby clothes" and coming from subsidized housing, felt they were ostracized. Veronica clearly decided to rebel rather than hang her head. "There was no place in that school that I was OK, except the library," she tells me. "I was a top student, that's part of what they couldn't handle. I didn't believe in God and I didn't believe in national anthems. But I read every book in that library. I started from the first book and I went through until I finished the last."

What made her such a reader? I ask. Veronica describes a very close relationship with her paternal grandfather, a learned man who always told her that she was smarter than anyone else. He told her to read, to learn and to believe in her intelligence. "He learned English when he was fifty-five years old," Veronica muses. "And you know why he did? Because he couldn't speak to his grandchildren because we didn't speak Italian. So if he wanted to know us, he had to learn."

The school librarian took to the voracious reader in Veronica. She encouraged the girl to do her homework in the library and asked Veronica to critique new books. Veronica loved the room, the books, and the elderly woman who made her feel so welcome. But outside that library door, she believed that she was under attack. She was getting into fights on the playground and by this time also fighting her father at home. In no time, she was in trouble with the school principal, who thought she was "some kind of juvenile delinquent . . . only like I pointed out, I was never absent and I was at the top of my class."

I ask Veronica how she managed that, to be so much the outsider and yet to achieve such high grades. She tells me that academic success was her revenge, it was her weapon against being "put down." Veronica believes that when her mother would come to the school to discuss her children's progress, the teachers were not respectful to the small, rotund lady who wore a kerchief around her head. Veronica, by then taller than many adults, thin as a twig, and so smart, would try to provoke "them" with her antireligious opinions and her refusal to pledge the American flag. She would construct intricate intellectual arguments on the most mundane matters to drive her teachers to a frenzy.

At the age of fifteen, after testifying against her violent father, Veronica left school and left her home too. "I had taken so many honors credits that I could graduate if I took one more year of English. But I was tired of all of it, I went to live in the street." Over the next decade, Veronica followed a path which seems explicitly outside the rules; in and out of some dangerous relationships, sometimes using drugs, sometimes engaging in illegal trade. In the weeks that we meet I find myself asking her again and again, "What drove you? What led you? What voice did you listen to while you made your radical way around in the world?" She gives me different answers, but finally she challenges me: "You want to know *why* I don't care for their laws, why I raise my children not to care. They taught me a long time ago that I don't belong, that they don't care what happens to me or my kids. So I do whatever I need to do." She has been called a juvenile delinquent, a welfare cheat, a prostitute. Veronica scoffs at the terms. "They are ignorant, ignorant, ignorant." Veronica, like Nemesis and some other women, seems to have constructed another way to understand her place in society, an insurgent way. She claims she understands how "mainstream" people think and sometimes she thinks that way too, but only when she can afford to.

Outside the doughnut shop we meet Veronica's eleven-year-old son and thirteen-year-old daughter. I notice that they both carry a stack of books under their arms. They have just come from the Cambridge Public Library.

On Seeing the Truth from the Corner: Marcia, Roxbury, 1994

When I first meet Marcia, a first-grader in one of Boston's public elementary schools, she talks about having to stand in the corner because her teacher doesn't like her crying. She cried a lot at school the first several months because she was uneasy, her mother explained, and not accustomed to being away from her mother's side. Marcia would try to hold back the sounds she made because if she could keep it all down she might get through the day not standing in the corner. But usually the sounds leaked out and then she was back into the corner. Ms. Gray would make Marcia stand with her back to the class mostly, but gradually Marcia would turn around. Just "little by little," she would turn until she could observe. Sometimes she stood watching the class for most of the morning, watching the boys clandestinely passing "gross stuff" and the girls waving to her, arms twisted behind their backs so no one in the front could see. And she could watch Ms. Gray telling the children to write their letters, to pronounce the vowels, to read out loud. She tells me that Ms. Gray does not like children and doesn't want to be a teacher. I ask Marcia how she knows this so absolutely. She shrugs. "I watch her face," she says. "You can tell by looking in her eyes when she don't know you are watching her. She looks mad and sad."

One day when I am waiting for the children to go to an afternoon class, I see Ms. Gray walking with Marcia. She is pulling the child along, angry and brittle. She speaks to another teacher, Ms. Constanza, complaining about Marcia and also about Marcia's mother, who is not there to pick up Marcia. I watch Ms. Constanza move firmly between Ms. Gray and the child. Halfway through her angry diatribe, Ms. Gray notices that Marcia is crying again. She shouts, "Sit down and look down. I don't want to see you cry once more today." As several other women quickly move closer, I see Marcia look up at Ms. Gray. And there it is, so clear, the reason why Marcia is detested by this teacher.

Frightened and sensitive, still Marcia sees this bitter woman undisguised. Her nature is made public by this child. Everyone can see it now.

By the week following this incident, Marcia's mother takes to being in the school most of the day. She is in the office, in the hall, around the cafeteria. Once, while I am chatting with her, she puts up her hand for silence. Indistinguishable to me in the din of a public school cafeteria, she discerns the sound of her child and is off like a shot. She returns in no time with Marcia by her side, her assignments in hand.

Eventually, Marcia's mother becomes a sore subject in the school, a source of discomfort. "I stay around here now," she tells me, "I keep watch." In time, and with help from Ms. Constanza and a few others, her mother's vigilance pays off. Despite his impatience with what seems to him a tedious episode, and despite the fact that moving a child is an unprecedented occurrence at this school of four hundred children, the principal moves Marcia to a new class.

Marcia clearly responds positively to the change. She seems happier, less anxious about leaving her mother. I notice her playing around with the other children. Marcia's mother tells me that both she and Marcia love Ms. Constanza because "she was willing to speak up," even when the administration told her it was none of her business. "It really helps," she says, "when another person from the inside speaks up."

Ms. Constanza tells me that she did not win many friends in that whole affair. "But I've got a little girl," she says. "How would it be for her if she was kept in the corner because she cried. I think sometimes you just have to choose where you stand, which side you are on. I choose children, even if that means breaking some unwritten rules."

The Inside World: Sometimes People at Home Are Wrong

In several interviews over the years, when women recalled how their mothers had been beaten by fathers or other men, they would, like Veronica, describe a counterattack launched by siblings. The first time I heard this tale I imagined a terrible picture of a beaten mother, terrified children, and then their pathetic attempt to defend. But twenty-five-year-old Leona, who is Irish, snuffs out this pitiful image.

"We didn't go into it with him like babies," Leona tells me. "Forget that. I got Collin's baseball bat and Maggie got a butcher knife. He went to the hospital, you hear what I am saying? He told nobody who done that 'cause he was too ashamed . . . and maybe scared." Leona pushes her point home. "When you have been watching a man beat, stamp on, and rape your mother, you either die inside, you get out as Collin did, or you finally get big enough to go to bat for her." Literally, it seems. Leona makes it clear to me she is done with femininity, what she refers to as "prissy-girl ways." She understands that her way of being female is much less attractive to most men. But she is blunt and unrepentant. Looking at me with just a touch of judgment, she lets it be known that raising timid daughters is dangerous.

I was to hear a similar analysis from some other women who face male violence. They often seemed proud of overcoming the abuse, but doing so almost always required a transformation, not only finding courage but also letting something go. Almost every woman and girl interviewed approached their lives as including an effort to find and even hold onto a man. They very much wanted fathers and partners to be there with them and were often willing to put up with a great deal to that end. Many women, particularly mothers of sons, express sympathy for men, an understanding that men have their problems too, sometimes big problems. Yet numerous women told me that holding onto a man and maintaining a man-centered household finally just cost too much.

Sometimes when women stand up to wrongful authority on home ground, they must face down community or cultural disapproval. Thirty-five-year-old Alicia described her extraordinary departure after years of abuse. She claimed that, "The eleventh commandment for Puerto Rican women is, 'Stand by your man, no matter what all he does.'" Alicia saw her decision to leave her abusive husband as a sin.

Her priest attempted to dissuade her, even "when I came to church with a bloody lip and a black eye." Along with all the rest of her battles, she found that she had to break with another authority, a church which she loved. In the end, she took her children and left "both those men, the husband and the priest." She told me that this was by no means easy. It was not only a rejection of two powerful male figures in her life, but also seemed to be a rejection of the ways her mother had taught her. With soft words, Alicia described her mother as a gentle, sympathetic woman whom she missed more than anyone. The idea that she had broken with her mother's ways was painful, but Alicia also told me that her mother's love, the idea that her mother would not want her to suffer so much abuse, was what led her at last to leave her husband and protect herself and her children.

The experience of abuse sometimes transforms young women in ways they still do not understand, nor claim, as teenagers. Seventeen-year-old Rosa, for example, was not certain how to feel about the story her friend Shareese told me about her. "I hate it when I get yelled at," Rosa told me. "I don't get mad like some girls do. I just get quiet . . . like I don't move a muscle." Her friend Shareese has seen this performance, especially when Rosa's stepfather loses his temper. He is, from all accounts, strict but not abusive. Rosa's response when he is angry is to become absolutely still, to avoid his eyes, to stand at attention. "Yeah," Shareese said, "but that day he hit Carmelita, you didn't stand so still."

Shareese loves the memory of her friend Rosa's reaction on that day. "She turned wild, I'm telling you *my girl was wild*." Apparently, Rosa's stepfather lost his temper with the more outspoken eight-year-old, Carmelita, and slapped her face. Rosa, who walked into the apartment just at that moment, "went off." She screamed at the astonished man and ran into the kitchen for a frying pan, a weapon of choice among the women in her family. Shareese, who had come home with her friend, was as surprised as Rosa's stepfather at the transformation.

Rosa attacked, Shareese reported, in a torrent of Spanish. "It was all 'something-ita' this and 'yo something that' . . . I mean I *knew* what she was saying even though I didn't know, you know?" Rosa brandished the frying pan over her head and shrieked at her stepfather. He ducked down under the table, Carmelita, cowering there with him. Rosa's mother came charging out of the bedroom and rescued her husband.

Rosa seemed both embarrassed and pleased by her friend's story. When Shareese finished talking, Rosa sat quietly for a moment. "My stepfather is not bad," she said at last. "But it was like when my father used to hurt us, like when I was that age, you know. So that came back and I saw Carmelita crying. *I felt something red come into my mind.* But I can't be like that . . . like just for me."

Rosa spoke as though she was uneasy with this version of herself, proud but uneasy. She described the infusion of rage and power as something almost separate from herself, something red, *rosa,* just as she is named. It was not a full presence residing in Rosa, not yet, but a presence which can emerge. "There's a tiger in there," Shareese said with glee.

Some of the stories of female rebellion against male abuse have taken on legendary status in families. Several women told me that it is "known" you don't mess with the Wilson sisters, or it is "known" that Annette "will cut up any man who hurts her daughters." One Wilson sister told me that, after the youngest of the six sisters was beaten by her boyfriend, the "girls went out." They found him playing basketball with several other men, but when the troupe of Wilson sisters approached, they broke ranks and ran, leaving the man to his fate. "He didn't look so good when we were done," she told me grimly.

Another woman related a tale about her mother's boyfriend. Her mother discovered that this new boyfriend was molesting her daughter. "She asked me why I didn't tell her . . . you see I told my aunt and she told Ma. So I said I didn't want to make you mad, and she said, 'I am mad and I am crazy mad, but not at you.' And then he disappeared, he was gone, just gone. My mother said he went away."

I heard another story from a young woman who reported that her mother came by her apartment the day after she had called her up and admitted that her man had hit her. "She came by all nice and sweet. She brought a pie." And then she asked her daughter and "son-in-law" if they wanted to see her new dress. Mystified, they said yes. Her mother pulled out a shiny black funeral dress. "And then she told him, 'The next time you hit my daughter, you will give me the chance to wear this.'"

These women spoke with rich pride and full smiles about acts of ferocious mothers and sisters. They voiced a determination to draw a firm and final line, to punish abusers, to resist violence that keeps them down. "You have to know when to leave gentle ways aside," Luscious told me, "because there's no white man on a horse coming. Or is the horse white?" she asked, laughing. "I never get that one straight."

EARLY COURAGE

I observed an early spirit of standing up to abuse in the littlest girls. One day in an elementary school where I was working, I ducked into the auditorium to listen to an opera singer who was performing for the children. In the front row of the audience, I recognized Dahlia, who was in the fourth grade, a little singer herself. She sat still as a stone, listening to the opera singer. Like Dahlia, the young woman with the heart-stopping voice was very dark-skinned, and she had caught the fidgeting children off guard with the first swelling note. Entranced, Dahlia hummed along, not knowing the song but knowing the powerful experience of singing unabashed.

Thirty minutes later, on line to leave the auditorium, Dahlia kept singing to herself even as Jose pushed her for the second time. But when he pushed her again and harder, she turned and pushed him back. In response, Jose punched, and he punched hard. Dahlia knew the futility of punching this big boy back, but she stuck her little face up close into his and told him, "*Anybody* can hit, but *I* can sing." No one could doubt who had won this round. As the teacher moved in to settle the conflict, Dahlia didn't even rub her sore arm. She kept her head held high.

Her Own Brand of Child Welfare: Adrienne, 1993

There is another way in which it became clear to me that some low-income women are resisting wrongful authority in their own world. Not through anger this time, nor a struggle to protect self, but by an insistence that humane ties not be undone.

Adrienne, in her mid-thirties, has an associate's degree and she plans for more education. She has told me about her children, a boy and a girl, both good students, generally content, and with plenty of friends. She has also mentioned to me that she informally adopted another child and may do so again. Coletta, one of Adrienne's girlfriends "from my wilder days," as she puts it, had become addicted to heroin and was unable to care for her four-year-old son, Dwight. He was put in foster care, but Coletta was able to reclaim him after she underwent a year of treatment and managed to set up a stable life. She told Adrienne that foster care had been bad for Dwight, he had been bounced around. The stability Coletta had built up crumbled as soon as her boyfriend, also an addict, was released from jail. "She shouldn't have let him back, of course," Adrienne tells me. "Like we all say, but there he was, nowhere to go, the father of her child and all that."

Coletta started using drugs again. She went to Adrienne and asked if Adrienne would keep Dwight for a few weeks while she straightened things out. Adrienne knew it would be longer than that, and when she agreed, she says, she thought of it as "a street adoption."

I ask her what this means. She explains this is social behavior learned at her mother's kitchen table. "My brother was eight or nine when he started to bring Mikey home, like a stray dog almost. Mikey was six or seven and he was a beaten-down kid. Ma started fixing a place for him at the dinner table. We didn't have much, we were on and off welfare ourselves. But she said, "We have enough for him." Mikey, "an Irish kid," was by Adrienne's account, almost feral. He would not sit down at the table at first, but stood by it and took food off the plate in an almost secretive way. They taught him, first, just to take food from his own plate, and then to sit down and eat. And to eat all that he wanted. "He looked better after a while," Adrienne says.

Pretty soon Mikey came home to the apartment each day, leaving when it became dark. When he came by with a black eye, Adrienne's mother asked him if he wanted to stay the night. She put a cot in "the boys' room" and Mikey was there to stay. Still, Mikey was worried. He was not sure of the ties which bound him into this new family, nor whether he could rely on the woman he had begun to call "Mom." He did not know if he had a contract which would stand up over the long haul.

"One day my mother saw him standing outside on the sidewalk, looking up at the window. He was all anxious. She met him at the door. And she told him, 'You don't ever have to hang around and look up and wonder if you're welcome. You can always come home to me.' When we moved the next year to another apartment, we just packed him up and took him along."

And what about his parents?

"Well, I don't know about them. You know my mother said that whatever was going on with them, they couldn't take care of that boy. So she did it and now I do it too."

When Adrienne's girlfriend Coletta asked her to take Dwight, Adrienne recalls, she felt a rush of memory. Taking on the responsibility for the little boy was both burdensome and satisfying, an affirmation of her small and indomitable mother, but also it was complicated. Dwight had always liked Adrienne, but the six-year-old was frightened and angry when he moved in. Adrienne and her kids "took a deep breath" and started the tedious process of helping out a difficult child. And how did her kids feel about the whole arrangement? They were not over-joyed, Adrienne admits. Her daughter was jealous of her mother's at-tention wandering and felt dubious about Dwight at best. There were also race matters embedded in this whole arrangement. Adrienne is white. Her children have a Black father from the Caribbean. Her daughter is fair and her son is very dark. And Dwight is a pale African American child. As I listen to Adrienne's catalog of colors, I laugh out-right and she laughs with me. "Why should anything be simple, right?" she asks. I shake my head. Adrienne acknowledges that it is confusing but, she says, here was a child who needed a home and someone who was willing. "I mean, that part is pretty simple, don't you think?"

Adrienne tells me that she does not believe in the legal child welfare system. She thinks that if they really wanted to take care of children, it would be fairly simple, at least in most cases. Most parents would do pretty well by their children if they were safe, had some basic security, and could get some help with emotional problems. I ask her if she thought that it was ever right for the child welfare people to intervene, maybe remove a child. Of course, sometimes, Adrienne answers me with some weariness in her voice. "But most of the time parents just need help handling their problems, getting healthy. That doesn't mean they don't love their kids. Most of them love their children better than anyone else, as far as that goes. I mean, how these kids get treated by the [child welfare] system, now is that showing how this society is sav-ing kids from their crappy parents?"

Adrienne is articulating what many women in these interviews de-scribed with more and more frequency from the mid to late 1990s. She says that in the communities where families are low-income, DSS (the Massachusetts child welfare agency) is like "big brother, out to get you, out to take your children away, 'cause then they can dump you" (off welfare and subsidized housing, among other services). DSS is a punishing presence, according to Adrienne and others, a threat, a foe. But what about the kids who get so badly abused, I ask again. Yes, Adrienne agrees, some parents should lose their parental rights, definitely. But she believes that most child abuse would disappear if families had some chance to be safe and stable. And so she goes ahead with her own small-scale, child welfare policy. I found out that she is not alone.

Quick Notes

One wintry day as Brenda and I leave the building where she works we run into Kathy, a tired-looking white woman who is heading into the clinic with three children. Brenda stops to chat with her, and then she speaks to each child. She turns to Kathy and asks how long she has been keeping Kevin's children. Kathy shrugs casually. Not long, she says. Brenda looks at her quietly and then says, "They look real good, Kathy," and just once the woman smiles and thanks her. We say goodbye. Brenda tells me that Kathy is covering for someone, this time a former boyfriend. Brenda says Kevin and Kathy broke off their relationship a year ago and that Kathy has sole custody of their baby. But she also seems to be taking care of Kevin's other children, children from a previous marriage. "It's not like a legal arrangement, she won't really discuss it, but they call her Momma and she sees to them. She hates foster care because she's been down that road herself . . . but she's not in health." Brenda is concerned about Kathy's ability to keep her fragile family arrangement going. I take a risk and ask Brenda if she, in her position at the clinic, is supposed to tell someone about . . . this unorthodox arrangement. Brenda smiles at me sweetly and I just smile back.

"He's my step-god-nephew and Ma cares for him now," Shareese explains to me matter-of-factly, as she introduces me to a little boy holding her hand.

Tilly, an African American woman in her thirties, tells me that when

she was a young mother, "living scared in a busted-up housing development," she came upon some little things left outside her apartment
one day. And more appeared another day. She would find tampons and
sometimes pampers or two jars of baby food. Proud and sad, Tilly did
not want to know who had left these things, was glad not to have to
express gratitude. But she figures that "it was the lady upstairs," an
older mother who subsequently moved on to another, better place. Several years later when Tilly had a part-time job, she began to leave the
odd box of cereal, a jar of peanut butter, some tampons outside the
door of "this child who moved in one night with a bag of clothes and
a baby and nothing else." When they exchanged greetings on the stairs,
Tilly never referred to her gifts, but "I think she knew and maybe she'll
do the same someday." Tilly seems to believe you can pass these ways
along.

Research on "kin work," often in low-income African American families, has examined the collective labor needed to sustain members and
keep the family intact.[1]

The importance of having more than one or even two parents to
tend to the many complicated needs of low-income families emerged in
very similar ways in this research on African American, white, and Hispanic families in Boston neighborhoods. Kin work here, as in other
studies, often fell to female members. And also similar to findings in
other research, such family care was often posited as part of a family
tradition, "the ways of my mother," as Adrienne put it, or sometimes
as a convoluted connection, "step-god-nephew," which established
claim and responsibility. These ways of explaining the use of family resources—that limited pool of time, money, and attention—were
framed as an extension of duty, bolstered by culture and kin ties.

But some people pushed beyond even the tenuous connection of
"steps," "gods," "cousins," and even "my people." Like Tilly, they
would look around the edge of a common definition of family and see

youngsters, young mothers, and other people who were barely holding on. These women knew about stigma, regulatory chaos, and the experiences vulnerable women and children face when isolated and friendless. Listening to these women, I realized that for some, alongside a hard-fought-for identity, a history remembered, and a name claimed, the definition of family had grown wide. The span of connection had stretched so far afield it hinted at the possibility that, for some people at least, all the world is kin.

Coda

Mission Hill, Boston, 1998

I have spent a fair amount of time in this vital city neighborhood over the past three years. About a year ago, all along Tremont Street, stickers decorated telephone poles and mailboxes advising people where to go to protest the growing "immigration inquisition." Other notices go up periodically, sometimes rallying people to speak against the English-only campaign that has reached this coast, sometimes publicizing a welfare "speak-out." Inside a local coffee shop people are discussing the latest twist of the HUD project which has torn down much of a major housing development, but may or may not build homes for all the people who were displaced. Cross over the street to the park and listen to a couple of women discussing the next tenants' meeting. One laughs as she says, "When they see me coming, they know they better stop the double-talk, 'cause I'll just keep asking, 'And what does *that* mean? OK, but what does *that* mean?'"

A block from the park, Blanca Bonilla is organizing a family theater in the local school. The playwrights, performers, prop designers, and stage managers are all children, parents, and grandparents from the neighborhood. "They don't miss a *single* rehearsal," she tells me. "They are stepping out, speaking up, losing their shyness. We use the plays to celebrate the people's culture." Beatrice Brown, whose children attend the local schools, has started an after-school program in which sixty children are getting their homework done and are also participating in arts programs. "Every child can learn," she warmly asserts, "every child can shine if we just give them that attention, that little lift. There is never an excuse not to help out a child." I have seen them shine in Ms. Brown's presence. Not too far away, Margarita Cintron is advising parents from the Mission Hill community how to apply for health insurance for their children. Patiently, she helps them manage the twists and turns of a difficult process. "Doesn't every child deserve health care?" she demands, looking you right in the eye.

Yarice Hidalgo is working with women who seek employment and some of whom face the imminent loss of welfare. She turns from one person's life to another, deftly designing strategies, encouraging them, listening to the complexities they face, sometimes holding down her anger at the chaos of rules which surround them. "They need child care, real educational opportunities, and they need respect, like everybody else does," Ms. Hidalgo tirelessly reiterates as she answers the inevitable inquiry about getting women on welfare into jobs. Sonia Beniquez is running a take-home library program for young children, encouraging them to carry books home, to share reading with parents and siblings, and to see themselves as readers. Ms. Beniquez is determined to see the service grow. "The dream is expanding the program, for more children to get their hands on books. That is what I am doing." And Dee Dee Costello, the very best kind of social worker, is working right alongside all of these women in Mission Hill. "We talk about everything now," she says, "about power and race and culture and the ways people get silenced. It is much bigger than just this place . . . right here . . . but this is where we are doing our piece of it. And we are doing it learning from each other." These women are teaching others: parents, children, community residents, even a visitor such as I am. The history which they make daily is largely untold. But the heart of many a neighborhood network, which springs up and spreads out in response to people's needs, is a group of women who have decided to make some change.

THE MAJOR THEMES: TAKING ADVICE FROM
WOMEN AND GIRLS

In the course of this book I have argued that there are certain themes which emerge in the lives of girls and women in poor America. I suggest these themes are a response to entrenched economic hardship and social troubles, conditions which give rise to complex family-care pressures and to divergent strategies for creating one's place in the world. Further, as so many women advised me, these profoundly different life-conditions make up another world, the economically segregated world of poor America. Those raising family and community in this other world must nurture their own ethical standards because their hard family work and devotion to other people is dismissed as dependency and dysfunction. They must develop their own knowledge of themselves because their true history is not told.

For most girls and women in poor America, family care is imperative in the face of chronic hardship. Insistently, people will care for each other even if the larger society does not, and in poor America as elsewhere, most family care falls to females. It is a pattern of life into which babies are born, girls are raised, and women carry forward. Simply counting the daily hours spent caring for low-income family life reveals that one person can not handle it all. These women try to care for children of an extended family, maintain battered public housing, do housework without basic appliances, grocery shop without a car—the list goes on and on and so do the people. As girls put it, "How do you think it gets done?"

If the young girls living in poor America were able to focus their attention on education, team sports and physical exercise, enriched summer camp, visual and performing arts, early leadership opportunities, and other youth development, they would integrate these experiences into their identity just as more privileged youth do. But they do not have access to most of these resources, and even if they did, they would be unable to take advantage of such opportunities unless they were granted a family-work release. The advice which I have received from these women and girls is clear. Low-income girls must be given the time and freedom away from family work if they are to "develop another picture of themselves" in the world. And that will only come about when the larger adult world, which controls the resources and has the power to choose, decides to choose to support the development of all youth. Until that time, low-income girls, and some boys too, will continue to shoulder the burdens of family care without money, without public support, and at the profound cost of attention to their own development.

Sometimes parents work long hours at low wages to avoid the chaos and stigma of state support. But there are some costs with absent parents. Jaylona, a young woman who was sexually abused as a child, told me that girls need adults around, need protection because people who prey on little girls are quick to recognize one that is on her own. But how are mothers to be there all the time, she and other young women pondered, if they have to "be about paying that rent" and have to hold down two jobs to do it? Several young women in an Interpretive Focus Group computed the actual income of a mother with two young children who takes a job at a minimum wage, without health insurance which is typical of such jobs. "How will it work, how can she take care of her business on this money?" they wanted to know. How many jobs will she need to pay bills and put food on the table, and then who will guard her children? I told them the truth as I know it, that she will not be able to support her family and her children will not be safe. They were very quiet for a while. Then Shareese asked, "But what are they thinking about with this?" I could not explain government policy which takes mothers away from children and makes no effort to promote them or protect their children. I cannot explain, but I will not back down from their questions. I will not pretend these are ethical answers to the troubles poverty creates.

This inquiry points out that many girls are drawn to boyfriends and sexual partnerships because these relationships are often the only tangible path to another phase of life. As do all young people, these young, low-income women want to cultivate something of their own, to differentiate, to break from family. It is a universal pattern of youth, to seek romantic and sexual partnerships during adolescence. In America, youth who are economically better off have many forums to test out their development. Through these experiences they gain pictures of themselves changing from a child in their family to a young woman or man in society in ways that do not revolve around pairing, making a home, caring for others. While all youth are engaged in the necessary task of exploring intimate relationships, and many are experimenting sexually, middle-class youth have other options for trying on adulthood. But I was asked again and again by low-income adolescent girls, "Why should I wait, what is coming?" They know how to run a family. It is knowledge that comes early, and they are confident of their competence. If these girls are to learn to imagine themselves as someone other than a young mother, then the adults must resolve to gather up resources and construct tangible opportunities for them. "Words are so cheap, aren't they?" I was asked. "Let's do the walk and get past the talk," they told me. Universally, the impact of choice, of having more than one way to imagine yourself in the world, is immeasurable. Yet as so many women recall, it was not until they had been mothers themselves for years that some found a pause, a hiatus from constant worry and work, a little time to consider their own lives.

Those years of poverty and public regulations—the welfare years— are a time of loss and loathing for parents and children. In-depth interviews, surveys, and focus groups with hundreds of women and children suggest that much of the hardship these families experience while on public aid is a result of abusive potentials hidden in the rules and terms of welfare policy. Living under welfare, women and their children face extreme stress, turmoil, and the risk of brutality.

"Is it a game, do you think?" women asked each other. As Luscious advised, you barter, trade, you earn money on the side. But if they actually want you to be "drawing inside the lines," to be abiding by the rules, then the rules must be fair. If the state sponsors regulations which obstruct a woman's ability to care for her children, well . . . as one woman said, "I'm going to say something rude." "Let some of them live on this for a few months, and then tell me about cheaters," Renata suggested.

Dealing with the bureaucracies which regulate poor family life is time-intensive work. Like it or not, if you do not want to end up homeless, without medical care, without money, without teeth, without papers required for your child to attend a decent school or a special program, without the most basic necessities, you must spend hours and hours in institutional waiting rooms, time that no one ever counts except as evidence of your "shiftlessness." Numerous women stated that the way in which they are treated by public institutions which monitor their own and their children's lives clearly expresses a conviction that "welfare mothers" are trash, are "low-lifes." As Ellen put it to her welfare worker, "How many mothers did you encourage today?" She and others argued that when officials and programs begin to treat women as people, as intelligent and ethical individuals who have contributions to make, the welfare experience will be transformed and so too the outcome.

Specifically, several participants in this research called for a critique of face-to-face treatment of low-income people, a watchdog or surveillance system in all the institutions which affect their lives. Several women suggested that, with their own growing expertise in collecting data, they should set up their own system of documenting the behavior of public officials and systems. I hope that some of them have undertaken this mission and will be making loud and public what happens behind closed doors.

If American society is interested in protecting children, and maybe even the mother of those children, then single mothers must have choices. And they need time and help to heal, I was reminded, because if you have been through "all that hell" you do not emerge unscathed. The women in this research offered scores of alternatives to current welfare policy, all of which suggested a social contract which allows all the opportunity to develop into the people they long to be.

They spoke of social security for families as well as the elderly. They discussed structured support for adolescent mothers that would allow them to hold onto their youth while also guiding them to become the mothers they hoped to be. The majority of women and girls mentioned the need for child-care programs. Not the cheap warehousing of children, "a hundred kids crammed into a basement," but child care that would work with mothers, encourage and praise them for their tenacious efforts, "like a family does," said one young single mother. They spoke of child development programs in housing projects, in public schools and churches, in all the places where low-income families come together. Many women spoke of the need for after-school programs where children would get help with their homework and working parents would know their children were safe. In all of their policy recommendations, women and girls spoke of the need for support groups, networks, advocates, and mentors, for people "who look like me," people who reflect the race, culture, or simply the common experience of poor women.

Some women demanded their history back.

They want to make public the people in their own families who had received assistance in the past, had carried on, moved up in their own ways, overcome extraordinary odds. As both girls and grown women pointed out, women from low-income families often need "hearts of iron" to make it, to move on from the welfare years. But they saw no public archive of this truth, no truth-telling commission about the history of their own lives. Without publicity, without the power of formal acknowledgment, this history remains known only in the outback of America.

"How long before 'they' learn?" Beatrice asked me. But the question was not really for me to answer. It was rhetorical, said to the whole company of women present, said to the sky that day: How does the truth get told? Claiming history such as this needs insistent speakers, local historians and those who will simply talk back, who will insist on a common woman's version of the truth.

The women and girls in these groups described the "self-sufficiency" pathways as constructed by public "training programs" as being largely designed to put women into inflexible, dead-end jobs. Real education, the opportunity to develop a career which would provide for families, is not even part of the national discourse about ending welfare and employing parents who are raising children in poor America. Tania put it bluntly, "Girls need employment skills early. Not bullshit typing courses, but real education for jobs like someone like *you* can get and, now, *I* can get. They need programs like 'working family programs,' not this thing they call welfare. It should be talked about as social security for family life. What is more important?" And Deborah reiterated, "We all need college. You got to change jobs six times, right, so you don't need to be trained, you need to be educated. And so there needs to be scholarships, lots of them, if women are going to be independent and teach their kids the same." Carmen argued for a packaging approach, working "part-time and getting some benefits and, say, Medicaid and some after-school program." This kind of approach she thought would reduce the need for welfare income gradually as labor market income improved, and would also build up a woman's sense of accomplishment and her belief that society is willing to invest in her family. She clearly separated the ongoing need for health insurance and child care from the issue of income. To Carmen and dozens of other mothers, health care and child care are an investment in children and

thus an expression of a society's moral stature. With no serious national policy investment in either, Carmen, alongside millions, was
looking elsewhere for a moral center.

And when I sit here today thinking about the policies these girls and
women proposed, and about the standard reaction that there is not
enough money to pay for their solutions, I have no doubt that somewhere today, in another part of Boston, Deborah is speaking out, loud
and clear: "Don't tell me there's not enough money because I am not a
fool. What did we all pay for that savings and loan crap? There's money
around, lots of it. We just got to decide who we are going to spend it
on, and when *we* start deciding, it will be spent on children first."

A CALL FOR A DIFFERENT PRACTICE

The final recommendation of this work is a call for a changed practice
in the building of American public policy. It is an assertion of the critical principle of self-representation and, thus, an assertion of the critical need for the presence of those people who have the immutable
knowledge which comes from life. Before the policy priorities are determined, before the reforms, investments, and programs are agreed
upon, the people who will live with the policy consequences must be at
the table. And they must be there from the beginning, not brought in
for the photographers after all the decisions are made.

This recommendation comes from an absolute belief in the demo-
cratic notion of self-representation, for all the paradoxes and vagaries
which plague it. And it comes from a more empirical source as well.
Over the years of listening to people speak about their lives, I have
come to know that the very act of facing unknown people holds great
power. The startling recognition of ourselves, of our shared humanity,
inevitably diminishes the distance between us and can become a deep
fracture in the unjust order of things. We are a nation of people forever
obligated to remember how segregation distorts humanity, how it

makes us monsters. If we were to reach back and forth across history, race, ethnicity, class, and community, we would touch something that changes us all. And might change the way we practice this democracy.

My work has taught me that people will speak up if they believe they will be heard, they will step forward if they have a respectful place to stand. They will do so in every neighborhood, housing development, community center, church, youth organization, public school, health center, food pantry, and playground. The truth is that, in these and a thousand other places, people are already engaged in the work of seeking a better society. In every one of these places, thinkers, activists, allies, and leaders emerge and engage. They are known in their world, daily they demonstrate ethical authority, they guide people, they take stands, and they raise a world of difference.

I have learned a great deal from people who decided to speak with me, some for only one afternoon, and some over the course of years. They have given me more than data, even more than their criticism and interpretations. Some people have pushed me to honor what I have learned, to hold onto the meaning and sentiment of people's lives. Gentle and intractable, Ellen, Arlette, Beatrice, Nemesis, Blanca, Yarice, Veronica, Annette, Mayisha, Dee Dee, Deborah, and too many others to name, pushed me to hold onto what I have been given, not to dilute or reform the truth. This book is my tribute to their example.

Notes

INTRODUCTION

1. Leatha Lamison-White, *Poverty in the United States: 1996,* U.S. Bureau of the Census, Current Population Reports, Series P-60–198, U.S. Government Printing Office, Washington, D.C., 1997. This report shows that there has been a significant improvement in the officially documented poverty rate since 1994. This improvement, in part, is fueled by the strong economy.

2. For a discussion of the concept of the feminization of poverty, see Diana Pearce, "The Feminization of Poverty: Women, Work and Welfare," *The Urban and Social Change Review* 11(1983): 28–36. Also Rochelle Lefkowitz and Ann Withorn, eds., *For Crying Out Loud: Women and Poverty in the United States* (New York: Pilgrim Press, 1986).

3. Rebecca M. Blank, *It Takes a Nation: A New Agenda for Fighting Poverty* (Princeton: Princeton University Press, 1997).

4. According to Mary Jo Bane and David Ellwood, "Slipping In and Out of Poverty: Dynamics of Spells," *Journal of Human Resources* (Winter 1986): 1–23, one way in which traditional statistics do not give a complete and accurate portrait of the poor is in terms of the dynamics of poverty. Poverty is not static; the problem is much more complex when one considers the duration and number of spells on welfare. Bane and Ellwood offer a hospital as an analogy: "Suppose one sat in the admitting room of a hypothetical hospital and observed people entering the hospital. One would quickly discover that the vast majority of those entering the hospital could expect very short stays. . . . But suppose one left the admitting room and walked around the hospital. One might be shocked to discover that the vast majority of beds

were occupied by people with chronic conditions. Even though they were a tiny fraction of people admitted to the hospital on any given day, they represented the bulk of patients in the hospital. . . . One person who enters the hospital and stays for fifty-two weeks will occupy as much bed time as fifty-two people who come in for one week. Thus if every week nine acute patients enter for a one-week stay, and one chronic person enters for a fifty-two week stay, 85% of the hospital beds will be filled with chronic care patients, even though they only represent 10 percent of hospital admissions."

Likewise, Patricia Ruggles, *Drawing the Line* (Washington, D.C.: Urban Institute Press, 1990) argues that who we consider to be poor depends on our definition of poverty itself. In the United States currently, we measure poverty in absolute terms with a poverty line. If you fall beneath the poverty line, you are considered poor. Our use of an absolute and rather arbitrary benchmark allows us to ignore the depth of the poverty problem as well as the notion of economic well-being. A fixed measurement ignores the relative poverty of households compared with the rest of society as well as an adequate standard-of-living. Additionally, over time, the benchmark becomes more and more arbitrary.

A relative income level measurement differs from the standard, absolute measurements of U.S. poverty. The poverty line, which is the traditional poverty measurement in the United States, defines poverty as having less than an absolute—and rather arbitrary—minimum measurement. A relative income level measurement, however, defines poverty as having less than or as not having a decent standard of living compared with others in society.

5. See chap. 3, "Who Are the Poor?" in Ruth Sidel, *Keeping Women and Children Last* (New York: Penguin Books, 1996).

6. Lamison-White, *Poverty in the United States*, x–xii.

7. Donald J. Hernandez, *America's Children: Resources from Family, Government, and the Economy*, (New York: Russell Sage Foundation, 1993). The discrepancy between these child-poverty estimates and the official poverty rate reflects an ongoing tension between official estimates and the experience of some families, relative to others, raising children in the United States. In this country, a family of three is *not* considered poor if their annual income exceeds $11,980, and for a family of four, the cutoff is $15,029. Near-poverty is defined as 150 percent of the official poverty line. For a detailed examination of the poverty line, see chap.1 in Blank, *It Takes*

a Nation. An additional reference to consider in analyzing relative family poverty is the now extinct U.S. Department of Labor *Quarterly Reports*, "Urban Family Budgets and Comparative Indexes for Selected Urban Areas," last undertaken in 1982. If those 1982 figures were updated to reflect current consumer-price levels, the income of what was referred to as a lower income family would today exceed $25,000.

8. Lamison-White, *Poverty in the United States*, vi.

9. Rebecca M. Blank, *It Takes a Nation*, 15.

10. Lamison-White, *Poverty in the United States*, 24. According to the U.S. Bureau of the Census, 1994, less than half (48 percent) of people below the poverty line in the United States are African American or Latino. However, while about 10 percent of white women are poor, about 30 percent of African American women and 30 percent of Latino women live below the poverty line. For a thorough and insightful overview of poverty distribution, see Randy Albelda and Chris Tilly, *Glass Ceilings and Bottomless Pits: Women's Work, Women's Poverty* (Boston: South End Press, 1997).

11. Kathryn Edin and Laura Lein, *Making Ends Meet: How Single Mothers Survive Welfare and Low-Wage Work* (New York: Russell Sage Foundation, 1997). Even if working in a low-wage job, single mothers still do not have enough money to make ends meet the majority of the time. Also see Sheldon Danziger and Harry J. Holzer, "Are Jobs Available for Disadvantaged Groups in America?" paper presented at the APPAM Research Conference, Washington, D.C., November 1997. Danziger and Holzer discovered through a survey of employers and households in four large major urban areas that disadvantaged workers (minorities, high school dropouts, welfare recipients, etc.) consistently receive exceptionally low wages and benefits.

12. Laurence Mishel, Jared Benskin, and John Schmitt, *The State of Working America 1996–1997* (Armonk, N.Y.: M. E. Sharpe, 1991).

13. For an ethnographic examination of employment issues in low-income inner-city neighborhoods, see Katherine Newman, "The Job Ghetto," *The American Prospect* 22 (Summer 1995): 66–68. For 1996 statistics on service sector and low-wage jobs, see the *Current Population Survey Bulletin: Income and Poverty* (Washington, D.C.: U.S. Department of Commerce/Bureau of the Census, March 1997).

14. For discussion on these issues, see Susan Houseman, "Job Growth

and the Quality of Jobs in the U.S. Economy," *Labor* 77 (1995): 593–5124. Employer-provided health insurance coverage decreased for all workers from 1980 to 1993, but particularly for workers with high school diplomas or less education. On the issue of family associated with ill children, see Jody Heymann, Alison Earle, and Brian Egleston, "Parental Availability for the Care of Sick Children," *Pediatrics* 98, no. 2 (1996). Nearly 60 percent of poor working parents did not have paid sick leave available through their employers at any time between 1985 and 1990.

15. For more information on inadequate child care in the United States, see NICHD Early Child Care Research Network, "Poverty and Patterns of Child Care," in *Consequences of Growing Up Poor,* eds. Greg J. Duncan and Jeanne Brooks-Gunn (New York: Russell Sage Foundation, 1997), 100–31; Barbara R. Bergmann, *Saving Our Children: What the United States Can Learn from France* (New York: Russell Sage Foundation, 1996); National Research Council Board on Children and Families, *New Findings on Children, Families, and Economic Self-Sufficiency: Summary of a Research Briefing* (Washington, D.C.: National Academy Press, 1995); Deborah A. Phillips, *Childcare for Low-Income Families: Summary of Two Workshops* (Washington, D.C.: National Academy Press, 1995).

16. See *State of the Nation's Housing* (Cambridge, Mass.: Joint Center for Housing Studies of Harvard University, 1997).

17. For more discussion of post-secondary education and employment opportunities for high school dropouts, see Richard J. Murnane, Kathryn Parker Boudette, and John B. Willett, *Does Acquisition of a GED Lead to More Training, Post-Secondary Education, and Military Service for High School Dropouts?* (Cambridge, Mass.: National Bureau of Economic Research, 1997).

18. Larry L. Bumpass, "Children and Marital Disruption: A Replication and Update," *Demography* 21 (1984): 71–82.

19. Sheldon Danziger and Peter Gottschalk, "Why Poverty Remains High," in *America Unequal* (New York: Russell Sage Foundation, 1995), 93–110, present an in-depth analysis of factors that perpetuate poverty. See also William Julius Wilson's major contribution to this debate, *The Truly Disadvantaged: The Inner City, the Underclass, and Public Policy* (Chicago: University of Chicago Press, 1987). Work by Sara McLanahan and Karen Booth,

"Mother-Only Families: Problems, Prospects, and Politics," *Journal of Marriage and Family* 51 (August 1989): 557–80 is dated but offers a detailed and sensitive overview of the complex problems such families face beyond economic hardship and suggests key themes for policy intervention. See also the "Children and Poverty" issue of *The Future of Children* 7 (Summer/Fall 1997), put out by the Center for the Future of Children. And, for an international comparison of child/family support programs, see Bergmann, *Saving Our Children from Poverty*.

20. There are several illuminating articles in Brooks-Gunn and Duncan, *Consequences of Growing Up Poor*, that examine the effects of poverty on children's academic and personal well-being, including: Jeanne Brooks-Gunn, Greg J. Duncan, and Nancy Maritato, "Poor Families, Poor Outcomes: The Well-Being of Children and Youth,": 1–17; Judith R. Smith, Jeanne Brooks-Gunn, and Pamela K. Klebanov, "Consequences of Living in Poverty for Young Children's Cognitive and Verbal Ability and Early School Achievement," 132–89; Linda Pagani, Bernard Boulerice, and Richard E. Tremblay, "The Influence of Poverty on Children's Classroom Placement and Behavior Problems," 311–39; H. Elizabeth Peters and Natalie C. Mullis, "The Role of Family Income and Sources of Income in Adolescent Achievement," 340–81; and Jay D. Teachman et al., "Poverty During Adolescence and Subsequent Educational Attainment," 382–418. See also the "Children and Poverty" issue of *The Future of Children* 7 (Summer/Fall 1997), put out by the Center for the Future of Children.

21. Both Charles Murray, *Losing Ground: American Social Policy* (New York: Basic Books, 1984) and Lawrence Mead, *The New Politics of Poverty: The Non-working Poor in America* (New York: Basic Books, 1992) offer a character analysis of "the poor" as key to the proliferation of American poverty.

22. For example, the sentiments of James Q. Wilson particularly capture this kind of perspective on poor familiaes in America. See his *Two Nations*, Francis Boyer Lecture of the annual dinner of the American Enterprise Institute, December 4, 1997. In this speech, Wilson expresses the belief that "bastardy has become more common, children more criminal and marriages less secure." He regards the nation of poor America as one in which child abuse, drug abuse, gang violence, personal criminality, and all the worst kinds of behavior proliferate.

23. William Julius Wilson, *When Work Disappears: The World of the New Urban Poor* (New York: Vintage Books, 1996). This is a powerful argument that the loss of work—particularly decently paid work which will support a family—is the basis for the social problems associated with inner-city family life. The argument is made that the effects of the ongoing isolation of millions of adults from decent work affects the whole society, not only people who are poor.

24. Michael Katz, *The Undeserving Poor: From the War on Poverty to the War on Welfare* (New York: Pantheon Books, 1989). Both this book and Katz's *In the Shadow of the Poorhouse: A Social History of Welfare in America* (New York: Basic Books, 1986) offer an in-depth historical analysis of the conceptualization and treatment of poor people in the United States.

25. Jacob Riis, *How the Other Half Lives: Studies Among the Tenements of New York* (New York: Charles Scribner's Sons, 1890).

26. Oscar Lewis, *The Children of Sanchez: Autobiography of a Mexican Family* (New York: Random House, 1961).

27. Edward Banfield, *The Unheavenly City: The Nature and Future of Our Urban Crisis* (Boston: Little, Brown, 1970). Daniel P. Moynihan, *The Negro Family: The Case for National Action* (Washington, D.C.: U.S. Government Printing Office, 1965).

28. Susan L. Thomas, "From the Culture of Poverty to the Culture of Single Motherhood: The New Poverty Paradigm," *Women and Politics* 14 (Spring 1994): 65–97.

29. Mimi Abramovitz, *Regulating the Lives of Women: Social Policy from Colonial Times to the Present* (Boston: South End Press, 1988).

30. Albelda and Tilly, *Glass Ceilings and Bottomless Pits,* 90.

31. Abramovitz, *Regulating the Lives of Women.* Also see Francis Fox Piven and Richard Cloward, *Regulating the Poor: The Functions of Public Welfare* (New York: Vintage Books, 1993), for a powerful and provocative analysis of the ways in which public welfare has been used to undermine organizing efforts of low-income peoples throughout American history.

32. For example, see Teresa Amott and Julie Matthaei, *Race, Gender, and Work: A Multicultural Economic History of Women in the United States*

(Boston: South End Press, 1996); Polly Callaghan and Heidi Hartmann, *Contingent Work: A Chart-Book on Part-time and Temporary Employment* (Washington, D.C.: Economic Policy Institute, 1991).

33. Sidel, *Keeping Women and Children Last*, 1.

34. Wahneema Lubiano, "Black Ladies, Welfare Queens, and State Minstrels: Ideological War by Narrative Means," in *Race-ing Justice, En-gendering Power: Essays on Anita Hill, Clarence Thomas and the Construction of Social Reality*, ed. Toni Morrison (New York: Pantheon Books, 1992): 323–63.

35. Doris Sue Wong, "Welfare Bill's Aim: ID Fathers or Payment for Child Could Be Withheld," *Boston Globe* (March 2, 1996): B1. The article opened, "Governor William F. Weld, saying some young people have come to view parenthood as a 'cheap joke' . . .". In considering America's derogatory view of low-income women, it is striking to compare policies directed at upper- and middle-class women with those directed at low-income women. Dorothy K. Seavey and Beth M. Miller, "Getting the Big Picture: Anti-Welfare Fertility Policies in Context," *Society* 33 (July–August 1996): 33–37, provides an excellent analysis of the role of class in public policy.

CHAPTER 1: DAUGHTERS' WORK

1. This poem appears in Elsa Aurbach, "Toward a Social-Contextual Approach to Family Literacy," *Harvard Educational Review* 59 (Spring 1989): 165–81. According to Aurbach: "As Rosa explains, she is more than a student; she is also a parent, wife, cook, neighbor, member of an extended family and community, and someone who is trying to balance the demands of these many roles."

2. Carol Stack, *All Our Kin: Strategies for Survival in a Black Community* (New York: Basic Books, 1974); Joyce Ladner, *Tomorrow's Tomorrow: The Black Woman* (Garden City, N.Y.: Doubleday, 1971). Both of these seminal works examine broad issues of race, survival, and women's lives in low-income America and are profoundly pertinent today.

3. Joyce Ladner, "Labeling Black Children: Some Mental Health Impli-

cations" (Washington D.C.: Howard University, Institute for Urban Affairs and Research 1979), vol. 5, 3.

4. Ann Oakly, *Woman's Work: Housewife Past and Present* (New York: Pantheon Books, 1974).

5. See Hilda Scott, *Working Your Way to the Bottom: Feminization of Poverty* (Boston: Pandora Press, 1984), and Barbara Bergmann, *The Economic Emergence of Women* (New York: Basic Books, 1986).

6. Debbie Ward, "Gender, Time, and Money in Caregiving," *Scholarly Inquiry for Nursing Practice: An International Journal* 4 (1990): 224.

7. Margery Garrett Spring Rice, *Working Class Wives: Their Health and Conditions* (London: Virago Books, 1981), 106.

8. Janet Finch and Dulcie Groves, *Labour of Love: Women, Work, and Caring* (London: Routledge and K. Paul, 1983), 26.

9. Michelle Fine and Nancie Zane, "Bein' Wrapped Too Tight: When Low-Income Women Drop Out of High School," *Women's Studies Quarterly* 19 (Spring/Summer 1991): 80.

CHAPTER 2: BOYFRIENDS, LOVE, AND SEX

1. Jean Baker Miller, *Toward a New Psychology of Women* (Boston: Beacon Press, 1976), Carol Gilligan, *In a Different Voice: Psychological Theory and Women's Development* (Cambridge, Mass.: Harvard University Press, 1982), and others have offered a perspective on human development and psychology that treats gender and socially prescribed gender roles as central to identity. The importance of this gendered perspective emerged throughout this research, as did other powerful themes of identity development such as race, ethnicity, and class status; these have not received the same degree of attention in women's and girls' studies. Their omission was an issue of concern among numerous participants who regarded their race, color, ethnicity, and some version of class status as also fundamental to their identity.

2. Lyn Mikel Brown and Carol Gilligan, *Meeting at the Crossroads: Women's Psychology and Girls' Development* (Cambridge, Mass.: Harvard University Press, 1992).

3. Mary Pipher, *Reviving Ophelia: Saving the Selves of Adolescent Girls* (New York: Ballantine Books, 1994).

4. Annie G. Rogers, "Voice, Play, and a Practice of Ordinary Courage in Girls' and Women's Lives," *Harvard Educational Review* 63 (Fall 1993): 265–96.

5. Sharon Thompson, *Going All the Way: Teenage Girls' Tales of Sex, Romance, and Pregnancy* (New York: Hill and Wang, 1996).

6. Lisa Dodson, *We Could Be Your Daughters; Girls, Sexuality and Pregnancy in Low-Income America* (Cambridge, Mass.: Radcliffe Public Policy Institute, 1996). The awareness of numerous girls of the prevalence of sexual abuse in American culture is rooted in reality. The incidence of reported sexual abuse has risen over the last two decades and those who work in disciplines in which they confront child sexual abuse have long recognized the profound impact of such abuse. Judith Herman, *Trauma and Recovery* (New York: Basic Books, 1992), challenges us to recognize the "post-traumatic stress disorder" of assaulted children (and women) much as one would survivors of wartime torture. These are wounds which need a society's response to fully heal. "Traumatic events destroy the sustaining bonds between individual and community. Those who survive learn that their sense of self, of worth, of humanity, depends upon a feeling of connection to others" 214.

7. Luce Irigaray, "When Our Lips Speak Together," *Signs* 6 (1980): 69.

8. See Bonnie J. Leadbeater and Niobe Way, *Urban Girls: Resisting Stereotypes, Creating Identities* (New York: New York University Press, 1996). Also see Joyce Ladner, *Tomorrow's Tomorrow* (Garden City, N.Y.: Anchor Books, 1971); Constance Willard Williams, *Black Teenage Mothers: Pregnancy and Child Rearing from Their Perspective* (Lexington, Mass.: Lexington Books, 1991); Niobe Way, "'Can't You See the Courage, the Strength I Have?': Listening to Urban Adolescent Girls Speak about Their Relationships," *Psychology of Women Quarterly* 19 (1995): 107–28. Rebecca Carroll's wonderful book *Sugar in the Raw: Voices of Young Black Girls in America* (New York: Crown Trade Paperbacks, 1997), speaks from the reflections and knowledge of girls themselves and offers an eloquent contrast with literature which suggests all girls lose themselves as they go through adolescence. All of these sources offer race perspectives (some provide class and

ethnic perspectives too) about girls coming of age, and all suggest that there are some significant developmental differences among girls who are not white and middle class.

9. Elijah Anderson, "Sex Codes and Family Life Among Inner-City Youths," in *The Ghetto Underclass*, ed. William Julius Wilson (Newbury Park, Calif.: Sage Publications, 1993).

10. Michelle Fine and Nancie Zane, "Bein' Wrapped Too Tight: When Low-Income Women Drop Out of High School," *Women's Studies Quarterly* 19 (Spring/Summer 1991): 77–99.

11. Pipher, *Reviving Ophelia.*

12. Girls seldom referred to their sexuality without speaking about relationships, about family and about race, ethnicity, and other roles they considered to be essential to their identity. For additional discussion about sex and relationships, see Michelle Fine, "Sexuality, Schooling, and Adolescent Females: The Missing Discourse on Desire," *Harvard Educational Review* 58 (Spring 1988): 29–53. As always, Fine offers a complex and provocative discussion of social responses to adolescent sexual feelings, particularly in the context of public education. Also see Deborah L. Tolman, "Doing Desire: Adolescent Girls' Struggles for/with Sexuality," *Gender and Society* 8 (June 1994): 324–42, and "Adolescent Girls, Women and Sexuality: Discerning Dilemmas of Desire," in Carol Gilligan, Annie Rogers, Deborah Tolman, eds., *Women, Girls and Psychotherapy: Reframing Resistance* (New York: Harrington Park Press, 1991): 55–70. For further reading see Sharon Thompson, "Putting a Big Thing in a Little Hole: Teenage Girl's Accounts of Sexual Initiation," *Journal of Sex Research* 27 (December 1991): 341–51. For a deeper exploration of female eroticism and political power, see Audre Lorde, "The Uses of the Erotic as Power," *Sister Outsider: Essays and Speeches* (Freedom, Calif.: Crossing Press, 1984).

13. There is no discussion herein of girls having sexual feelings for other girls, but it is important to note that none of the study guides or questions specifically *asked* girls/young women about sexual identity or sexual feelings other than heterosexual feelings. It is very unlikely a girl would introduce this into sex talk if the women in charge do not. This was a considerable oversight which, as several older women in the Interpretive Focus Groups

reminded me in no uncertain terms, colludes in keeping adolescent lesbians in silence.

CHAPTER 3: CHOICE AND MOTHERHOOD IN POOR AMERICA

1. For a thorough examination of these issues, see the work of the Alan Guttmacher Institute (AGI), in particular, *Sex and America's Teenagers* (New York: AGI, 1994). Also see Childtrends, Inc., *Facts at a Glance,* 1994 95. As examined in the literature, sexual activity among all American adolescents has increased considerably over the past twenty-five years. Fifty-six percent of adolescent women under the age of eighteen (more than three-quarters of young men) were sexually experienced in 1988; in contrast, in the mid-1950s, less than one-quarter of girls were sexually active. In the past, many of the sexually active teens were also married teens, but that is no longer the case. In 1988, 96 percent of women who had sexual intercourse as teens were unmarried when they first had sex.

2. AGI, *Sex and America's Teenagers.*

3. "Overwhelmingly, pregnant teenagers either have an abortion or give birth and raise the child themselves; adoption is rare. White adolescents and those from more advantaged backgrounds generally elect to terminate their pregnancies. Childbearing . . . is concentrated among teenagers who are poor." Ibid., 55.

4. For an examination of the association between early adolescent sexual activity and involuntary or forced sex, see Kristin Anderson Moore, Christine Winquist Nord, and James L. Peterson, "Nonvoluntary Sexual Activity Among Adolescents," *Family Planning Perspectives* 21 (1989): 110–14. Experiences of involuntary sex or rape are more common among women who have had intercourse in their early teens. AGI, *Sex and America's Teenagers,* reports that "some 74% of women who had intercourse before age 14 and 60% of those who had sex before age 15 report having had sex involuntarily" 22. The findings of the Girls Project survey (see methodology section) are similar in that girls who had intercourse before the age of fifteen were three times more likely to report lack of "readiness" for sex than were the adolescents who had sex after the age of sixteen.

5. Self-esteem is an issue which often arises when teen childbearing is discussed. For more information on self-esteem and teenagers in general, see Marc A. Zimmerman, "A Longitudinal Study of Self-Esteem: Implications for Adolescent Development," *Journal of Youth and Adolescence* 26 (April 1997): 117–42; Michael T. Maly, "Socioeconomic Status and Early Adolescent Self-Esteem," *Sociological Inquiry* 62 (Summer 1992): 375–83; Juliet T. Harper, "Adolescents' Problems and Their Relationship to Self-Esteem," *Adolescence* 26 (Winter 1991): 800–10. For an analysis of the relationship between self-esteem, early sexual activity, and teen pregnancy, see Liana R. Clark, "Teen Sex Blues," *Journal of the American Medical Association* 273 (June 28, 1995): 1969–71; Kathy Dobie, "Hellbent on Redemption," *Mother Jones* 20 (January-February 1997): 50–55; Delores E. Smith, "Pregnancy Status, Self-esteem, and Ethnicity: Some Relationships in a Sample of Adolescents," *Family and Consumer Sciences Research Journal* 23 (December 1994): 183–98; Rachel B. Robinson, "The Relationship Between Self-Esteem, Sexual Activity, and Pregnancy," *Adolescence* 29 (Spring 1994): 27–36.

6. See the discussions in *The Ghetto Underclass*, ed. William Julius Wilson (Newbury Park, Calif.: Sage Publications, 1993), in particular Elijah Anderson, "Sex Codes and Family Life Among Poor Inner-City Youths," and Mercer L. Sullivan, "Absent Fathers in the Inner City." Also see Ross D. Parke and Brian Neville, "Teenage Fatherhood," in *Risking the Future: Adolescent Sexuality, Pregnancy and Childbearing*, eds. Cheryl Hayes and Sandra Hofferth (Washington, D.C.: National Academy Press, 1987): 145–73. For readings on fatherhood, see Judith Bruce et al., *Families in Focus: New Perspectives on Mothers, Fathers, and Children* (New York: The Population Council, 1995).

7. Constance Willard Williams, *Black Teenage Mothers: Pregnancy and Child Rearing from Their Perspective* (Lexington, Mass.: Lexington Books, 1991).

8. Arline T. Geronimus, "Why Teenage Childbearing Might Be Sensible: Research and Policy Implications," paper presented at the annual meetings of the American Association of the Advancement of Science, New Orleans, 1990.

9. Kristin Luker, *Dubious Conceptions: The Politics of Teenage Pregnancy* (Cambridge, Mass.: Harvard University Press, 1996).

10. Carol Stack, *All Our Kin: Strategies for Survival in a Black Community* (New York: Basic Books, 1974). Also see Andrew Billingsley, *Black Families in White America* (Englewood Cliffs, N.J.: Prentice Hall, 1968).

11. Julia Danzy and Sondra M. Jackson, "Family Preservation and Support Services: A Missed Opportunity for Kinship Care," *Child Welfare* 76, no. 1 (1997). In this article the authors examine kinship care, particularly in the African American family tradition, as an alternative model for child welfare out-of-home placement. While exposing the reluctance of bureaucratic agencies to accept creative family structures, the authors do not address the issue of just who is responsible for all the family labor inevitably involved when children are facing out-of-home placement and will need considerable attention. Family care is generally a pseudonym for female care, usually mothers, grandmothers, and daughters.

12. For discussion on childbearing and educational attainment, see Kristin A. Moore, Charles L. Betsey, and Margaret C. Simms, *Choice and Circumstance: Racial Differences in Adolescent Sexuality and Fertility* (New Brunswick, N.J.: Transaction Books, 1986) and Dawn Upchurch and James McCarthy, "The Timing of a First Birth and High School Completion," *American Sociological Review* 55 (April 1990): 224–35. For a discussion of intergenerational influences, see Mark D. Hayward, William R. Grady, and John O. G. Billy, "The Influence of Socioeconomic Status on Adolescent Pregnancy," *Social Science Quarterly* 73 (December 1992): 750–73.

13. AGI, *Sex and America's Teenagers,* 41.

14. Geronimus, "Why Teenage Childbearing Might Be Sensible."

15. See all the work of Frank F. Furstenberg, in particular with Jeanne Brooks-Gunn and S. Phillip Morgan, *Adolescent Mothers in Later Life* (Cambridge, England: Cambridge University Press,1987). For an exhaustive overview of the arguments and counterpoints on teen childbearing, see "As the Pendulum Swings: Teenage Childbearing and Social Concern," *Family Relations* 40 (April 1991): 127–38.

CHAPTER 4: LOSSES AND LOATHING IN THE WELFARE YEARS

1. See Vickie Steinitz, *The Interim Report* (Cambridge, Mass.: Welfare and Human Rights Monitoring Project, 1996), 13.

2. For a discussion of extreme examples of abuse as a reflection of state-structured human rights violations, see Mary M. Brabeck, Theresa Ferns, M. Brinton Lykes, and Angela Radan, "Human Rights and Mental Health Among Latin American Women in Situations of State-Sponsored Violence," *Psychology of Women Quarterly* 17 (December 1993): 525–44. While the degree of abuse reported is extreme, the notion of unmonitored state authorities sexually abusing women who have relatively little power and are therefore likely to remain silent, bears some comparison.

3. Judith Herman, *Trauma and Recovery* (New York: Basic Books, 1992), discusses the dynamics of recovery from traumatic abuses as requiring a community-wide response—the antithesis of exclusion, shame, and silence. She points out that "trauma shames and stigmatizes; the group bears witness and affirms. Trauma degrades the victim; the group exalts her" 214. I believe that many women experience degrading, perhaps even overtly abusive exchanges over the course of their time on welfare, but there are no witnesses, at least no witnesses who will speak up. The affirmation and exaltation of survival of welfare, too, needs some public forum to break that silence.

4. Kathryn Edin and Laura Lein, *Making Ends Meet: How Single Mothers Survive Welfare and Low-Wage Work* (New York: Russell Sage Foundation, 1997); Mark Rank, *Living on the Edge: The Realities of Welfare in America* (New York: Columbia University Press, 1994).

5. See discussion of employment patterns and obstacles in Margaret G. Brooks and John C. Buckner, "Work and Welfare: Job Histories, Barriers to Employment, and Predictors of Work Among Low-Income Single Mothers," *American Journal of Orthopsychiatry* 66 (October 1996): 526–38. See also Kathleen Mullan Harris, "Work and Welfare Among Single Mothers in Poverty," *American Journal of Sociology* 99 (September 1993): 317–53. S. Jody Heymann and Alison Earle, *Working Conditions: What Do Parents Leaving Welfare and Low-Income Parents Face?* (Cambridge, Mass.: Malcolm Weiner Center for Social Policy, 1997), examines some of the "work-family conflicts"—in particular, sick-child care—which are exaggerated for low-income, single mothers. Edin and Lein also examine these issues in *Making Ends Meet*.

6. Phoebe Kazdin Schnitzer, "'They Don't Come In!': Stories Told, Lessons Taught About Poor Families in Therapy," *American Journal of Orthopsychiatry* 66 (October 1996): 572–83.

7. Much of the literature on women and depression has focused on gender role issues, abuse, and on the context of middle-class women's lives. However, the work of Deborah Belle addresses the dynamics of poverty, stress, and stigma as vital factors in depression among low-income women. See Belle, *Lives in Stress: Women and Depression* (Beverly Hills: Sage Publications, 1982). See also Belle, "Poverty and Women's Mental Health: Psychology in the Public Forum," *American Psychologist* 45 (March 1990): 385–90; Belle, "Attempting to Comprehend the Lives of Low-Income Women," in *Women Creating Lives: Identities, Resilience, Resistance,* eds. Carol E. Franz and Abigail J. Stewart (Boulder, Colo.: Westview Press, 1994). For additional discussion on mental well-being and low-income women, see Sheryl L. Olson, Elizabeth Kieschnick, Victoria Banyard, and Rosario Ceballo, "Socioenvironmental and Individual Correlates of Psychological Adjustment in Low-Income Single Mothers," *American Journal of Orthopsychiatry* 64 (April 1994): 317–32.

8. Nancy Marshall, "The Public Welfare System: Regulation and Dehumanization," in Belle, *Lives in Stress.*

9. Belle, *Lives in Stress,* 197.

10. Marta Elliot, "Impact of Work, Family, and Welfare Receipt on Women's Self-Esteem in Young Adulthood," *Social Psychology Quarterly* 59 (March 1996): 80–95.

11. Ann Withorn, "'Why do They Hate Me So Much?': A History of Welfare and Its Abandonment in the United States," *American Journal of Orthopsychiatry* 66 (October 1996): 496–510. Also see Withorn and Diane Dijon, *For Crying Out Loud: Women's Poverty in the United States* (Boston: South End Press, 1996).

12. Mary Ann Allard, Randy Albelda, Mary Ellen Colten, and Carol Cosenza, *In Harm's Way?: Domestic Violence, AFDC Receipt, and Welfare Reform in Massachusetts* (Boston: McCormack Institute, U of Mass., February 1997), examined the prevalence of domestic violence among women receiving AFDC, and their findings pinpoint this as a critical issue. Also see Ellen Bassuk et al., "The Characteristics and Needs of Sheltered Homeless and Low-Income Mothers (Caring for the Uninsured and Underinsured)," *Journal of the American Medical Association* 276 (August 28, 1996): 640–46.

13. Edin and Lein, *Making Ends Meet,* discuss the issue of the gap between both welfare payment and low-wage jobs and actual cost of living for a family.

Chapter 5: Moving On: "Don't Call Me Out of Name"

1. Hearing low-income women's voices is a fairly recent inclusion in most research, even when they are the "subject" of the discussion. Robin L. Jarrett raises the question, "But where are the people?" in her article, "Living Poor: Family Life Among Single Parent, African-American Women," *Social Problems* 41 (February 1994): 30–50. She describes focus group research in which women discuss the dominant themes and problems of "living poor" from their own perspective. See also, Pamela Trotman Reid, "Poor Women in Psychological Research: Shut Up and Shut Out," *Psychology of Women Quarterly* 17 (June 1994): 133–50. Reid argues that much research, but particularly feminist research which honors the "voice" of women in fact refuses to contend with the "confounds of class and race." A specific pursuit of the voices of welfare recipients can be found in Mark Rank, "A View from the Inside Out: Recipients' Perceptions of Welfare," *Journal of Sociology and Social Welfare* 21 (June 1994): 27–48. His exploration of recipients' perception of public stigma and their own attitudes about welfare receipt offers intriguing discussion of both commonality and difference in perspective.

For another, more critical perspective on the issue of the systematic exclusion of poor women from the welfare reform debate, see Lucie E. White's wonderful article, "Making Welfare Work for Women: Notes From the Field," *Loyola Poverty Law Journal* 1 (1995), in which she offers a historical critique of the nonalliance between middle-class working mothers and women on welfare/women moving into low-wage jobs.

2. Randy Albelda and Chris Tilly, *Glass Ceilings and Bottomless Pits: Women's Work, Women's Poverty* (Boston: South End Press, 1997).

3. William Julius Wilson, *When Work Disappears: The World of the New Urban Poor* (New York: Vintage Books, 1996). Also see his groundbreaking analysis in *The Truly Disadvantaged: The Inner City, the Underclass, and Public Policy* (Chicago: University of Chicago Press, 1987). While the impact of family labor and community caretaking work of many low-income women and girls has little presence in his analysis, Wilson offers a powerful overview

of the loss of decent, stable employment in urban neighborhoods and the associated losses to communities and to families.

4. For a bold assertion of the father as the real solution for preserving the family and for most social problems, see David Blankenhorn, *Fatherless America: Confronting Our Most Urgent Social Problem* (New York: Basic Books, 1995).

5. See Lawrence Mead, *The New Politics of Poverty: The Non-working Poor in America* (New York: Basic Books, 1992), for a discussion of non-workers and dependency.

6. For a fine overview of the issues embedded in the "self-sufficiency" rhetoric of welfare reforms, see Hilda Kahne, *Low Earning Single Mothers and Self-Sufficiency: What Can Help?* (Waltham, Mass.: Brandeis University Women's Studies Program, 1997). For some general background on distinguishing the discussion of welfare and poverty, see discussion of poverty and low wages in Kathryn Edin and Laura Lein, *Making Ends Meet: How Single Mothers Survive Welfare and Low-Wage Work* (New York: Russell Sage Foundation, 1997). Also see Douglas Massey and Nancy A. Denton, *American Apartheid* (Chicago: University of Chicago Press, 1993), for a broad discussion of racial divisions and poverty in America. Ruth Sidel, *Keeping Women and Children Last* (New York: Penguin Books, 1996), examines antipoverty policies and their meaning.

7. For a wonderful individual account of "moving on" through family effort, individual strength, and through the availability of welfare, see Rosemary L. Bray, "So How Did I Get Here?" *The New York Times Magazine* (November 8, 1992): 34. While insisting that no one woman's account should be used to set a standard for other women, Ms. Bray points out that she, her mother, and siblings managed family life and achieved, in time, remarkable individual successes.

8. Maria Cancian and Daniel R. Meyer, *Life After Welfare: The Economic Well-Being of Women and Children Following an Exit From AFDC* (Madison, Wis.: Institute for Research on Poverty, 1996).

9. For discussion of this, see Erika Kates, "Educational Pathways Out of Poverty: Responding to the Realities of Women's Lives," *American Journal of Orthopsychiatry* 66 (October 1996): 548–56.

10. Marilyn Gittell et al., *From Welfare to Independence: The College Option* (New York: Ford Foundation, 1990). Also see Gittell et al., *Building Human Capital: The Impact of Post-secondary Education on AFDC Recipients in Five States* (New York: Ford Foundation, 1993).

11. See Lillian Rubin, *Worlds of Pain: Life in the Working-Class Family* (New York: Basic Books, 1976), for a class-based analysis of women juggling and struggling with private and public roles. For a description of the barriers that women face as they attempt to pursue work-preparatory classes or education, see Marilyn Gittell and Janice Moore, "Denying Independence: Barriers to Women on AFDC," in *Job Training for Women: The Promises and the Limits of Public Policies*, eds. Ronnie J. Steinberg and Sharlon L. Harlan (Philadelphia: Temple University Press, 1989). As they report, "[Women] speak often of jealousy from their boyfriends when they start education, training programs, and jobs. 'He just ripped my books up one day,' a young woman told us. Some are beaten or verbally abused. Others are discouraged by jealousy or resentment," 461.

Chapter 6: A Common Woman's Resistance

1. Carol Stack, *All Our Kin: Strategies for Survival in a Black Community* (New York: Basic Books, 1974) and Stack, *Call To Home: African Americans Reclaim the Rural South* (New York: Basic Books, 1993), examine the strength of kin connections and the importance of the collective effort to maintain families. See also Carol B. Stack and Linda M. Burton, "Kinscripts," *Journal of Comparative Family Studies* 24 (Summer 1993): 157–70 for a discussion on sociological perspectives on the life course and study of kinships.

Micaela Di Leonardo examines "kin work" as collective labor which is expected of family members and is used to maintain households in, "The Female World of Cards and Holidays: Women, Family and the Work of Kinship," *Signs* 12 (1986): 440–53. In her analysis, in contrast to some kinship discourse, the gender nature of such labor is identified.

Methodology

I have many people to thank for their collaboration, advice, and challenges in the course of this research. In the Acknowledgments, I have thanked people whose hard work in community-based programs has been the source for some of the data used in this book. I mention there only those people who worked with me directly in the research process. But it is always important to note that without those who organize programs, mobilize communities, teach children, provide health care, watch over neighbors and playgrounds, and do all the other jobs, paid and unpaid, which make up community life, there would be no place to go to conduct this and a thousand other research efforts.

Before describing the specific studies that support this book, I want briefly to state some principles about conducting research across contemporary American class borders. These principles are founded in the mission of gaining knowledge which will be used to promote the development of all of our people.

It has traditionally been argued that the canon of objectivity in social research requires a researcher to maintain a position of neutrality. This requirement dictates that one can cross over into poor America only as the neutral stranger. Many critics of this methodological position point out that neutrality is a false assumption for anyone, researcher or not. I would push this counterargument further.

It is my position that social research which aims at gaining knowledge and deepening understanding requires consciousness of a divided society. It requires that the researcher acknowledge crossing over to an economically segregated place where things are more than just different or diverse. It means recognizing that this difference is infused with historical and structural in-

equity and for people who live the contemporary class, race, and ethnic version of that inequity, there is no such thing as neutrality. Important research
has often been undertaken without the investigator ever actually meeting the
people who are the subject of the research. Crossing over, however, is another
kind of investigation. It seeks out another kind of information and builds a
different knowledge.

Crossing over means spending considerable time with people; being observed, being tested, revealing before you get to collect revelations. This is
sometimes hard to do, one inevitably blunders, I continue to, but that is part
of gaining knowledge. Above anything else, it means declaring yourself where
neutrality does not exist. Long before I started this book I had learned lessons
of engagement. I learned when I helped someone compose a letter to a bureaucracy, when I accompanied someone to a welfare case-review or to a doctor's office, and when I discussed the power of race and ethnicity not as distant history, but as vitally affecting the here and now. More often, lessons in
engagement have been a matter of learning to say what I think back to people
who are respectful enough to say what they think to me, instead of suggesting that I am without an attitude and have no opinion about the conditions
they describe and endure in poor America. Learning to cross over has required seeing that beyond what *I* think, there is the other side of every contact, each interview, each focus group; and that side is the way people assess
me or any other researcher who does not currently live in poor America.
When you look into the faces of women raising their children in the outback,
you see that neutrality is not recognized as some professional practice. In the
face of stigma, irrational regulations, peril to children, and a woman's despair, neutrality is known only as collusive silence.

People do not share with those who are unwilling to declare their ethical
position across this kind of divide. History teaches people who are a nation's
"other" class, race, tribe, religion, or ethnic minority that being questioned
may be experienced as a humane and respectful inquiry into valued people's
lives or it may be felt as an inquisition. When facing inquisitors, people develop marvelous skills to resist imparting real knowledge.

The other critical aspect of social research that crosses over is the authoritative participation of members of whatever community or population
is investigated to the greatest extent possible in the actual research process.
This means systematically incorporating people who have knowledge which

comes from life, even if they have very little practical background in social research. It means incorporating them at different stages of the research, including the interpretive stages. It means compensating people appropriately for the contribution they make. This practice is complicated to design, near-impossible to get decent funding for, and devilishly hard to implement. But it is fundamental to gaining the reflective and critical analyses of those historically left out and to building with them another kind of discourse.

Four Studies and a New Study Technique

The four studies which provided most of the data for this book were conducted in and around the city of Boston between 1989 and 1997. Beyond these studies, I had the opportunity to conduct ethnographic research through other work in different Boston community-based agencies. I was able to present and discuss my data in various settings, both with people who were clients of these agencies and with staff members, many of whom identified with the local community. All the women and girls who participated in some way in the research come from Dorchester, Roxbury, South Boston, Mattapan, the South End, Jamaica Plain, Mission Hill, Waltham, and Central Square in Cambridge. Each study separately and all studies combined included women who are African American, white (largely Irish and Italian with less than one third calling themselves "just white"), Latino (almost all Puerto Rican), and from Haiti and Jamaica.

Life-History Study

I began the fifty Life-History interviews as part of my doctoral research in 1989. I started that process with several discussion groups of women with whom I had worked in Boston neighborhoods. Based upon their advice and my own years of experience, I conducted five pilot interviews and then an additional thirty interviews, which made up the interview data for my dissertation. I continued to do interviews over the next three years, in some cases following individuals who were willing to continue to meet with me. I met participants through my past work in several community organizations in Boston neighborhoods and also by presenting workshops, primarily on health issues. These workshops were offered in health center waiting areas, churches, child-care centers, and housing development common areas, after which I would ask if anyone was interested in being interviewed about managing family/life as single mothers without a lot of money. All of the women involved were between the ages of twenty-four and forty-nine and had received AFDC at some time but not necessarily at the time of the interview. The total sample of fifty women reflected the population of women receiving Aid to Families with Dependent Children in the Boston area during the early 1990s, in terms of major demographic variables (race/ethnicity, marital status, level of formal education, years of employment history, fertility, etc.)

Every person was paid twenty dollars for each interview which was helpful in encouraging second interviews. Very few people ever called me to stay in touch, but in a few cases I was given a mother's or grandmother's address or phone number as a source for finding someone. I lost track of most people very quickly, but I stayed in touch with several individuals over the years.

I have altered specific, distinguishing features in the histories of some women in ways which disguise their identity but do not alter the content of their accounts. I also removed four women from the original total of fifty-four because these individuals became co-workers or friends. Three of those four women eventually participated in the interpretation of some of the data, and their own intimate knowledge of how I interview was very helpful in critiquing the results.

I changed every woman's name as I explained to participants that I would. However, every name used is the name of someone I have met in the course this work. It was only after I was several years into this research that I understood how powerful is the issue of naming, so wrapped into the knowledge I was seeking and trying to share. I discovered the truth of what Elliot Liebow discusses in the research for his wonderful book, *Tell Them Who I Am,* that the names given to these life histories were not mine to choose but should be self-chosen, and so thereafter, people named themselves. Women generally picked family names, often the names of their mothers, grandmothers, or their own daughters. But many women in the book had already been named by me and should not have been.

The interviews included a review of childhood, which generally took an hour to two hours. I asked women about the place from which their families came, the family's movement over the course of their early years, sibling relationships, changes in families, school days, and teachers remembered. The histories covered their high school years, partnerships with men, and transitions away from birth families. I included questions about education, years of work, and years receiving AFDC, but most of the inquiry was a kind of oral history which almost every individual took over herself. And thus my own role changed with each person as did the follow-up questions, depending upon how the individual chose to uncover her memories. The interviews ranged in length from one and a half hours to eight hours.

I analyzed the data, primarily by drawing out themes which were emphasized and reiterated, as well as by looking at numeric information. The findings gradually took on a rough life-stages structure, which ultimately became the structure for this book.

As many researchers agree, life-history interviews are particularly complicated ethically and personally. They are deeply revealing, and when you listen to the lives of poor women in America, the revelations often call for a response. When conducting such interviews, it is common practice to keep a list of referrals, to the extent that any exist. I always offered a list of services to the women I interviewed, services for domestic violence and substance abuse, local counseling services, child opportunity programs, health/reproductive services, and local GED programs, among others. But few woman showed interest in these services, and in one case, when I placed a call for an individual, the service was full and had no referrals to offer.

The truth is that in roughly half of the interviews, I left someone who, beyond her clear need for material resources, was obviously in need of other services, support, and attention. Often, her children were as well. And in most cases, I was convinced that neither she nor her children would receive any such help.

The Girls Project

The Girls Project was a two-stage, participatory survey and focus group study conducted by a racially/ethnically diverse staff of volunteers and researchers at the Women for Economic Justice (WEJ), a not-for-profit organization, in Boston. The first part, the survey, was conducted in the summer of 1993, and the second stage started a year later and was completed in the winter of 1995. The board of directors of WEJ (I was on the board) was interested in conducting an action research project in which girls played a key role in defining and interpreting the meaning of the data. The mission of the survey was to identify the issues low-income girls consider priorities in their lives and to elicit their insight and opinions on these issues. The methodology included structuring the involvement of adolescent women at the design, implementation, and analysis stages of the study. This research was partially supported through a grant from the Remmer Family Fund, but much of the work was done on a volunteer basis.

THE SURVEY

Altogether nine young women: Sherly, Holly, Alfreda, Juna, Flor, Melissa, Daniele, Debby, and Nora, participated in the survey part of the Girls Project through the Cambridge Commission on the Status of Women in Cambridge, Massachusetts. Under the coordination and wise guidance of Terri Small and Charlene Gilbert, project co-coordinators, young women designed, wrote, and tested a survey with eighty respondents in Boston. The survey was revised by five of the girls and co-coordinators, resulting in a final instrument consisting of closed and open-ended questions on: relationships, gender issues, sexual choices, education, and a broad array of issues affecting communities in which respondents live. Beginning in the summer of 1993, the survey was administered by five young women to a convenience sample of 250 girls, ages twelve to nineteen, in parks, common areas, and other places youth congregate in low-income neighborhoods in Cambridge. Respondents filled out the questionnaire with one of the surveyors or arrangements were made to pick up the questionnaire within a few hours. By the end of the summer, 250 surveys were completed and the team analyzed major findings, which completed the first stage of the investigation.

Subsequently, all the numeric data and, where possible, coded qualitative data were input into a data base and reviewed. During the summer and fall of 1994, a team of two or three investigators, Liliana Silva, Terri Small, and myself, presented the major themes and findings in five focus groups of (altogether forty) adolescent girls in Boston high schools or community centers. Participants were demographically similar to both the survey respondents and the five girls who designed the original survey. In the groups, girls discussed their own experiences, their beliefs, and their knowledge of other young people, to dissect the findings in the survey and to interpret the themes which emerged. I presented some of the findings of the combined survey and focus group research in a paper ("'We Could Be Your Daughters': Girls' Sexuality and Pregnancy in Low-Income America," Radcliffe Public Policy Institute, 1996).

The High School Study

From 1993 to 1995 I worked as the senior researcher and evaluator of the Healthy Transitions/Health Futures Program, a comprehensive program of Tufts/New England Medical Center which worked with high school students in Boston High School. This W. K. Kellogg Foundation–funded project served one hundred ninth and tenth grade students, young men and young women, who were identified through all kinds of outreach and publicity techniques. The services were available to anyone (until all the slots were filled) and drew a sample of youth who reflected the whole range of the school population: the academically strongest to the weakest students, those with disciplinary problems and those without, students who came because they would jump at any opportunity for a better future to students who would jump at any opportunity to miss an occasional class. The program offered these young people comprehensive and integrated services: career exploration and job opportunities, academic support, mentors, health promotion services, leadership opportunities, and ongoing team-building activities. Three staff people, Liliana Silva, Tony DeJesus, and Ceronne Berkeley, and later a fourth, Marcus Agard, worked hard and long with these young people.

In the course of my two years working with this program, I conducted interviews (as did all of the above staff) and ran focus groups with the young women about issues they faced: juggling school, family, and relationship obligations and managing without much money as they neared the end of their high school years. (There were almost as many young men in the project, but they tended to work more with the men on staff and I interviewed only five of them.) The information gathered from both interviews and focus groups was discussed by staff with the students. Later, I took the data and their analyses to other high school interpretive focus groups as well.

The interviews inquired about family work, sibling responsibilities, sexual attitudes and choices, all kinds of relationships, and internal and external forces significant to these young people. We asked about conflicts with adults, their beliefs about the future, and their definitions of achievement and ethical behavior. These were long, open-ended interviews which were repeated over time and, in some cases, girls simply kept the dialogue going with each other and with the adults with whom they worked. Key informants (such as mentors, teachers, job supervisors) were also interviewed and contributed their thoughts, and I might add, their deep commitment to many individual young people over years.

The Women in Transition Study

The goal of this focus group project was to inquire into and gather data about the supports, tools, and resources which made a difference in the success of low-income women who set for themselves a goal of finishing school (either high school or post-secondary school) as a way to attain their chosen path and to advance their own lives. Most of the women were contacted through programs specifically designed to support the progress of women receiving welfare or high school students in urban schools. These focus groups took place in local colleges: Roxbury Community College, North Shore Community College, University of Massachusetts, Bunker Hill Community College, and the Urban College in Boston. Women who were in the process of seeking apprenticeships in the building trades were also interviewed through the Women in the Building Trades program. Younger women were interviewed in focus groups in Fenway Community High School and Boston High School.

In teams of two or three (either with Terri Small, Liliana Silva, or Pamela Westcott) and sometimes with the assistance of someone working in the school or college, we conducted two-hour focus groups which explored the following questions: How can girls/women be assisted in their own pursuits, particularly when they are handling parenthood? What/who stands in the way most? What/who helps the most? What goes into making the commitment to stick it out (either high school, college program, or some other post-secondary effort)? What do they do/need right now to keep on with their goals? What effect(s) do children have on their endeavors? What would they recommend to others coming up along the same paths? What would they design as policy for other women/girls?

An additional area of analysis was a general discussion on the economic impact of getting to where they have chosen to go, and conversely not succeeding. Lengthy notations were taken at each focus group or they were taped. Data from these focus groups previously have not been reported.

Interpretive Focus Groups: A New Study Technique

I have developed this approach in my research as part of the process of interpreting the meaning of qualitative data. In some cases, this involves the triangulation of qualitative and quantitative data as a way of bridging the information of one study with that of another. In the research for this book, I used this approach in all but the Life-History Study. Interpretive focus groups differ from conventional focus groups in that the focus is on data previously collected and then methodically presented to groups of women and/or girls for their analysis. Major themes as well as numeric data were presented, sometimes in verbal and sometimes in written form. Over the course of all the research for this book, I have conducted (often with a companion) more than thirty interpretive focus groups, some carefully planned with transportation, food, and child care provided and some quite spontaneous, as when a community program, school, or health center brought together a group of women/girls who were willing to examine the findings of some of my current research. The inclusion of people who possess primary knowledge and who also were willing to engage in a reflective and critical conversation was essential to my own interpretation and to completing this book.

Selected Bibliography

Abramovitz, Mimi. *Regulating the Lives of Women: Social Policy from Colonial Times to the Present.* Boston: South End Press, 1988.

Albelda, Randy, and Chris Tilly. *Glass Ceilings and Bottomless Pits: Women's Work, Women's Poverty.* Boston: South End Press, 1997.

Amott, Teresa, and Julie Matthaei. *Race, Gender, and Work: A Multicultural Economic History of Women in the United States.* Revised edition. Boston: South End Press, 1996.

Bane, Mary Jo, and David T. Ellwood. *Welfare Realities: From Rhetoric to Reform.* Cambridge, Mass.: Harvard University Press, 1994.

Baxter, Janeen, and Diane Gibson. *Double Take: The Links Between Paid and Unpaid Work.* Canberra: Australian Government Publishing Service, 1990.

Belle, Deborah. *Lives in Stress: Women and Depression.* Beverly Hills: Sage Publications, 1982.

Bergmann, Barbara R. *The Economic Emergence of Women.* New York: Basic Books, 1986.

———. *Saving Our Children From Poverty: What the United States Can Learn From France.* New York: Russell Sage Foundation, 1996.

Betsey, Charles L., Kristin A. Moore, and Margaret C. Simms. *Choice and Circumstance: Racial Differences in Adolescent Sexuality and Fertility.* New Brunswick, N.J.: Transaction Books, 1986.

Billingsley, Andrew. *Black Families in White America.* Englewood Cliffs, N.J.: Prentice Hall, 1968.

Blank, Rebecca M. *It Takes a Nation: A New Agenda for Fighting Poverty.*

New York: Russell Sage Foundation, and Princeton: Princeton University Press, 1997.

Blankenhorn, David. *Fatherless America: Confronting Our Most Urgent Social Problem*. New York: Basic Books, 1995.

Brooks-Gunn, Jeanne, and Greg J. Duncan. *Consequences of Growing Up Poor*. New York: Russell Sage Foundation, 1997.

Brooks-Gunn, Jeanne, Frank F. Furstenberg, Jr., and S. Phillip Morgan. *Adolescent Mothers in Later Life*. New York: Cambridge University Press, 1987.

Brown, Lyn Mikel, and Carol Gilligan. *Meeting at the Crossroads: Women's Psychology and Girls' Development*. Cambridge, Mass.: Harvard University Press, 1992.

Bruce, Judith et al. *Families in Focus: New Perspectives on Mothers, Fathers, and Children*. New York: The Population Council, 1995.

Callaghan, Polly, and Heidi Hartmann. *Contingent Work: A Chart Book on Part-time and Temporary Employment*. Washington, D.C.: Economic Policy Institute, 1991.

Carroll, Rebecca. *Sugar in the Raw: Voices of Young Black Girls in America*. New York: Crown Trade Paperbacks, 1997.

Cloward, Richard A., and Francis Fox Piven. *Regulating the Poor: The Functions of Public Welfare*. Updated edition. New York: Vintage Books, 1993.

Danziger, Sheldon, and Peter Gottschalk. *America Unequal*. New York: Russell Sage Foundation, and Cambridge, Mass.: Harvard University Press, 1995.

Denton, Nancy A., and Douglas S. Massey. *American Apartheid: Segregation and the Making of the Underclass*. Chicago: University of Chicago Press, 1993.

Dujon, Diane, and Ann Withorn. *For Crying Out Loud: Women's Poverty in the United States*. Boston: South End Press, 1996.

Edin, Kathryn, and Laura Lein. *Making Ends Meet: How Single Mothers Survive Welfare and Low-Wage Work*. New York: Russell Sage Foundation, 1997.

Ellwood, David T. *Poor Support: Poverty in the American Family*. New York: Basic Books, 1988.

England, Paula, and George Farkas. *Households, Employment, and Gender:*

A Social, Economic, and Demographic View. New York: Aldine Publishing Company, 1986.

Finch, Janet, and Dulcie Groves. *Labour of Love: Women, Work, and Caring.* London: Routledge and K. Paul, 1983.

Franz, Carol E., and Abigail J. Stewart. *Women Creating Lives: Identities, Resilience, and Resistance.* Boulder, Colo.: Westview Press, 1994.

Garfinkle, Irwin, and Sara S. McLanahan. *Single Mothers and Their Children: A New American Dilemma.* Washington, D.C.: Urban Institute Press, 1986.

Gilligan, Carol. *In a Different Voice: Psychological Theory and Women's Development.* Cambridge, Mass.: Harvard University Press, 1982.

Gilligan, Carol, Annie Rogers, and Deborah Tolman. *Women, Girls and Psychotherapy: Reframing Resistance.* New York: Harrington Park Press, 1991.

Gittell, Marilyn et al. *From Welfare to Independence: The College Option.* New York: Ford Foundation, 1990.

Gordon, Linda. *Women, the State, and Welfare.* Madison: University of Wisconsin Press, 1990.

Harlan, Sharlon L., and Ronnie J. Steinberg. *Job Training for Women: The Promise and the Limits of Public Policies.* Philadelphia: Temple University Press, 1989.

Herman, Judith Lewis. *Trauma and Recovery.* New York: Basic Books, 1992.

Hernandez, Donald J., with David E. Meyers. *America's Children: Resources From Family, Government, and the Economy.* New York: Russell Sage Foundation, 1993.

Hernes, Helga Maria. *Welfare State and Woman Power: Essays in State Feminism.* New York: Oxford University Press, 1987.

Jargowsky, Paul A. *Poverty and Place: Ghettos, Barrios, and the American City.* New York: Russell Sage Foundation, 1997.

Jencks, Christopher. *Rethinking Social Policy: Race, Poverty, and the Underclass.* Cambridge, Mass.: Harvard University Press, 1992.

Jencks, Christopher, and Paul E. Peterson. *The Urban Underclass.* Washington, D.C.: Brookings Institute, 1991.

Katz, Michael B. *In the Shadow of the Poorhouse: A Social History of Welfare in America.* New York: Basic Books, 1986.

————. *The Undeserving Poor: From the War on Poverty to the War on Welfare.* New York: Pantheon Books, 1989.

Kuttner, Robert. *The Economic Illusion: False Choices Between Prosperity and Social Justice.* Boston: Houghton Mifflin, 1984.

Ladner, Joyce A. *Tomorrow's Tomorrow: The Black Woman.* Garden City, N.Y.: Doubleday, 1971.

Leadbeater, Bonnie J. Ross, and Niobe Way. *Urban Girls: Resisting Stereotypes, Creating Identities.* New York: New York University Press, 1996.

Liebow, Elliot. *Tell Them Who I Am: The Lives of Homeless Women.* New York: Penguin Books, 1993.

Lorde, Audre. *Sister Outsider: Essays and Speeches.* Trumansburg, N.Y.: Crossing Press, 1984.

Ludtke, Melissa. *On Our Own: Unmarried Motherhood in America.* New York: Random House, 1997.

Luker, Kristin. *Dubious Conceptions: The Politics of Teenage Pregnancy.* Cambridge, Mass.: Harvard Univerity Press, 1996.

Miller, Jean Baker. *Toward a New Psychology of Women.* Boston: Beacon Press, 1976.

Morrison, Toni. *Race-ing Justice, En-gendering Power: Essays on Anita Hill, Clarence Thomas and the Construction of Social Reality.* New York: Pantheon Books, 1992.

Morrison, Toni, ed. *Collected Essays: James Baldwin.* New York: Library of America, 1998.

National Research Council Board on Children and Families. *New Findings on Children, Families, and Economic Self-Sufficiency: Summary of a Research Briefing.* Washington, D.C.: National Academy Press, 1995.

National Research Council Panel on Adolescent Pregnancy and Childbearing. *Risking the Future: Adolescent Sexuality, Pregnancy, and Childbearing.* Washington, D.C.: National Academy Press, 1987.

Newman, Katherine S. *Declining Fortunes: The Withering of the American Dream.* New York: Basic Books, 1993.

Oakly, Ann. *Woman's Work: Housewife Past and Present.* New York: Pantheon Books, 1974.

Phillips, Deborah A. *Childcare for Low-Income Families: Summary of Two Workshops*. Washington, D.C.: National Academy Press, 1995.

Pipher, Mary. *Reviving Ophelia: Saving the Selves of Adolescent Girls*. New York: Ballantine Books, 1994.

Rank, Mark Robert. *Living on the Edge: The Realities of Welfare in America*. New York: Columbia University Press, 1994.

Rice, Margery Garrett Spring. *Working Class Wives: Their Health and Conditions*. Second edition. London: Virago Books, 1981.

Rubin, Lillian Breslow. *Worlds of Pain: Life in the Working-Class Family*. New York: Basic Books, 1976.

Ruggles, Patricia. *Drawing the Line: Alternative Poverty Measures and Their Implications for Public Policy*. Washington, D.C.: Urban Institute Press, 1990.

Schein, Virginia E. *Working from the Margins: Voices of Mothers in Poverty*. Ithaca, N.Y.: ILR Press, 1995.

Schorr, Lisbeth B. *Common Purpose: Strengthening Families and Neighborhoods to Rebuild America*. New York: Anchor Books, 1997.

Scott, Hilda. *Working Your Way to the Bottom: The Feminization of Poverty*. Boston: Pandora Press, 1984.

Sidel, Ruth. *Keeping Women and Children Last: America's War on the Poor*. New York: Penguin Books, 1996.

Stack, Carol. *All Our Kin: Strategies for Survival in a Black Community*. New York: Harper and Row, 1974.

Thompson, Sharon. *Going All the Way: Teenage Girls' Tales of Sex, Romance, and Pregnancy*. New York: Hill and Wang, 1996.

Williams, Constance Willard. *Black Teenage Mothers: Pregnancy and Child Rearing from Their Perspective*. Lexington, Mass.: Lexington Books, 1991.

Wilson, William Julius. *The Truly Disadvantaged: The Inner City, the Underclass, and Public Policy*. Chicago: University of Chicago Press, 1987.

———*The Ghetto Underclass: Social Science Perspectives*. Updated edition. Newbury Park, Cal.: Sage Publications, 1993.

———. *When Work Disappears: The World of the New Urban Poor*. New York: Vintage Books, 1997.

Acknowledgments

There are many people I want to thank for their contribution to this work. Foremost, I want to express my deepest appreciation to the women and girls who spent time with me over the last decade, not only giving information but also sharing their knowledge. I want particularly to thank those individuals who were willing to push me, who encouraged me to resist the old welfare talk about women and girls, people who pushed me to cross over and reckon with the world from the other side.

I also want to express my sincere appreciation to the following people with whom I have worked over the years as co-investigators, *compañeras*, and critical friends: my grandfather John Abt, Yvonne Anthony, BarbaraNeely, Blanca Bonilla, Myrna Boucage, Beatrice Brown, Margarita Cintron, Dee Dee Costello, Elba Crespo, Cyndi Daniels, Roz Feldberg, David Gil, Yarice Hidalgo, Hilda Kahne, Deb Karlan, Lois McLoskey, Judith Palmer, Liliana Silva, Terri Small, Beverly Smith, Candace Waldron, and Lucie White.

For reviewing some or all of this book on a tough schedule, I gratefully thank Cyndi Daniels, Roz Feldberg, Pam Joshi, Meg Lovejoy, and Lois McLoskey.

For ongoing support throughout this effort I want to give warm thanks to Paula Rayman, Director of the Radcliffe Public Policy Institute, a place where I was able to sit and write with little distraction, for the first time in my life. I also want to thank the community of scholars, fellows, and staff of the Public Policy Institute, who offered encouragement, humor, and an occasional lunch.

Some of the information which I used for this book came through my work or association with people and programs in greater Boston. Particularly I want to thank all the women past and present of Women for Economic

Justice; the staff and individual residents of sheltering projects of Casa Myrna Vasquez; Sharon Rosen, principal investigator of the Healthy Transitions/ Healthy Futures program of Tufts/New England Medical Center, as well as the staff, Marcus Agard, Ceronne Berkeley, Tony DeJesus, and Liliana Silva; women of the organizing project "Homeless Organization for Women"; Martha Kurz, director of the Center for Perinatal and Family Health of Brigham and Women's Hospital; and in the Maurice Tobin School in Roxbury, the Tobin Brigham Family Support Center staff, all of whom are mentioned in the text, as well as the teachers, family members, and community friends who support their work.

My sincere gratitude to Helene Atwan, my editor and the director of Beacon Press, as well as the entire Beacon editorial board, all of whom believed in this book immediately. I also want to thank Melissa Gibson in the Women's Studies Program at Harvard University, who thoughtfully assisted me in the final stages of the work.

I am always grateful to Judith Ware Dodson, Dorian Dodson, and Francesca Bang for life-long conversations about carrying on. Finally, I thank John Fontana, Odessa Cole, and Clara Fontana for seeing this through with me and for their love.